C000072195

Critics

against

Culture

Critics
against
Culture

Anthropological Observers of
Mass Society

RICHARD HANDLER

THE UNIVERSITY OF WISCONSIN PRESS

The University of Wisconsin Press
1930 Monroe Street
Madison, Wisconsin 53711

www.wisc.edu/wisconsinpress/

3 Henrietta Street
London WC2E 8LU, England

5   4   3   2   1

Printed in the United States of America

Library of Congress Cataloging-in-Publication Data
Handler, Richard, 1950–
Critics against culture: anthropological observers of mass society /
Richard Handler.
p. cm.
Includes bibliographical references and index.
ISBN 0-299-21370-6 (cloth: alk. paper)
1. Ethnology—History. 2. Anthropologists' writings. I. Title.
GN308.H34 2005
306′.09—dc22
2005011175

For

GEORGE STOCKING,

and In Memory of

DAVID SCHNEIDER

CONTENTS

ACKNOWLEDGMENTS
AND SOURCES

I have for some time wished to bring together a series of essays that I published over the years concerning Boasian anthropologists as cultural critics. I felt, however, that such a collection needed to include an essay on Alexis de Tocqueville's *Democracy in America*, one that I finally drafted in the summer of 2002 and revised the following summer. Like the introductory essay and chapter 7, on Jules Henry and Richard Hoggart, it appears here for the first time. Original publication information for the other chapters follows in the separate acknowledgments for each. All have been at least minimally revised for this book.

I would like to thank Maria Lepowsky and George Marcus, who read the manuscript of *Critics against Culture* for the University of Wisconsin Press and provided a wealth of critical commentary. I am also grateful to Steve Salemson of the Press, who has been unfailingly enthusiastic about this work and a stalwart supporter of the ongoing publication of related work in the *History of Anthropology* series.

Introduction: Critics, Teachers, Observers

I adapted the middle section of the introduction from a paper that I presented at the 102nd annual meeting of the American Anthropological Association (November 2003, Chicago), in a session called "Culture-at-Large with John Guillory" that was sponsored by the Society for Cultural Anthropology. Ira Bashkow, Eric Gable, Daniel Segal, and Pauline Turner Strong commented on various drafts of the introduction, for which I thank them.

The Dainty and the Hungry Man: Literature and Anthropology in the Work of Edward Sapir

I presented earlier versions of chapter 2 as a paper, at the February 1981 meeting of the Chicago Group in the History of the Social Sciences (sponsored by the Morris Fishbein Center for the Study of the History of Science and Medicine) and at the fourteenth annual meeting of the Cheiron Society in June 1982. I would like to thank the participants in those sessions for their helpful comments. In addition, Franci Duitch, Dell Hymes, Richard Preston, and George Stocking read the paper as it progressed through various versions, and I found their critical suggestions stimulating. This chapter was first published in George Stocking, ed., *Observers Observed: Essays on Ethnographic Fieldwork*, 208–31 (Madison: University of Wisconsin Press, 1983).

Antiromantic Romanticism: Sapir's Critique of American Individualism

I presented an early version of the first part of chapter 3, on Sapir and Matthew Arnold, to the Charles Darwin Society of Purdue University in September 1985. I thank Myrdene Anderson and her colleagues for their constructive responses to that presentation. I also would like to thank George Stocking and Dell Hymes, who commented extensively on an initial draft of the final version that appeared in *Anthropological Quarterly* 62, no. 1 (January 1989):1–13.

Vigorous Male and Aspiring Female: Poetry, Personality, and Culture in Edward Sapir and Ruth Benedict

The research upon which I based this essay (chapter 4) was made possible by a summer grant from the National Endowment for the Humanities in 1985. I would like to thank James Clifford, Michael Ebner, Dell Hymes, Daniel Segal, Laurie Shrage, George Stocking, and Jennifer Wallace for critical commentaries while I was researching and writing it. It was first published in George Stocking, ed., *Malinowski, Rivers, Benedict and Others: Essays on Culture and Personality*, 127–55 (Madison: University of Wisconsin Press, 1986).

Ruth Benedict and the Modernist Sensibility

I presented a brief version of this paper, which forms the basis of chapter 5, at the Ruth Benedict Centennial held at Vassar College, April 2–3, 1987.

I would like to thank Lilo Stern and Judith Goldstein for inviting me to participate. Clifford Geertz's and James Boon's contributions to the conference provided much stimulation as I was rewriting this chapter for publication (Geertz's paper is now published in Geertz 1988, Boon's in Boon 1999). Patricia Wallace, of the English Department at Vassar College, offered insightful commentary on the original paper, particularly with respect to Benedict's feminism; I have incorporated many of Wallace's suggestions in this chapter. Finally, Marc Manganaro worked with me steadily on various drafts of this essay, generously sharing his expertise on literary modernism. This chapter originally appeared in Manganaro's edited volume, *Modernist Anthropology: From Fieldwork to Text*, 163–80 (Princeton, NJ: Princeton University Press, 1990).

American Culture in the World:
Margaret Mead's *And Keep Your Powder Dry*

David Hollinger provided helpful commentary on an initial draft of chapter 6, a longer version of which was published as "Boasian Anthropology and the Critique of American Culture" in *American Quarterly* 42 (1990):252–73.

Critics against Culture: Jules Henry, Richard Hoggart,
and the Tragicomedy of Mass Society

I first presented chapter 7 as a paper, to the Department of Anthropology at the University of Illinois in September 1999. I thank Matti Bunzl for the invitation to visit, and the members of the department for their many useful comments. I especially want to thank Derek Pardue, who prepared a challenging and thoughtful response. I presented a much shorter version at the annual meeting of the American Anthropological Association in Chicago on November 19, 1999, and a longer, revised version to the Department of Anthropology at New York University in September 2003. I thank Fred Myers and his colleagues for their stimulating responses on that occasion.

Raymond Williams, George Stocking, and
Fin-de-siècle U.S. Anthropology

I originally wrote this article that forms the basis of chapter 8 for a May 1995 conference honoring George Stocking that was sponsored by the Morris Fishbein Center for the History of Science and Medicine and the

Department of Anthropology, both of the University of Chicago, and organized by Robert Richards. I presented a shorter version at the 1997 annual meeting of the American Anthropological Association, held in Washington, DC, in a session organized by Ira Bashkow and Matti Bunzl titled "The Historian's Magic and the Remaking of Anthropology: Papers on the History and Anthropology of George W. Stocking Jr." In February 1998 I presented a revised, longer version to the Department of Anthropology at York University in Toronto, Canada. I would like to thank the various participants in those sessions, including Clifford Geertz and Ken Little, for their comments on the material. I am pleased also to acknowledge the students in my seminar, "Cultural Studies and Culture Theory," offered in 1994 and 1998 at the University of Virginia, who have helped me to think about the relationship between anthropology and cultural studies. Finally, I would like to thank Daniel Segal, editor of *Cultural Anthropology*, and his anonymous (to me) readers. This chapter first appeared in *Cultural Anthropology* 13 (1998):447–63.

Critics

against

Culture

Introduction

Critics, Teachers, Observers

The cast of mind of doing "being ordinary" is essentially this: Your business in life is only to see and report the usual aspects of any possible scene. That is to say, what you look for is to see how any scene you're in can be made an ordinary scene. . . . You can come home day after day and, asked what happened, report without concealing, that nothing happened. And were you concealing something, if it were reported it would turn out to be nothing much.

—HARVEY SACKS (1992:218–19)

When we read about another culture, we have to remember to read every word; we have to forget our habits of fast reading, because, when we begin a sentence, we can never predict what its end will be.

—DOROTHY LEE (1959:3)

Critics

The wisdom I've borrowed from Harvey Sacks and Dorothy Lee is at first glance a commonplace wisdom among anthropologists. Natives everywhere live in a world made real, familiar, and known to them by culture, and they often seem strange and unpredictable to us (as we do to them). Most natives are storytellers, but they tell the same stories over and over. Culture makes storytelling, and "creativity" in general, possible, but the creativity of most people in most situations is rather severely limited. That is to say, the price we pay for being able to function at all in an infinite universe is to create for ourselves a quite finite world and then to pretty much stick to it.

But I intend my paired epigraphs to mean more than those commonplaces. It is true, as Lee says, that when we encounter a strange culture, we "can never predict" what the natives will tell us. But it is also true that we can never predict with certainty what our friends, neighbors, and family will tell us. When someone I know well begins a sentence, I can "never predict what its end will be" (nor, perhaps, can the speaker), although all of us involved in familiar conversations, or in conversations with familiars, can usually surmise what is going to be said. So Lee's observation about anthropological reading is on the surface incomplete, or even misleading, but at the same time, it is startlingly insightful about cultural criticism as practiced by anthropologists, as I will argue in this book. It is correct in what it teaches us about the anthropological practice of learning "to forget our habits." Anthropological cultural criticism stems from a particular "cross-culturally" induced practice of forgetting.

There is more than meets the eye in the passage from Sacks, too. Although we tend to think of "the ordinary" as a neutral term, one that must be applicable to all cultural worlds, Sacks is talking *not* about natives everywhere but about us, that is, about citizens of societies like the contemporary United States and England. "Doing 'being ordinary'" describes the practices of selves as these are constituted in modern, individualistic, mass societies. But "being ordinary" would not necessarily occur to people elsewhere as a good or reasonable thing to do. Much anthropological cultural criticism, especially that of the writers whom I discuss in this book, has attacked the problem of the ordinary—and not simply the generic ordinary but the ordinariness that modern individualism creates.

I have been implying that there is a distinction between cultural critics and anthropological cultural critics. There is nothing mysterious here: no single discipline or field owns the title "critic." There are critics in the humanities and arts, and in politics, religion, and society (to use our common labels for social arenas as we constitute and inhabit them). Moreover, the term "cultural criticism" has been in use in the United States for at least a century (see chapter 3). As I see it, anthropological cultural critics are anthropologists who expend at least some of their professional effort in dissecting the commonsense presuppositions of their own world and in disseminating the results of that work to as wide an audience of other citizens as they can reach. As anthropologists, they have a distinctive style, or method, of generating critical insight, one born of the historically given tasks of the discipline, its commitment to the comparative study of the variety and particularity of cultural experiences around the globe, and of the fieldwork methods developed to accomplish that task. In my opinion, anthropological training and work make anthropologists particularly insightful cultural critics. But we anthropologists should remember that other scholars, writers, and citizens draw critical insight from other sorts of experiences and disciplines.

Anthropological cultural critics may well be insightful, but have we been politically and socially effective or influential? In the United States in the summer of 2004 (as I write this), it is easy to respond with despair to such a question. With "W" in the White House, the U.S. Army in Iraq, and far too much bile, bible, sycophancy, and inanity in the endlessly segmenting news media, we anthropologists do not seem to be doing much to help Americans penetrate the fog of the U.S. cultural imaginary. There are, of course, anthropologists who have entered the fray. But despite our participation in discussions in our own institutions, and perhaps in specialist publications (for example, Ghosh 2001; Nader 2001; Mascia-Lees and Lees 2002), we seem to be almost completely absent from the popular media. This lament is heard from scholars in many fields—it is sometimes discussed as the demise of the public intellectual. Among North American anthropologists, that lament may be particularly heartfelt, as we have great disciplinary ancestors (whose work we continue to study), who even long after their deaths seem to cast a longer media shadow than we current practitioners are able to do. Indeed, the two most remarkable media appearances by anthropologists that came to my attention recently were those of Ruth Benedict, in Alexander Stille's *New York Times* article (July 19, 2003), and Franz Boas, in Claudia Roth Pierpont's *New Yorker* essay (March 8, 2004).

Sketching the history of Benedict's work for the Office of War Information in the 1940s, Stille honored her success in conveying to American policy makers an understanding of Japanese culture that they could use to construct a lasting peace between the two countries: "With considerable sensitivity, she managed both to stress the differences in Japanese society of which American policy makers needed to be aware and to debunk the stereotype of the Japanese as hopelessly rigid and incapable of change" (Stille 2003:A17). He noted as well the enduring success that *The Chrysanthemum and the Sword*, the book that came out of Benedict's war work, has had in Japan (see Kent 1999). But, reading Benedict against the Bush administration's repeated assertions that the American mission in Iraq is analogous to the tasks that the United States accomplished in Japan and Germany after World War II, Stille's parting observation is ominous: "As the occupation of Iraq appears more complex by the day, where are the new Ruth Benedicts, authoritative voices who will carry weight with both Iraqis and Americans?"[1]

Pierpont's capsule biography of Boas is more hopeful; indeed, Boas assumes heroic proportions in her moving essay. Pierpont discovered Boas when she was working on an essay about Zora Neale Hurston (Pierpont 2000:138), and, struck by his influence, as propagated by his students (especially Benedict and Margaret Mead), Pierpont decided to bring the by-now forgotten Boas to *New Yorker* readers. In her essay, subtitled "How a Rebel Anthropologist Waged War on Racism," Pierpont takes Boas from his German homeland (where he had been imbued with the political liberalism of 1848 and the scientific liberalism of Alexander von Humboldt, but in which anti-Semitism had become increasingly potent by the 1880s) to the United States (with its "wretched history" of racial subjugation [Pierpont 2004:50] coupled to its apparently vast opportunities for European immigrants). Sketching Boas's participation in the 1893 World's Columbian Exposition in Chicago, and his subsequent move to the American Museum of Natural History and Columbia University, Pierpont shows Boas developing his antiracist understanding of human potential even as his new homeland became ever more frenzied in its pursuit of scientific racism—"separate but equal," eugenics, nativism, anti-immigration legislation, and then the tepid American response to the rise of anti-Semitic fascism in Europe. Indeed, after outlining the influence of the American eugenics movement in Germany, Pierpont describes Boas in 1929 as "wearing down" after "a lifetime of arguments." And then, in the most chilling passage of the essay,[2] she imagines Boas pondering the world situation in terms that invite her readers to meditate on the contingencies of history:

> He spent summers in Germany; his sisters were alarmed by the number of votes being cast for the Nazis, but he clearly thought that sense would prevail. Was there less reason to have faith in Germany than in America? Hitler had

1. Stille's question hauntingly recalls Dorothy Lee's obituary of Benedict in the *Journal of American Folklore*, in which Lee imagines social scientists, educators, philosophers, and "men in governmental offices" asking, 'To whom do we turn with our questions now?' I do not know the answer. Ruth Benedict is irreplaceable" (Lee 1949:345).

2. I am indebted to Matti Bunzl for pointing out the power of this passage. For the trajectory of German anthropology from liberal humanism to fascism, see Penny and Bunzl 2003.

written admiringly of U.S. immigration policy in "Mein Kampf," but the Germans had passed no national or racial immigration restrictions; German eugenicists had gained government approval only for a program of consensual sterilization. Who could have been sure, as the thirties began, which of these economically plummeting nations would go racially mad? (61)

Pierpont nonetheless ends on a hopeful note. Boas, she asserts, was "uncontestably right" about race, culture, and human potential, and "American society has been reaping the benefits [of his work] for decades" (63). Such a conclusion returns readers, with glass-half-empty–glass-half-full sentiments, to the discouraging present. Though Pierpont cannot be wrong to conclude that Boas did much to change the terms of racial debate in the United States, or at least to formulate and disseminate a progressive position, he did not vanquish modern racism—which, in the broadest perspective, has to be seen as integral to the rise and spread of global capitalism (Holt 2000). And although it seems clear that the development of a large African American middle class means that class and race intersect somewhat differently today than they did in Boas's time, the foundations (both American and global) of the racist social order remain firmly in place. How else to account (for example) for the lack of value placed on the lives of individual African Americans, as evidenced by the dismaying incarceration rates of blacks in the United States, or for the virulent prejudice that, in some sense, has made it possible for the U.S. government to justify two Iraq wars (to its citizens, if not to the world) and for the "developed" world to tolerate the plight of the Palestinians (Nader 2001)?

Perhaps the civic engagement and public presence of Boas and Benedict seem beyond the capabilities of anthropologists today because ancestors always assume heroic proportions in the eyes of their descendants. Or perhaps their success in institutionalizing anthropology in North American universities inevitably led to the routinization of their charisma. In their day, a handful of anthropologists, a Boasian "school" (Stocking 1974a:17–18), had an intellectual mission that transcended mere institutional survival. In these fallen days, thousands of anthropologists work at North American colleges and universities (although the discipline is small compared to the other social sciences), and it is easy enough to see ourselves as comfortably middle-class, salaried professionals in the employ of the state or of nonprofit corporations and unwilling to rock those boats (Grimshaw and Hart 1993). On the other hand, depending on our age, we wrestled as undergraduate and graduate students with the great political issues of the day, at least as troubling, I'm sure, as Iraq is now: the cold war, McCarthyism, civil rights, Vietnam. And although many professors of anthropology are also social activists, we mostly choose to work "inside" the system, perhaps because most of us, like most people everywhere, lack the creativity and optimism required to work beyond it. The question then becomes, can we function as cultural critics even as we remain good citizens of a key institution in the American system of social privilege? And the answer is a qualified yes, if we are willing to consider our students, particularly our undergraduate students, as an important audience of citizens.

Teachers

The American Anthropological Association worries a good bit about the discipline's lack of public voice and profile. It also worries about anthropology and education, that is, anthropology in the classroom at all levels, from elementary school to graduate training. But the association connects those two sets of concerns less readily than one would imagine. Or perhaps I should say that we anthropologists (especially those of us whose professional identity is geared to research) place less stock in our potential influence as teachers than we should. We may not figure as media pundits, but, as a discipline, we routinely teach tens of thousands of students at the top of the American educational system. And some of those students are influenced, sometimes profoundly, by our teaching—or, at least, so they have told my colleagues and me over the years. Thus, although we may regret our failure to measure up to our forebears as public intellectuals, we tend to forget that the institutionalization of anthropology means that we teach far more students, collectively, than they ever did.

The united front of the association notwithstanding—its public face of unity across subfields and across theoretical orientations, and its notion that anthropology as such is "good for" the public—it matters which version of anthropology we teach. Although anthropology is probably the most left-wing of all U.S. social science disciplines (saying so is damning with faint praise, I fear), and although very few, if any, anthropologists today would teach the kind of socioevolutionary racism that Victorian anthropologists were instrumental in fomenting, the varieties of anthropology, and of scientific or humanistic orientations, that coexist in our field are not all culturally critical or provocative in the same way. That is, differing anthropological orientations matter in and of themselves, to us as practitioners, but they are perhaps more important in relationship to the presuppositions that our student audiences bring to the classroom.[3]

I regularly teach Anthropology 101, "Introduction to Anthropology," to groups of 250 students. I teach it nominally as a four-field course, but the structure of the course stems not from the disciplinary subfields but from two sets of opposed concepts: "interpretation" and "explanation," and "culture" and "race." (Those opposed pairs are ultimately transformations of each other.) "Interpretation versus explanation" is of course the 1970s version (Geertz 1973; Rabinow and Sullivan 1979) of a dichotomy that is much older, and, indeed, I take students back to Boas's 1887 essay, "The Study of Geography," which lays out the distinction between what he saw as the natural (or physical) and historical (or cosmographic) sciences, the first being explanatory, the second interpretive (Boas 1887; see also Stocking 1989, 1996). In Boas's discussion, interpretation and explanation, however different, are nonetheless both scientific orientations; as such, neither entails a particular political or moral stance. That is, the interpretation and explanation of cultural phenomena (in Anthropology 101, for example) need not be accompanied by "value judgments." Yet questions of "judgment" and "value" (value not in the sense of a neutral description of the values of a culture but value as "evaluation," differential judgments about relative merit) are not absent from Anthropology 101. The students return to such questions with relentless anxiety, as, indeed, do some of the canonical texts I use, such as Benedict's *Patterns of Culture* and Montaigne's essay "Of Custom." The interpretation of cultures is all well and good, the students say, but don't we need scientific facts to determine questions of value? And isn't such factual determination of value judgments precisely the role of the social sciences?

So the stage is set, after a few lectures, for a struggle that will last the rest of the semester. The students want explanations based on facts, or "true" answers for test questions, as for life; the instructor wants to muddy the distinction between interpretation and explanation, and question the notion that facts (and truth) can exist (for humans) outside a cultural frame. This also has a political dimension. The students expect that the knowledge that comes packaged in a university course is "objective" and nonpolitical; the instructor wants to convince them that the very structure of

3. For two important discussions of the complicated relationship of U.S. anthropology to U.S. citizenship and public knowledge, see di Leonardo 1998 and Segal 2000.

knowledge production in the university is historically particular and saturated with political values. To put the matter differently: the students' understanding of terms like "explanation," "judgment," "value," and "fact" is structured by a hegemonic narrative of scientific and civilizational progress that almost all of them know ("by heart," as it were) and almost none has thought to question. Paraphrasing my colleague Peter Metcalf, another tiller of this field at the University of Virginia, the students come into 101 believing in cultural evolution and not believing in biological evolution, and it is our job to reverse that. Leaving out for now the work that such a course may do to teach about Darwinian evolution and the place of *homo sapiens* within it (not to mention the struggle of "creationism" against it), let me just remark that for these students, questions of value are not simply questions about mobilizing scientific facts to discover appropriate values. *Their* questions of value always begin with the assumption that "our" values are "better" than those of all others, indeed, that "human nature" itself is governed by our values. Or, to put this another way, they do not see their own values as values but as facts.

Enter that much maligned, much misunderstood concept, anthropological relativism. It appeals too easily to the students' democratic individualism, so that, no matter how carefully I build my discussion of relativism, the students interpret it to mean "every person is as good as every other [period]." But relativism, as I understand it, has to do not with the equal standing of individuals, defined a certain way in a certain kind of society, but with the grounding of all human thought in historically particular languages and situations. "Barbarians are no more marvelous to us than we are to them, nor for better cause," as Montaigne put it (1580–88:80). Or, in a famous passage from Benedict's *Patterns of Culture*, "No man ever looks at the world with pristine eyes. He sees it edited by a definite set of customs and institutions and ways of thinking. Even in his philosophical probings he cannot go behind these stereotypes; his very concepts of the true and the false will still have reference to his particular traditional customs" (1934a:2).

To confuse these issues further, my primary text in Anthropology 101 is Benedict's *Patterns of Culture*, a paradigmatic statement for the discipline that wavers between two possible readings of the passage just quoted (see chapter 5). On the one hand, with its constant probing of modern American values, facilitated by Benedict's readings of other people's worlds, *Patterns of Culture* models cultural interpretation as a hermeneutic "tacking

back and forth" between meaningful positions. The work of cultural interpretation not only crosses cultural boundaries, it unsettles them, as it allows
readers to stand aside from their own culture and think about it critically.
This is why Dorothy Lee's remark about the surprises in store for readers
when they read or hear other-cultural sentences is directly relevant to the
work of cultural criticism. Interpreters like Lee and Benedict always turn
the surprise that they discover in others' unpredictability back on their own
commonsense presumptions, showing readers how surprising and unpredictable they are too. And in those moments of surprise, of interpretive
unsettling, it is at once possible to take a moral stance (war is an "asocial
trait," and rivalry is "notoriously wasteful," to mention two of Benedict's
examples [1934a:32, 247]) and to learn and teach about other people's moral
stances.

In the kind of hermeneutic exercise that I have just described, *Patterns
of Culture* provides a demonstration of why a culture is less aptly described
as a bounded collection of similar individuals than as an ongoing discussion (sometimes harmonious, sometimes acrimonious, sometimes phatic)
among people who speak similar languages. Benedict's discussions are *never*
about one and only one culture, even when she seems to be writing mere
descriptive summaries of some other world. On the other hand, to convince people of the reality of those other-cultural worlds, and of anthropology's legitimacy as the science that studies them, Benedict places at the
center of *Patterns of Culture* portraits of three apparently neatly bounded
cultural groups, apparently scientifically described. Never mind that she
cautions readers that her central interpretive concepts (like "Dionysian" and
"Apollonian") are not scientific terms that can be applied universally but
poetic metaphors drawn from specific authors, commenting on specific traditions (Nietzsche, on the "ancient" Greeks). Never mind, also, that her
chapters on Zuni and Kwakiutl blur the distinction between named peoples ("Zuni," "Kwakiutl") and culture areas ("the Southwest," "the Northwest Coast"), each of which is home to many communities and traditions
that have been borrowing from one another for hundreds of years. Despite
those features of her argument, *Patterns of Culture* is structured with three
individualized cultural portraits at the center of its narrative. Readers can
guess that Benedict chose the three (Zuni, Dobu, Kwakiutl) for maximal
contrast: she inserts a Melanesian portrait between those of the two North
American groups, and the metaphors she uses to distinguish those two—
in addition to the Greek terms, she uses a psychiatric term (of Greek

derivation!), "megalomaniac paranoid" (222)—move them further apart, for the reader's viewing, than other strands of Benedict's analysis (not included in *Patterns of Culture*) would warrant. Immediately upon completing the three portraits, Benedict tells her readers that Zuni, Dobu, and Kwakiutl are cultures "travelling along different roads in pursuit of different ends, and these ends and these means in one society cannot be judged in terms of those of another society, because essentially they are incommensurable" (223).

Now, that statement can be interpreted in terms of each of the two epistemological positions that *Patterns of Culture* makes possible. The incommensurability of language games does *not* mean that translation is not possible, nor does it mean that judgment is not possible. It means only that one has to do the hard work of translation, and interpretation, before making judgments of moral value or aesthetic merit or social utility. It means, literally, that one cannot understand the "means" and "ends" of an "exotic" culture if one insists on interpreting those means and ends solely in one's own language, from one's own perspective.

But the statement can also be fitted into the kind of objectivist scientific epistemology that the students in Anthropology 101 presuppose. From that perspective, the "fact" of cultural difference is not an invitation to translation but an allegory of democratic individualism (see Rosenblatt 2004). Just as the students are relentless in their anxiety about others' values, they are relentless at reinterpreting anthropological relativism as a rule of consumer choice (the world is made up of sovereign individuals, each of whom has the inalienable right to see the world from his or her point of view, and to act accordingly, without criticizing the views, or purchasing decisions, of others). Transposed to the collective level, this means: each culture is different, we must value each culture equally, or, rather, we must refuse moral judgment of cultures altogether. (Remember, Benedict said, "One society cannot be judged in terms of [the values] of another society.") And such reasoning gives rise, in class, to the inevitable question about Hitler ("how, then, from an anthropological perspective, is it possible to condemn Hitler?").

The epistemological culprit here is one that preys not only on students but on anthropologists. For despite all criticisms of the culture concept since the 1970s, not to mention similar criticisms that were elaborated at the beginning of the last century, American social scientists, including anthropologists, have a deep affinity for the idea that "culture" and "society" (and also "identity" and "community") are built upon similarity, not difference. John Guillory has brilliantly analyzed this position in his 1993 book, *Cultural Capital*, where he shows that many literary-social expositions of the idea of "value" depend, in the end, on the notion of a bounded community of people who hold "the same" values and who, therefore, will make "the same" judgments. The result is a form of argumentation wherein any differences of value (such as those expressed in disputes about literary canons) must be attributed to communities, subcommunities, communities-within-communities. In other words, value judgments emerge from, and define, homogeneous communities of like-minded individuals. And analysis of value disputes presupposes what Guillory calls an "implicit subjectivism" or "individualism" (1993:286) in which difference is attributed to individuated communities, communities that differ one from another but that, internally, are homogeneous. This is not far from Benedict's second epistemology, in which the world is made up of discrete cultures. And in Anthropology 101, this leads to the students' anxiety-ridden conclusion that because all value systems are equal, no value judgments are possible.

There are at least two ways out of this trap. Guillory's position turns on an analysis of "those social conditions which structure the society as a whole"—"structuring conditions . . . that . . . affect different social groups differently as a consequence of their very universality [within a given society]" (286–87). In such a model, social difference is not an essential property of individuated groups but a function of social inequalities and relationships in a wider system. Here is the turn to questions of "power" that some anthropologists have developed since the mid-1980s, particularly as a way out of the epistemological (and political) trap of the objectivist approach to culture, Benedict's second epistemological position. In Anthropology 101, this requires that students think about their own access to power and the privilege that their place in the classroom promises. (This discussion, in turn, usually elicits some students' self-assured contempt for "affirmative action." No longer, for the moment, newly converted relativists, they know what true standards are and who doesn't live up to them.)

Another way out of the trap created by the presupposition that similarity defines community is to consider that culture always makes possible, and indeed gives rise to, metacultural commentary. Here it is useful to remember that anthropology itself is a cultural activity, and anthropological interpretations of cultures contribute to the culture of those being studied, as well as to the culture of those who are the students or analysts. Those professional, scholarly disciplines that study human beings must always, first, engage in conversation (of some sort) with the objects of their study and, second, erect a second-order language to analyze those conversations. But such second-order languages are also a feature of all culture; indeed, they are one variety of what Boas termed "secondary reasoning" (1911b:67; see also Urban 2001). All cultural activities arise out of the tension between the unconscious categories that make thought possible and consciously articulated attempts to "get at" those categories, or to find them in the world, or to organize the world in terms of them. Such attempts may be more or less "rational," but they must always be "rationalizing," precisely to the degree that humans must draw on unconscious cultural categories to think at all (Handler 2004). So the conventional notion that communities are composed of people who share the same way of thinking can never account for the fact that, as people think, they sometimes think about thinking and, in so doing, change their relationship to their conventional way of thinking.

Here, then, is one final lesson that I try to teach students in Anthropology 101. They start with a naive belief that disciplines study the world in objective fashion and, moreover, that the disciplinary division of labor that they find in the university is merely a function of the structure of reality. Anthropology 101 tries to teach them not only that disciplines are historical precipitates but also that disciplinary activities are part of the very world that social scientists and humanists study. There is no value-free language to analyze human values. The students learn, then, not only that the social-evolutionary, progressivist assumptions that they brought into the classroom can be challenged but also that they have both the responsibility and the possibility to challenge a world of preconceptions. Benedict's first epistemological position, in which her anthropological voice cannot resist engaging critically with the common sense of her own world, cannot give students the "objectivity" that they think they want. But it can make them "culture conscious," to use Benedict's phrase (1934a:245), and such modes of thought sometimes help them (they tell me) to become wiser, more tolerant citizens.

Observers

The essays collected in this volume speak of teachers and students, ancestors and descendants, all, in one fashion or another, cultural critics and anthropological observers of mass society. The essays speak especially of the Boasian "lineage" of anthropologists, one that derives in my experience from teachers and texts, or, more precisely, from teachers who pointed the way to particular texts, authored perhaps by disciplinary totems or by people the teachers considered to be their ancestors. In any case, I remember Robert Murphy's telling us, his students in a senior seminar for anthropology majors in Columbia College in the spring of 1972, that the department had always been Boas's department and still was Boas's department (see Murphy 1991:65)—this in an era when another teacher in an introductory anthropology course told us that Columbia and Michigan were the best places in the country for the field, because they were the only places that took seriously both ecology and structuralism. (And I still remember the excitement in the department when Levi-Strauss came to deliver a lecture at Barnard College, one ostensibly uniting ecological and structural approaches, that Marvin Harris boycotted [Levi-Strauss 1972].)

At that stage of my education, I had little understanding of the meaning of all this—of theoretical schools and disputes and of the peculiar relevance that anthropologists (more than the practitioners of most other scholarly disciplines, as far as I can tell) attach to their intellectual genealogy. I knew little at all about the anthropology department at the University of Chicago, other than that it was considered to be an excellent department, when I began the doctoral program there in the fall of 1973. At Chicago, David Schneider and George Stocking, the teachers I consider my mentors, directed me (sometimes indirectly) to the anthropologists and cultural critics who are the subjects of this book.

Schneider admired the work of Louis Dumont. Dumont's approach to modern ideology (in particular, to individualism and nationalism) became crucial to my study of Quebecois nationalism (at the time, my dissertation topic). More to the point of this book, through Dumont I came to Alexis de Tocqueville and his monumental *Democracy in America* (hereafter, *Democracy*). I do not know why Tocqueville had not been included in the iterations of the various great-books courses that I had taken at Columbia, but, in any case, Schneider gave me a photocopy of Dumont's 1965 essay "'The Individual' in Two Types of Society," taken from *Contributions to Indian Sociology*. The original publication included introductory remarks and a chapter from *Democracy*, "Of Individualism in Democratic Countries," both of which were omitted from later republications of the essay (Dumont 1983, 1986). In the 1965 presentation, Dumont justified his reproduction of Tocqueville's chapter in the following words: "The parallelism is so close between the comparison we shall attempt [between Indian and modern ideologies] and that provided by one of our greatest forebears, Alexis de Tocqueville, of aristocratic and democratic society, that it seems fitting to reproduce a short chapter of his as an opening salute or invocation" (1965:9).

Tocqueville proved helpful to me in thinking through the problem of nationalist culture theory, but I drew less on him than on Dumont. Only much later, when I began to teach *Democracy*, did I come to appreciate the theoretical leverage that Tocqueville can offer us today. I now find it almost impossible to teach a course without including Tocqueville on the reading list. For graduate students, I select chapters from *Democracy* that can be brought to bear on particular theoretical problems, but I ask the hundreds of undergraduates to whom I regularly teach introductory anthropology to read most of the second volume as a superb ethnography of American culture. When I ask those undergraduates whether any has read *Democracy*, a few raise their hands. Typically, their acquaintance with Tocqueville will have come from government classes, at either the high school or college level, or perhaps from a college course in American studies.

Despite the influence of Dumont, I do not find that anthropologists today routinely draw on Tocqueville. They have left him pretty much to the political theorists, who typically have read Tocqueville as a traditional political philosopher whose closest ancestors are Pascal, Montesquieu, and Rousseau (Aron 1965: 242–44; Ceaser 1990:68; Cohler 1988:170–90; Mansfield and Winthrop 2000:xxx–xxxix), all members of a wide-ranging lineage whose apical ancestors are Plato and Aristotle. In a concise discussion of "traditional political science" (which "began with Plato and Aristotle . . . and which continued until well into this century"), James Ceaser notes that the concern of such people as Tocqueville and Montesquieu for "historical sociology" distinguishes these "traditional" philosophers from practitioners of a modern political science devoted to "the elaboration of actual causal connections among social phenomena" (1990:41–43, 71). It is not that Tocqueville was not interested in causality; he was. But he undertook discussions of causality in relationship to specific historical sequences and specific social and cultural formations; for the most part, he did not formulate abstract social-scientific laws understood to be universally valid (see chapter 1).

Recent interpretations of Tocqueville have paid more attention than earlier readings to his comparative method and, especially, the epistemological assumptions that derive from it. (See, above all, Sheldon Wolin's superb *Tocqueville between Two Worlds* [2001].) As Dumont noted in the passage quoted earlier, his anthropologically comparative study of Indian and modern ideologies (Dumont 1977, 1986, 1994) can find a great precursor in *Democracy*. And Boasian anthropology can do the same. Whether that makes Tocqueville a Boasian, or Boasians Tocquevillians, will depend on those who write and rewrite disciplinary genealogies (e.g., Darnell 2001). For my present purpose, it is enough to explore the similarities and differences in the ways that Tocqueville and the Boasians about whom I write—Boas himself, Edward Sapir, Ruth Benedict, Margaret Mead, Jules Henry—approach the general problem of cross-cultural translation and the particular puzzle that modern mass society presents to anthropological interpretation.

The Boasian possibilities of my lineage, suggested by Murphy, Abraham Rosman, and Paula Rubel at Columbia and Barnard, became more compelling to me at Chicago. While Schneider's admiration for Dumont stemmed in part from the interest of both in "modern ideology," Dumont represented one strand of a broader French structuralism that catalyzed great debates in North American anthropology departments beginning in the mid-1960s (Murphy 1971; Sahlins 1976). (Dumont was of special interest as well to the South Asianists in the Chicago department, for obvious reasons.) In both my undergraduate and graduate department, grand theoretical battles were waged about idealism and materialism (to use two of the most general terms available to sort out the various "isms" of the time), leading to what some of us who became Boasians called "symbolic anthropology" and, a bit later, "interpretive anthropology" (Handler 1997). The anthropologists who promoted a renewed symbolic anthropology may or may not have called themselves Boasians, and certainly many of them would have considered themselves connected to the culture concept most proximately through the sociologist Talcott Parsons and thus through the Weberian strand of that same neo-Kantian idealism that had nurtured Boas a generation before Weber wrote *The Protestant Epic* (Bunzl 1996:52–63). Nevertheless, they drew explicitly (even when critically) on such ancestors as Boas, Benedict, Mead, Sapir, and Alfred Kroeber. Schneider, for example, admired Benedict and directed me as well to Kroeber, whom he had known at Harvard and Berkeley (Schneider 1968:1; 1995:78–83).[4]

But my personal connection to the Boasian anthropologists derives as

4. It was also an oblique reference in Schneider's *American Kinship* (1968:109) that prompted me to take note of Henry's *Culture against Man* (1963).

much from George Stocking as it does from Schneider. Stocking accomplished the difficult feat of profoundly affecting a discipline (anthropology) in which he was not trained and to which he does not consider himself to belong (other than in an honorary fashion). He did this by transforming anthropologists' long-standing interest in their intellectual ancestors into a flourishing subdiscipline, called history of anthropology, which has itself had a significant effect on theoretical discussions within the field (Yelvington 2003; also see chapter 8). As a beginning graduate student, I found that Stocking's essays on Boas (gathered in Stocking 1968) made anthropological ideas and practices accessible to me more readily than did most anthropological writing by anthropologists. But I was drafted to become a Boasian, or chose to graft myself onto my version of the lineage, as a consequence of Stocking's seminar in the history of anthropology, which I took in the fall 1975 term. The topic of the seminar was anthropology between the world wars (Stocking 1976), and each student was assigned, or chose, a prominent anthropologist of the period to represent to the class. I ended up with Sapir, and that semester read most of his oeuvre (other than his considerable body of technical linguistic work).

Sapir is one of the few anthropologists whom people in the field call a genius, probably because virtuoso linguistic skill strikes us as both scientific and artistic in a way that, say, skill in writing ethnographies (or, better yet, the skill in human relationships that allows us to write ethnographies) does not. In any case, reading Sapir for me was like reading Jane Austen or George Eliot: readers experience, or are tricked into thinking that they experience, a direct connection to the narrator or author—to a keen mind that seems to be speaking directly to them. The seminar paper that I wrote in response to my conversation with Sapir concerned the connection of his writings on art and literature to his work in culture theory (see chapter 2).

Alongside Sapir's essays on aesthetics were essays in social and cultural criticism. In all this work, as in his work on anthropological culture theory, Sapir was concerned with "culture, genuine and spurious" (1924a) and especially with the social and cultural grounding of individual self-expression. Such concerns place him not only in a grand tradition of modernist social science but also in a centuries-old tradition of European social philosophy. Although Tocqueville, too, must be read in relationship to the various strands of that tradition, in this book I begin with him and move to the Boasians. Because Tocqueville straddled the divide between "traditional" Europe and "modernity" in a way that the first generations of professional social scientists who followed him did not, Tocqueville, I will argue, was able to provide a more radical critique of Western individualism than most of the numerous and celebrated twentieth-century critics of mass society—among whom I include the Boasians I write about here. The Boasian anthropologists drew on their research among and knowledge of non-Western peoples to distance themselves from modernist values, but individual self-expression remained a foundational value for the Boasians, and in their culture theories, in a way that it was not for Tocqueville. Thus, although Tocqueville can sometimes seem naive or dated from the perspective of Boasian cultural relativism—especially when he discusses Native Americans, whom he regarded as representing a barbarism that was inferior to European civilization and hence destined to disappear—his reading of modernity in some sense encompasses almost all modernist social science theory, including that of Boas and his students.

The essays drawn together in this book start with Tocqueville, move on to the Boasians as critics, or observers, of mass society, and pursue these issues into the present by bringing cultural studies, in the work of Richard Hoggart and Raymond Williams, into dialogue with the Boasian tradition. I have used the term "mass society" instead of "American society" even though most of the works that I discuss focus on the United States. The practical reason for this is to include Hoggart and Williams, whose work is focused on England. But "mass society" is, I think, theoretically justifiable in this case. It suggests a fundamental feature of modern democracies, one of concern to the writers I discuss: the horizontal aggregation of large numbers of people who, however disparate in fortune, are presumed to be equal as individuals and who, as a result of their equality and individuality, are at once uniquely valued and anonymously lumped (or "massed") together. Such equality and individualism struck Tocqueville as central to American democracy and to democracy in general, for he was as interested in social types and theoretical models as he was in specific nations like the United States, England, and France. The same can be said of Sapir, Benedict, Mead, and Henry. From one point of view, of course, those American anthropologists sometimes conflate "America" and "mass society" or "modern society" (another term I could have chosen). On the other hand, all the authors considered here belong to a critical tradition, stemming from individualism and modernity, that has never been confined within the borders of particular nation-states, even when particular authors focus their attention on their country of residence.

A related problem, in my analysis and in the works of these authors, is that a concept like "mass society" makes it easy to neglect "internal" cultural variation. Although the authors discussed here attend at times to issues of race, gender, and class, those are not their main concern, at least not in the works that I have chosen to analyze (for an extensive critique of Mead in this regard, see di Leonardo 1998:163–98). Yet I find their work useful nonetheless—indeed, even crucial to an understanding of "difference"—precisely because modern conceptions of social and cultural difference are constructed from individualistic premises (as Guillory's work, discussed earlier, shows). Thus an understanding of individualism—of the hegemonic cultural principles of "mass," or "modern," societies—is a prerequisite for a critique of the politics of difference in the contemporary world. Another way to say this is to ask readers to suspend their disbelief: the authors considered sometimes traffic in generalizations that may be too broad. But the fact that their interpretations do not apply as widely as they think does not mean we cannot learn from them.

A final terminological and conceptual problem concerns the word "observer." The term has become suspect in cultural anthropology since the 1980s because of the positivist connotations of the specialized use of the term to refer to the scientific "gaze" and its results (e.g., "experimental observations"). That is only one among many uses of the word. Concocting the subtitle of this book, *Anthropological Observers of Mass Society*, I found myself drawn back to another use of the verb "to observe" that I recalled from Jane Austen's novels. For example, in a highly charged scene from *Pride and Prejudice*, as Elizabeth Bennett and Mr. Darcy dance together for the first time, she explains to him the rules of conversation at a ball: "Perhaps by and by I may observe that private balls are much pleasanter than public ones" (Austen 1969:91; see Handler and Segal 1990:99). Elizabeth's "observation" is as much a social judgment as a description of fact. Indeed, according to the *Oxford English Dictionary*, more than a century before the scientific meaning of "observe" and "observation" began to congeal, the words were used (as they still are today) to indicate adherence to custom, celebration of religious rites, and worshipful attention. Thus the evaluative overtones of Elizabeth's use of the term suggest approaches to experience that are more frankly "subjective" than the scientific practice of measuring sensory data. To observe is a social and moral activity, and one's observations are by definition value laden. Something of this semantic tension, between objectivity and subjectivity, prompted anthropologists to invent that awkward term "participant-observation." Anthropologists and other cultural critics observe the world around them, but their observations grow out of social relationships and are deeply tinged by a moral sensibility.

If "observer" is a term that anthropologists rarely claim these days, "moralist" might seem even quainter, or less apt, as a term for what we do. Nor does "critic" fare much better, for it suggests, still today, a person who writes reviews of aesthetic (high-cultural) products, that is, a person not fully engaged by the range and diversity of culture as anthropologists understand it. Alternatively, when construed more broadly, "critic" seems related to "moralist," in the case of a social or cultural critic who reflects on, and argues with, common sense across a variety of social domains. Yet it is precisely a moral stance, combined with anthropological understanding, that distinguishes the critics of mass society whom I have chosen to study. My notion of "critics against culture" draws less from recent theoretical attacks on the anthropological culture concept (as in Abu-Lughod's brief [1991] for "writing against culture") than it does from the title of Jules Henry's great moral (and comedic) tract, *Culture against Man* (1963). For Henry, culture was to be understood in terms of both geographic and historical diversity and particularity, but he also considered culture generically, as humankind's adaptive tool (to use the language of the neo-evolutionary synthesis of the 1950s). It was with regard to that latter sense of the term that Henry could write about culture "against" man, that is, about the problems that humans create for themselves as they invent convoluted and troublesome cultural patterns to solve what would seem to be fairly simple human problems. And, taking on his own culture—American culture—in *Culture against Man*, Henry had plenty of room to express the full range of his convictions.

The critics, considered in the essays that follow, who wrote about and against culture were writing about "our" culture, that of contemporary "mass society" and its social practices and philosophies (including its theories about "culture"). If there is an art in my critical analysis of the works of these critics, it is the art of explication de texte, taking apart individual works and connecting their pieces to the pieces of other, related works while at the same time placing the interpreted works in larger social and historical contexts. Not least among my aims is to raise the voices of these critics. It is a privilege to quote from them, and I have done so extensively, both to explicate their arguments and to bring their authorial voices to life for new audiences.

CHAPTER I

Individualism Inside Out

Tocqueville's *Democracy in America*

Democracy in America is a comparative ethnography. Its primary focus is the United States of the 1830s, where Alexis de Tocqueville (1805–1859) traveled as a social and political observer. But it is a *comparative* ethnography because Tocqueville concerns himself, above all, with the nature of a new type of society, "democracy," which he delineated (both theoretically and ethnographically) in opposition to another type of society, "aristocracy." Tocqueville's comparative analysis is at once ideal-typical and historically particular. He is interested in understanding democracy and aristocracy as ideal types (in Weber's sense, that is, as analytic models of social formations as they would be, had they been constructed by rational actors and if they could exist beyond the contingencies of history). At the same time, Tocqueville's observations are drawn from particular historical examples of those two great types. Illustrating, then, the general comparison of democracy and aristocracy, we find an ongoing comparison of three contemporary nations that Tocqueville knew from experience, the United States, England, and France, and that differed, in his analysis, in the historical paths that had led each, in different ways and to different degrees, from aristocracy to democracy. Aristocratic France was a fourth social formation, dying but not dead in Tocqueville's lifetime, of which he had direct experience. Finally, feudal Europe, China, and ancient Greece and Rome provided him with other historically particular examples, known to him from his studies of literature, history, and philosophy.

Tocqueville scholars and biographers have extensively discussed his aristocratic roots (his father was imprisoned during the Terror but lived to be made a count in 1820), his political career, and his nine-month voyage through North America with his friend Gustave de Beaumont (1802–1866) in 1831–32.[1] The "pretext" of their expedition, as Tocqueville put it, was to study American penal institutions, and in 1833 they published their results, *On the Penitentiary System in the United States and Its Application to France* (Mansfield and Winthrop 2000:xl; Wolin 2001:102). But Tocqueville's journey can be seen, as Wolin has argued, though in somewhat different terms, as the classic anthropological rite-de-passage of first fieldwork. "Owing to the contingencies of his genealogy," Wolin notes, "Tocqueville began as an outsider to his own society. He was about to have that status doubly confirmed by his two voyages, one to an alien land, the other the return to a homeland where aristocracy had lost much of its political status" (2001:103). Indeed, Wolin frames his book-length meditation on Tocqueville by noting "that 'theorist' derives from the Greek *theoros*, which was the name for an emissary who traveled on behalf of his city to other cities or societies. . . . Traveling is, of course, an encounter with differences. We might think of Tocqueville as a traveler in time" (5).

That Tocqueville may be said to have traveled "in time" probably corresponds to his own sense of the passing of the aristocratic world and the irresistible emergence of the democratic. The expression nonetheless denies coevalness (Fabian 1983), that is, it mystifies the fact that aristocracy and democracy overlapped in Tocqueville's experience. Indeed, from the perspective of anthropologists, the "culture shock" that Tocqueville experienced, perhaps even courted, must be seen as generative of the remarkably astute cultural consciousness (to use Ruth Benedict's phrase [1934a:249]) that Tocqueville displayed in *Democracy*. He developed his growing cultural consciousness by working in two directions, from the Old World to the New and back. As Eduardo Nolla, editor of a magnificent critical edition of *Democracy*, has suggested, Tocqueville and Beaumont realized almost immediately upon arrival in New York that "their desire to . . . understand American society would require . . . a serious knowledge of French society, which

1. For the itinerary of their voyage, and much other useful material on *Democracy in America*, consult the website of the American studies program at the University of Virginia: http://xroads.virginia.edu/~HYPER/DETOC/TOUR/itin.html. The literature on Tocqueville is vast; in addition to the work of Louis Dumont (cited in chapter 1), I have drawn mainly on the following works: Aron (1968), Bradley (1945), Ceaser (1990), Cohler (1988), Eisenstadt (1988), Jardin (1988), Lamberti (1989), Manent (1994, 1996), Pierson (1938), Schleifer (1980), and Wolin (2001).

they lacked" (Nolla 1990:xxv). Thus, for example, during his American journey Tocqueville wrote to a French friend that what most hindered him in
understanding a particular detail of the American scene was his complete
ignorance of its French counterpart. Nolla points out as well that Tocqueville's brief trips to England in 1833 and 1835, like his longer American
voyage, served as exercises in cultural estrangement that he put to good use:
"If England is not strictly speaking a reference point for the American and
French situations, it was nonetheless one of the keys to understanding
America. England is evoked throughout *Democracy in America*" (xxxv).

Tocqueville scholars have long argued about the continuity between the
first and second volumes of *Democracy*, published in 1835 and 1840, respectively (Drescher 1988; Richter 1988). The most recent American translators
see the first volume as a "lively picturing of America" and the second as
a "somber analysis of democracy" (Mansfield and Winthrop 2000:xli).
The lively/somber distinction is a version of an interpretive dispute about
whether Tocqueville was a friend or foe of democracy, optimistic or pessimistic about its future, liberal or conservative in his political orientation.
In his foreword to the second volume, Tocqueville himself described its
focus as "civil society," or American "sentiments and opinions," as opposed
to the focus of the first volume on "the political world" of "laws and political mores" (2:399).[2] Here I will not frame the discussion in the dichotomous
terms employed by Tocqueville scholars but will take Tocqueville more or
less at his word. For my purposes, the more interesting volume is the second, not because it is more ethnographic than the first (it isn't—both make
use of the telling vignette) but because its focus is, indeed, what Tocqueville calls mores and what anthropologists call culture (see Wolin 2001:129).

Democracy is usually presented today as a two-volume work bound as
one book. Each volume is divided into "parts"—two in the first volume
and four in the second—and the parts are divided into chapters. The two
parts of the first volume are untitled, but the four parts of the second are
titled "Influence of Democracy on Intellectual Movement in the United
States," "Influence of Democracy on the Sentiments of the Americans,"
"Influence of Democracy on Mores Properly So-Called," and "On the Influence That Democratic Ideas and Sentiments Exert on Political Society."

2. Citations to *Democracy* are to the Mansfield and Winthrop translation (Tocqueville 2000). I have drawn extensively on Nolla's critical edition (Tocqueville 1990)
and an earlier English translation by Henry Reeve (Tocqueville 1945). All translations
from Nolla's edition are mine.

(Taken together, those titles constitute a twentieth-century definition of "culture," including patterns of thought, feeling, practice, and sociopolitical organization, and the mutual influences of all these on one another.) The first volume has eighteen chapters, and many are divided into titled sections (for instance, chapter 8 of part 1, "On the Federal Constitution," is divided into twenty-three sections, on such topics as "Federal Powers," "Legislative Powers," "Mode of Election," and so on). The four parts of the second volume contain seventy-five short, titled chapters, each consisting of a few pages devoted to particular topics ("On the Literary Industry," "On the Taste for Material Well-being in America," "Education of Girls in the United States," and so on).

Many chapters in the second volume are structured in terms of a comparison: in an aristocracy, Tocqueville tells his readers, literature, or religion, or family, or . . . , is organized in one way, but in a democracy, the phenomenon in question looks different. In such comparisons, Tocqueville relies only rarely on universalistic definitions. Although he occasionally posits apparent universals such as "natural" family bonds (2:561), his delineations of aristocratic and democratic social and cultural forms emerge, as it were, from the process of comparison itself. Democratic "culture traits" come into view, in *Democracy*, only in contrast to their aristocratic analogues and vice versa (see Wolin 2001:235). The work has, as a result, a back-and-forth rhetorical movement (and a deep relativistic epistemology) that should be more than familiar to anthropologists.

The Uses of Abstraction

The nineteenth-century social theorists who figure as ancestors for anthropology, sociology, and political science—Marx, Weber, Durkheim—all wrote about religion, but none, so far as I know, includes his notion of God's vision among his comparative reference points. Tocqueville does. A central component of democratic culture, in his analysis, is the affinity of its people for "general ideas," or categories and abstractions. Tocqueville argues that members of democratic cultures are more prone than those of aristocratic cultures to make use of such ideas. But, as a good student of the French Enlightenment, with its abiding concern for theories of language and thought (Rosenfeld 2001), Tocqueville knew that "general ideas" are more than a trait of a particular type of culture, for all human thought depends on them. And he sees this—or asks his reader to see it—by comparing human thinking to the workings of the divine mind:

God does not ponder the human race in general. At a single glance he sees
separately all of the beings of which humanity is composed, and he perceives
each of them with the similarities that bring [each one] closer to all and the
differences that isolate [each one] from [everyone else].

God therefore has no need of general ideas; that is to say, he never feels
the necessity of enclosing a very great number of analogous objects under the
same form so as to think about them more conveniently. (2:411)

"It is not so with man," Tocqueville continues. The finite human mind
cannot control the infinite detail that reality presents: to attempt to com-
prehend "all the particular cases that strike it" would overwhelm it and
make thought impossible. Thus must humans have recourse to general
ideas: noting "superficial" resemblances among objects, they group or clas-
sify them under "the same name." For Tocqueville, this reliance on general
ideas is at once a weakness and a strength, a sign of human "insufficiency"
and ingenuity: "General ideas are admirable in that they permit the human
mind to bring rapid judgments to a great number of objects at one time;
but on the other hand, they never provide it with anything but incomplete
notions, and they always make it lose in exactness what they give it in
extent" (2:411). Indeed, Tocqueville has clearly in mind the necessary gap
between word and object, thought and the world, that many twentieth-
century semiotic theorists (including the Boasians) have considered central
to the human condition: "Man is uncovered enough to perceive something
of himself and veiled enough so that the rest is sunk in impenetrable darkness, into which he plunges constantly and always in vain" (2:462–63). Or,
as he put it in a discarded passage, "Men grasp fragments of the truth, but
never truth itself. This being admitted, it follows that any man who presents a complete and absolute [theoretical] system, by that fact alone . . .
is almost certainly in a state of error" (1990, vol. 2:20, n. f).

On the one hand, then, with its reliance on general ideas, the human
mind is capable only of flawed, incomplete knowledge. Moreover, people
are prone to rest content with easily acquired generalizations, those "born
of a first rapid effort of the mind" that "lead only to very superficial . . .
notions" (2:414). (As Sapir once put it, "It is almost as though at some
period in the past the unconscious mind of the race had made a hasty
inventory of experience, committed itself to a premature classification that
allowed of no revision, and saddled the inheritors of its language with
a science that they no longer quite believed in nor had the strength to

overthrow" [1921a:100].) On the other hand, general ideas make learning, and the accumulation of knowledge, or "enlightenment," possible. Starting, therefore, with inexact abstractions, humans explore the world and discover "new facts" and "particular truths" (2:411). The accumulation of such knowledge leads to more comprehensive general ideas, or theories, and these, Tocqueville seems to think, become better or truer as civilization progresses. (Boas takes up a similar argument in his sketch of the history of anthropology, beginning with the too-grand abstractions of evolutionism that his historical ethnology had to overcome in order for anthropology to progress: "The brilliant theories in which the whole range of problems of a science appears simple . . . have always preceded the periods of steady empirical work which makes necessary a complete revision of the original theories, and leads . . . to a more strictly inductive attack of the ultimate problems" [1904:34].)

For Tocqueville, the accumulation of knowledge is a social process, and this in several senses. First, humans are social creatures, or, to rephrase it with respect to the present topic, the individual human mind can develop only by drawing on a given cultural heritage: "There is no philosopher in the world so great that he does not believe a million things on faith in others or does not suppose many more truths than he establishes" (2:408). Second, "as societies age," as he puts it, people develop bodies of knowledge that lead to an ever-greater understanding of those aspects of reality that they examine in systematic fashion. Practice and theory interact and correct one another. But third, and most interesting for the project of comparative culture theory, Tocqueville argues that beyond the need that all humans have for general ideas, democratic culture encourages people to make wider use of such abstractions than other kinds of culture, especially the aristocratic. To understand his argument, we need to look first at his analysis of individualism as a cultural system.

Culture, Individualism, and Authority

Tocqueville does not use the word "culture," but among the many definitions of culture that Kroeber and Kluckhohn (1952) collected fifty years ago, Tocqueville's definition of "mores" would fit easily: "the whole moral and intellectual state of a people." More fully, he defines "mores properly so-called" as "habits of the heart," by which he understands such things as sexual morality, the tenor of family life, and manners. But beyond this narrow use of the term, Tocqueville intends it to refer to "the different notions that men possess, . . . the various opinions that are current in their midst, and . . . the sum of ideas of which the habits of the mind are formed" (2:275).

Following Rousseau and Montesquieu (Richter 1970:90–91), Tocqueville considered mores, or culture, to be first among several "principal causes" underpinning the "maintenance" or stability of democratic society in the United States—more powerful than "accidental or providential causes," such as the geographic isolation and natural resources of North America, and more powerful than democratic laws and political institutions themselves (1:264–65). This is a typical formulation for Tocqueville, the historical particularist. Again and again in *Democracy,* Tocqueville points out that cultural causality is always multifaceted and contingent: the Americans, for example, share much of the cultural heritage of the English, but the two peoples differ in their geographic environments and "social states" (2:541), and one cannot expect a common culture to generate identical social forms in differing circumstances. Similarly, the French and the Americans share egalitarian political ideals, but the French enacted those ideals only after a violent revolution, whereas American society, Tocqueville thought, was born already embracing them—two histories that make all the difference. And, in a sardonic critique of a common variety of monocausal argument, climatic determinism, Tocqueville remarks, "This is getting out of the difficulty [of explaining cultural differences] cheaply, and by this account a globe and a compass would suffice to resolve in an instant one of the most difficult problems that humanity presents" (2:567).

For Tocqueville, individualism is the central cultural fact of the United States, and of democratic societies in general (the key chapters are in volume 2, pt. 1, chaps. 1–2, and pt. 2, chaps. 1–2). He summarizes the cultural principle of American individualism in a phrase: "In most of the operations of the mind, each American calls only on the individual effort of his reason" (2:403). Americans' appeal to individual reason is simultaneously, and more or less self-consciously, a rejection of traditional authorities, privileges, and relationships:

> To escape from the spirit of system, from the yoke of habits, from family maxims, from class opinions, and, up to a certain point, from national prejudices; to take tradition only as information, and current facts only as a useful study for doing otherwise and better; to seek the reason for things by themselves and in themselves alone, to strive for a result without letting themselves be chained to the means, and to see through the form to the foundation:

these are the principal features that characterize what I shall call the philosophic method of the Americans. (2:403)

This "philosophic method" is, of course, the anthropologist's "culture."
And although Americans can be self-conscious about their rejection of
traditional authorities, they are (like natives everywhere) not particularly
self-conscious of their habits of thought qua cultural system: "America is
therefore the one country in the world where the precepts of Descartes are
least studied and best followed." Tocqueville refers here to Descartes's *Discourse on Method* and a few paragraphs later to Luther, Bacon, and Voltaire,
all of whom contributed to a grand revolution in culture wherein "received
formulas, . . . the empire of traditions, and . . . the authority of the master"
were overturned in favor of "the individual effort" of each person's reason
(2:404). Tocqueville equivocates (as we all do) on which came first, the cultural revolution or the social conditions that made it possible, but in general he sees the two proceeding together: the earlier modern philosophers
propounded their ideas "in a period when men were beginning to be equal
and to resemble each other," but their ideas could become dominant only
as the aristocratic social order gave way to the democratic (2:405; see also
the fragments and discarded passages of notes m–s in Tocqueville 1990,
vol. 2:15–17).

Although the rejection of authority is a central principle of American
culture, Tocqueville argues (as I noted in the discussion of "general ideas")
that humans depend on socially transmitted knowledge. In his terms, such
implicit cultural knowledge constituted an "authority": "It is always necessary . . . that we encounter authority somewhere in the intellectual and moral
world. . . . Individual independence can be more or less great; it cannot be
boundless. Thus, the question is not that of knowing whether an intellectual authority exists in democratic centuries, but only where it is deposited
and what its extent will be" (2:408). And Tocqueville finds democratic
authority, in a paradox that the natives rarely appreciate, in subservience to
mass, or public, "opinion." Thus the consequences of the privileging of
individual reason are out of all proportion to the apparent simplicity of the
fundamental cultural principle, nor are those consequences, as Tocqueville
comparatively construes them, those that the natives themselves imagine.
Modern individualists (if I may so call them), from Luther, Bacon, and
Descartes on, imagine that the reasoning individual progressively abandons superstition and approaches truth; Tocqueville, by contrast, sees that

individualism leads to conformity, even totalitarianism. His key formulation comes, as is so often the case in *Democracy*, in a comparison of the structuring of moral authority in the aristocratic and democratic worlds:

> When conditions are unequal and men are not alike, there are some individuals who are very enlightened, very learned, and of very powerful intellect, and a multitude who are very ignorant and very limited. People who live in aristocratic times are therefore . . . brought to take the superior reason of one man or one class as a guide for their opinions, while they are little disposed to recognize the infallibility of the mass.
> The opposite happens in centuries of equality.
> As citizens become more equal and alike, the penchant of each to believe blindly a certain man or class diminishes. The disposition to believe the mass is augmented, and more and more it is opinion that leads the world. (2:409)

Developing further the paradoxical implications of this cultural formation, Tocqueville argues (here, and repeatedly in *Democracy*) that the privileging of individual authority leads to the insignificance of the individual and to each individual's sense of impotence. All individuals, as individuals, are in theory empowered, but, in a mass society of equal citizens, no one has any more standing than anyone else, and, further, each person is insignificant in comparison to the mass: "When the man who lives in democratic countries compares himself individually to all those who surround him, he feels with pride that he is the equal of each of them; but when he comes to view the sum of those like him and places himself at the side of this great body, he is immediately overwhelmed by his own insignificance and his weakness" (2:409).

One consequence of the individual's linked autonomy and impotence is the notion of majority rule, which, as Tocqueville construes it, comes naturally to citizens of a democracy: "In times of equality, because of their similarity, men have no faith in one another; but this same similarity gives them an almost unlimited trust in the judgment of the public; for it does not seem plausible to them that when all have the same enlightenment, truth is not found on the side of the greatest number" (2:409). Majority rule is the celebrated (and largely unexamined) consequence of individualism, but uncelebrated, even unacknowledged, is the overwhelming power of public opinion to constrain the apparently free play of individual thought:

The same equality that makes him independent of each of his fellow citizens in particular leaves him isolated and without defense against the action of the greatest number.

The public therefore has a singular power among democratic peoples, the very idea of which aristocratic nations could not conceive. It does not persuade [one] of its beliefs, it imposes them and makes them penetrate souls by a sort of immense pressure of the minds of all on the intellect of each. (2:409)

We must never forget that in Tocqueville's analysis, individualism and what modern citizens see as its positive corollaries—personal independence, choice, majority rule—are indissolubly linked to conformity and the potentially negative power of public opinion. In democracies, as Tocqueville saw it, individuals are at once independent and, because of their independence, weak.

Public Opinion and the Concept of Society

Here I want to open a parenthesis in the discussion of Tocqueville, to make good on my claim that he was able to view democracy from outside modernity in a way that the great, ancestral (to us) social scientists who followed him were not. Tocqueville's description of the workings of public opinion in a democracy is strikingly similar to a commonsense model of society/culture, or, more specifically, the relationship between society/ culture and the individual, that almost all twentieth-century sociology and anthropology presupposes. But there is this crucial difference: Tocqueville sees as culturally specific the relationship of individual and society/culture that we presuppose and hence project as a universal feature of the human condition. Aristocracies do not imagine or structure the world in such terms.

Consider Benedict's *Patterns of Culture* as a paradigmatic statement of this commonsense (and social-scientific) model. The book establishes a model of cultures as socially (nonbiologically) transmitted, aesthetically "patterned" lifeways that are historically "fortuitous" (1934a:5), that emerge and develop over generations, even centuries, and that present individuals with a ready-made world, without which they could not think or function. With her much-discussed use of psychological metaphors, the book treats individual cultures as if they had the structural or aesthetic unity of individual personality formations (although Benedict cautioned her readers not to misinterpret her psychological metaphors as universal cultural types

[78–80, 238]). Only after she presents the general model, and three exquisitely drawn case studies, does she come, in the final chapter, to the
problem of "the individual and the pattern of culture." There she engages
the intractable chicken-and-egg question of the individual and society/
culture, insisting: "Society and the individual are not antagonists" (251).
That modern Americans presuppose such an antagonism is explained by
Benedict as a function of their rejection of the restrictions of government.
But as a "basic philosophical and political notion," the modern presupposition "is naive indeed" (252), because society/culture and the individual
are interdependent:

> Society . . . is never an entity separable from the individuals who compose it.
> No individual can arrive even at the threshold of his potentialities without a
> culture in which he participates. Conversely, no civilization has in it any ele-
> ment which in the last analysis is not the contribution of an individual. Where
> else could any trait come from except from the behaviour of a man or a
> woman or a child? (253)

And not only, she continues, are society and the individual not antagonists, they are mutually reinforcing. This leads to a discussion of her (and
Margaret Mead's) theory of the deviant as the person unluckily born into
a society to which he or she cannot adjust. For our purposes, however, it is
not the deviant but the concept of adjustment itself that is crucial:

> The vast proportion of all individuals who are born into any society always
> and whatever the idiosyncrasies of its institutions assume . . . the behaviour
> dictated by that society. This fact is always interpreted by the carriers of that
> culture as being due to the fact that their particular institutions reflect an
> ultimate and universal sanity. The actual reason is quite different. Most people
> are shaped to the form of their culture because of the enormous malleability
> of their original endowment. They are plastic to the moulding force of the
> society into which they are born. . . . The great mass of individuals take quite
> readily the form that is presented to them. (254–55)

Now, what is this but an image of what Tocqueville describes as the
relationship between mass opinion and the culturally defined individual—
with the difference, of course, that Benedict universalizes the model that
Tocqueville saw as peculiar to modernity? Recall Tocqueville's depiction of

public opinion: "It does not persuade [one] of its beliefs, it imposes them and makes them penetrate souls by a sort of immense pressure of the minds of all on the intellect of each" (2:409). This is Benedict's vision of society "moulding" plastic individuals—society imagined as a disembodied but real and omnipresent force floating somewhere (perhaps, as Kroeber argued [1917], constituting a distinct "superorganic" level of reality) above individual humans even as it marks and constrains them.[3] Tocqueville thought that such a phantasm came naturally to the members of a democratic culture: "Men being equal and weak, people see no individuals who force them to march in the same path. They must therefore imagine a great cause which acts separately but in the same manner on each of them" (1990, vol. 2:25, n. a). And in the second volume of *Democracy*, he gives many examples of such reasoning—with its reifications, personifications, and generalizations—in the art, architecture, literature, historiography, and language of democratic societies.

This brings us back to Tocqueville's notion of the peculiar affinity of democratic culture for "general ideas." In such cultures, people consider themselves equal, and they expect their institutions (governments, laws) and the natural world itself to act uniformly and directly on each of them:

> The man who inhabits democratic countries finds near to him only beings who are almost the same; he therefore cannot consider any part whatsoever of the human species without having his thought enlarge and dilate to embrace the sum. All the truths applicable to himself appear to him to apply equally and in the same manner to each of his fellow citizens and to those like him. Having contracted the habit of general ideas in the one study with which he most occupies himself and which most interests him, he carries this same habit over to all the others, and thus the need to discover common rules for all things, to enclose many objects within the same form, and to explain a collection of facts by a single cause becomes an ardent and often blind passion of the human mind. (2:412–13)

From such habits of mind, we might say, Western social science is born. It is not that Western philosophers before the mid-nineteenth century were

3. Hence Durkheim on collective sentiments: "They dominate us; they are, so to speak, something superhuman, and, at the same time, they bind us to objects which are outside of our temporal life. They appear to us as an echo in us of a force which is foreign to us, and which is superior to that which we are" (1933:100).

not interested in general principles concerning human nature and human communities; they were. But they did not necessarily imagine such principles as real-world forces (like "gravity" and even "society") that simultaneously permeated all aspects of the universe and acted equally on each constituent unit (Cassirer 1932:41). To anthropology, "the science of custom" (Benedict 1934a:1), fell the intractable problem of reconciling global human diversity and the types of uniform causality (either "racial" or "cultural") that science demanded (Geertz 1966).

Civic Associations

Returning to Tocqueville's notion of the necessary link, in democratic culture, between the individual's autonomy and impotence, we come to his famous discussion of civic associations, a discussion that has preoccupied students of American culture ever since (see Bellah et al. 1985; Putnam 2000). Tocqueville remarked upon the extraordinary number of civic associations that flourished in the United States ("civic," that is, above and beyond the political associations spawned by the system of government and party politics).[4] His explanation of the phenomenon was simple: in an aristocracy, "men have no need to unite to act because they are kept very much together," under the control of the feudal lord. In other words, the lord and his dependents constitute "a permanent and obligatory association," ready to undertake the civic projects the lord deems necessary. Such an association, of course, is hierarchical; although it undertakes civic works that may benefit all, those works benefit all unequally—that is, according to their stations. Individuals' interests are not equivalent. In a democracy, by contrast, individuals who are equal but weak in their isolation come together to form associations on the basis of freely chosen self-interests, interests that all members of the association perceive to be equivalent. Tocqueville captures the combination of individuals' isolation and their perceived equivalence of interests in a striking ethnographic vignette about temperance: "The first time I heard it said in the United States that a hundred thousand men

4. Consider some examples compiled by the artist Tom Parker (1984): the National Hot Dog and Sausage Council, Aromatic Red Cedar Closet Lining Manufacturers Association, Council of Societies in Dental Hypnosis, Amputee Shoe and Glove Exchange, National Association of Horseradish Packers, Organization of Advanced Disabled Hobbyists, American Cricket Growers Association, Thermometer Collectors Club of America.

publicly engaged not to make use of strong liquors, the thing appeared to me more amusing than serious, and at first I did not see well why such temperate citizens were not content to drink water within their families [i.e., on their own]." Recovering (or profiting) from culture shock, he came to realize the foundational role of associations in a democracy: once united by common interest, in pursuit of a common goal, individuals are no longer weak, "but a power one sees from afar, whose actions serve as an example; a power that speaks, and to which one listens" (2:492). Associations, we might say, are a form of Dumont's "collective individuals" (Dumont 1970, 1977).

Tocqueville linked his discussion of civic associations to his analysis of newspapers, which he saw less in terms of the free expression of ideas than of the necessity for "mediation" to facilitate the association of weak individuals in a mass society. In this, once again, Tocqueville saw beyond or through the "natives' rationalizations," which are phrased in terms of a celebration of freedom ("freedom of the press"), to the less obvious but arguably more significant organizing, even "disciplining," functions of newspapers. In a penetrating analysis that political science and anthropology rediscovered only in Benedict Anderson's notion of the relationship between "print capitalism" and the "horizontal" solidarity of nation-states (1983), Tocqueville hinted at the totalitarian (or "brain-washing") potential of democratic media. Among isolated and weak democratic citizens, "only a newspaper can come to deposit the same thought in a thousand minds at the same moment. A newspaper is a counselor that one does not need to go seek, but that presents itself of its own accord and speaks to you briefly each day and of common affairs" (2:493).

A newspaper, in short, both *is* and *represents* an association. The total readership of a newspaper *is* an association, defined precisely by the fact (as Anderson depicted it) that each reader independently reads the same material at the same time as all the others, and they do so with some awareness of their participation in this group activity. As Tocqueville puts it, "One can say that it [a newspaper] speaks to each of its readers in the name of all the others," and, he adds, "It carries them along the more easily as individuals are weaker" (2:495). We can also say that the newspaper *represents* an association, an interest group, founded for a particular purpose and held together, in part, by the mediation of the newspaper itself. In one sense, the "local" newspaper represents communities (villages, towns, neighborhoods, cities) all across the United States. But "newsletters" also represent and hold together the myriad civic associations that Tocqueville noted, as Erving Goffman suggested in his brilliant book, *Stigma* ("often those with a particular stigma sponsor a publication of some kind. . . . No matter how small and how badly off a particular category is, the viewpoint of its members is likely to be given public presentation of some kind. It can thus be said that Americans who are stigmatized tend to live in a literarily-defined world" [1963:25]).

In addition to the totalitarian overtones of newspapers (dropping "the same thought in a thousand minds at the same moment"), Tocqueville saw potential dangers in government itself as the most permanent and powerful of all associations in a democratic society. In a brilliant analysis of the interaction of citizens' interest groups and government growth, he went a long way to explain one of the contemporary paradoxes of American politics, wherein conservative opponents of "big government" nonetheless preside over constant governmental expansion. As Tocqueville saw it, citizens are ceaselessly forming new interest groups to pursue particular goals. While they abjure government aid as a general rule, they seek it on behalf of their own cause. Such interest groups are temporary, but government "endures" and even "increases its prerogatives" as it takes on projects that vital but ephemeral interest groups initiate (2:644).

Indeed, as Tocqueville pointed out, despite Americans' suspicion of government aid and activity, the structure of democratic society, an agglomeration of isolated, equivalent individuals, makes it "natural" for them to accept the reality of a single, great power hovering above them, whether they imagine such a power as "society," "government," or "the nation":

> The idea of secondary powers, placed between sovereign and subjects, naturally presented itself to the imagination of aristocratic peoples. . . . This same idea is naturally absent from the minds of men in centuries of equality . . . whereas they conceive, so to speak without thinking about it, the idea of a lone central power that leads all citizens by itself. (2:640)

When they imagine that hovering power as their government, they demand of it "uniformity of legislation" (2:641), that is, they demand that the laws apply equally to all individuals (no matter how inadequate such a practice might be, given the different needs and situations of people). When they imagine that hovering reality as the nation itself, they thrill to see their own features reproduced and magnified in the collective individual, as Tocqueville suggests in his analysis of the "sources of poetry in democratic nations." Given the equivalence of individuals, he argues, when people see themselves, they see "all the others" as well. Moreover, the insignificance of any one of these equivalent individuals makes each an unlikely subject for poetry. But poets in democratic societies are drawn to "the nation itself," which encompasses all the equivalent human individuals who compose it: "The similarity of all individuals . . . permits poets to include all of them in the same image and finally to consider the people itself" (2:460–1). Thus the grandest association of all, the people as a nation—as a collective individual and a collection of individuals (Dumont 1970, 1977)—comes into view.

The Culture of Aristocracy

If Tocqueville helps us to see that our social-scientific and commonsense models of the individual in relation to society and nation are peculiar to modern, egalitarian democracies, what can we learn from his depiction of the corresponding model in aristocracies?

Tocqueville's model of aristocracy rests on an idea that modern individualists might find paradoxical. In an aristocracy, people are unlike (there are vast differences, socially and religiously legitimated, among rich and poor, noble and commoner, master, servant, slave), but they are tightly linked in relationships of hierarchical dependence. Moreover, people are not individuals, not, at least, in the democratic sense. Rather, superiors "encompass" inferiors, to use Dumont's term (1977:53), and thus the latter are (from the modern perspective) less than complete independent entities, while the former are greater than such entities.

Tocqueville stresses that aristocracies are divided into a multitude of distinct classes, guilds, and local groups. Within such communities there is cultural commonality, but beyond them there is both difference and an expectation of it: "In an aristocratic people each caste has its own opinions, sentiments, rights, mores, and separate existence. Thus the men who compose it do not resemble everyone else; they do not have the same manner of thinking or of feeling, and they scarcely believe themselves to be a part of the same humanity" (2:535; on artisan guilds, see 2:439). "In addition," Tocqueville argues, "aristocratic institutions have the effect of binding each man tightly to several of his fellow citizens." People "perceive" society to be a hierarchy. They are always aware that there are others beneath them of whom they can expect "cooperation," and others above them whose "protection" they need (2:483).

Morever, people living in aristocratic times do not think in terms of an abstract humanity, or the human race. They owe service to particular socially constituted beings, not to humankind in general; to empirical individuals, certainly, but not to individuals whom they conceptualize as embodiments of "man": "It was not to a man that one believed oneself bound to lend support; it was to a vassal or a lord" (2:536).

The implications of hierarchical dependence are spelled out in a remarkable chapter, "How Democracy Modifies the Relations of Servant and Master." There Tocqueville argues that, on the one hand, aristocratic masters and servants have, as it were, different cultures. They "have no natural resemblance between them; . . . on the contrary, fortune, education, opinions, and rights place them at an immense distance on the scale of beings" (2:548). On the other hand, these separate cultures are structured by the same values concerning hierarchy: "They are two societies superimposed on one another, always distinct, but regulated by analogous principles" (2:546). Thus there is a social hierarchy of servants, coupled to a set of values, that parallels or mimics that of the masters: "These men whose destiny is to obey undoubtedly do not understand glory, virtue, honesty, or honor in the same manner as the masters. But they have made for themselves a glory, virtues, and an honesty of servants, and they conceive . . . a sort of servile honor" (2:547). Moreover, masters and servants are bound together over the generations: "Not only are there hereditary families of valets as well as . . . of masters, . . . the same families of valets are settled for several generations beside the same families of masters." Thus "time binds them together . . . and however different they may be, they assimilate." They become, in short, "a community of memories" (2:548).

Tocqueville goes on to give a convincing account of the way in which superiors are thought, in aristocracies, to encompass inferiors:

> Among aristocratic peoples, the master therefore comes to view his servants as an inferior and secondary part of himself, and he often interests himself in their lot by a final effort of selfishness.
>
> For their part, servants are not far from considering themselves from the same point of view, and they sometimes identify themselves with the person of the master in such a way that they finally become his accessory in their own eyes as in his. . . .
>
> In this extremity, the servant is in the end uninterested in himself; he becomes detached from himself; in a way he deserts himself, or rather he

transports himself entirely to his master; there he creates an imaginary personality for himself. (2:548)

The notion of a person "uninterested in himself" is striking, especially given the importance that Tocqueville attributes to self-interest as a motive in democratic cultures. The contrast between this hierarchical world and democratic egalitarianism could not be clearer. In an aristocracy, there is little sense of a common humanity and no presumption that all human individuals are equal, in the sense of embodiments of the same human nature, partaking of the same human condition. A religiously sanctioned vision of cosmic hierarchy assigns authority to certain highly ranked beings (kings, nobles, priests), and the opinions of inferiors are neither valorized nor counted (aggregated); "public opinion" is unknown. People differ along axes of rank and locale, but sociopolitical integration grows out of the hierarchical organization of difference and, indeed, out of the encompassment of inferiors by superiors.

In Tocqueville's aristocracy, people are not driven (as are the citizens of democracies) by materialism, social mobility, or a sense of linear time. Although the upper ranks may enjoy considerable material luxury, they do so by virtue of birth. They do not live in dread of losing their wealth, and they do not conceive of themselves as pursuing it: "Material well-being is . . . not the goal of life for them; it is a manner of living" (2:506). Similarly, the poor, whose life conditions may be wretched, do not imagine themselves bettering their lot: "In nations where the aristocracy dominates society and holds it immobile, the people in the end become habituated to poverty. . . . [They] do not think about [material well-being] because they despair of acquiring it and because they are not familiar enough with it to desire it" (2:507).

In sum, aristocracies are "immobile." Moreover, Tocqueville suggests that they imagine time, too, as immobile, or perhaps that time is less important to them than the connections between generations and, ultimately, those between this world and the next. In the upper ranks, "families remain in the same state for centuries, and often in the same place. That renders all generations so to speak contemporaries. A man almost always knows his ancestors and respects them; he believes he already perceives his great-grandsons and he loves them" (2:483). And among the lower orders, where people have little chance to improve their fortunes, "the imagination . . . is thrown back upon the other world" (2:507).

The Pursuit of Happiness

The restlessness of Americans and their constant, worried movements (both across the continent and up and down the ladder of poverty and wealth) struck Tocqueville as much as anything he saw in the United States: "All privileges being destroyed, ranks are mixed and all men are constantly falling and rising on the social scale" (2:440). Closely linked to this social mobility was American materialism, the pursuit of wealth and "well-being." Individualism and materialism are inextricable in his analysis, and as he composed the second volume of *Democracy*, he wavered as to which to present first: "Perhaps," he wrote in a note to himself, "I should begin the entire book by the chapters on individualism and on the taste for material pleasures. Almost everything follows from there" (1990, vol. 2:13, n. a).

Materialism, then, like individualism, is for Tocqueville an irreducible cultural fact of American democracy. In an aristocratic society, as we have seen, social action is not consistently motivated by the desire to achieve material well-being: superiors presuppose their possession of wealth, and inferiors do not aspire to it. In a democracy, by contrast, people "discover ... that nothing limits or fixes them and forces them to content themselves with their present fortune" (2:431). There ensues a mad scramble for wealth, a restless, unhappy pursuit of happiness: "Love of well-being has become the national and dominant taste; the great current of human passions bears from this direction; it carries everything along in its course." Moreover, Tocqueville emphasizes that all Americans, rich and poor alike, participate in this passion:

> When ... ranks are confused and privileges destroyed ... the longing to acquire well-being presents itself to the imagination of the poor man, and the fear of losing it, to the mind of the rich. A multitude of mediocre fortunes is established. Those who possess them have enough material enjoyments to conceive the taste for these enjoyments and not enough to be content with them. They never get them except with effort, and they indulge in them only while trembling. (2:507)

And, in a remarkable passage that prefigures both contemporary "career" mobility and the twentieth-century vacation, he gives a haunting portrait of the inability of Americans to stay in one spot, to rest content with what they have:

In the United States, a man carefully builds a dwelling in which to pass his declining years, and he sells it while the roof is being laid; he plants a garden and he rents it out just as he was going to taste its fruits; he clears a field and he leaves to others the care of harvesting its crops. He embraces a profession and quits it. . . . And when toward the end of a year filled with work some leisure still remains to him, he carries his restive curiosity here and there within the vast limits of the United States. He will thus go five hundred leagues in a few days in order better to distract himself from his happiness.

Death finally comes, and it stops him before he has grown weary of this useless pursuit of a complete felicity that always flees from him. (2:512)

Linked to such restlessness, as Tocqueville sees it, is an unreasonable idea of what he calls "the indefinite perfectibility of man." Aristocracies are relatively immobile societies; they can imagine incremental "improvement" in worldly conditions, but, given human imperfection, they do not envision "change." In democracies, by contrast, "continual changes . . . pass at each instant before the eyes of each man," and people are thus led to conceive "the image of an ideal and always fugitive perfection" (2:427). Tocqueville depicts this as a deep-seated cultural belief, presupposed by Americans and thus invisible to them but nonetheless "prodigious" in its "influence" on their actions:

I meet an American sailor and I ask him why his country's vessels are built to last a short time, and he replies to me without hesitation that the art of navigation makes such rapid progress daily that the most beautiful ship would soon become almost useless if its existence were prolonged beyond a few years.

In these words pronounced at random by a coarse man concerning a particular fact I perceive the general and systematic idea according to which a great people conducts all things. (2:428)

Americans' belief in indefinite perfectibility is coupled to their sense of time. The sense of cosmic hierarchy and time that Tocqueville attributes to people in an aristocracy—the contemporaneousness, as it were, of people with their ancestors and descendants—is little felt in democracies. In search of the next product, the next invention, the next career, the next residence, the citizens of a democracy are restless and oriented to the future. But theirs is a near-sighted vision of a short-term future. American democracy, with its individualism and materialism, leads people to shut themselves up in their own little worlds: "It tends to isolate them from one another and to bring each of them to be occupied with himself alone." Worse, "it opens their souls excessively to the love of material enjoyments" (2:419). Thus Tocqueville argues that religion is a crucial institution in democracies to counter the excessive narrowness of their people's vision.

For Tocqueville, the religious motivations of the American founders, and the subsequent deep religiosity of American culture, are among the most important of the historical contingencies that contribute to the "maintenance" (the success, health, or functioning, in other metaphors) of democracy in North America. His analysis of religion prefigures Weber more than Durkheim: for Tocqueville, the social utility of religion derives not merely from any impetus it may lend to common action or to any effects it may have on social solidarity. Rather, religion is useful to society because it provides humans with meaningful coherence on precisely those issues where they most need guidance:

> There is almost no human action, however particular one supposes it, that does not arise from a very general idea that men have conceived of God, of his relations with the human race, of the nature of their souls, and of their duties toward those like them. One cannot keep these ideas from being the common source from which all the rest flow. (2:417)

He goes on to argue that religion in the United States (unlike state religions in Europe) is socially effective because it remains apart from politics and government. Religion combats Americans' narrowed vision, but, confined within its own domain, it does not intrude on the free play of the economic and political domains.

Consumer Culture

Tocqueville traces the effects of the American coupling of individualism and materialism across the range of domains of what we would today call consumer culture. The key arguments are articulated in a chapter entitled "In What Spirit the Americans Cultivate the Arts" (vol. 2, pt. 1, chap. 11) that concerns not simply high-cultural "arts" (such as literature and theater, which he discusses in subsequent chapters) but "artisanship," or the mass production of consumer goods. Aristocracies do not have free markets; the use, consumption, and display of goods are at once regulated by, and an index of, hierarchical social distinctions. Artisans produce customarily defined goods for a specified, and small, group of consumers. They do not think to expand their market, nor have they any motivation to discover short-cuts in the production process.

In democracies, by contrast, both consumers and producers "dream only of the means of changing their fortune or of increasing it," and thus "every new method that leads to wealth by a shorter path, every machine that shortens work, every instrument that diminishes the costs of production . . . seems to be the most magnificent effort of human intelligence" (2:436). This leads in particular to the mass marketing of what we might call "cheap imitations":

> Artisans who live in democratic centuries not only seek to put their useful products within the reach of all citizens, they also strive to give all their products brilliant qualities that they do not have.
>
> In the confusion of all classes each hopes to be able to appear what he is not and engages in great efforts to succeed at this. (2:441)

This is a striking passage, suggesting the influence of Rousseau and his concern for the authentic self masked by social forms (see Mansfield and Winthrop 2000:xxxvi–xxxix; Manent 1994:66–67). At first glance, it might seem difficult to reconcile the centrality of social mobility in democracies, on the one hand, with the notion expressed here of a person's appearing to be "what he is not" by wielding products that appear to have qualities "they do not have," on the other. If, in other words, social mobility is central to democratic culture, how, then, can people cling to the notion that they have a fixed identity—albeit an identity that they must mask as they climb the social ladder? The answer is found at the heart of the cultural ideology of individualism, in the notion of the self as an independent, self-contained unit, one that exists in a sense before social distinctions. An egalitarian mass democracy is (in its own cultural terms) a collection of individuals (to use Dumont's 1977 phrase), all having equal rights and all sharing the same humanity, whatever their fortune or circumstances. The self is simultaneously a complete and a unique self, although such selves take on a variety of social roles in their lives. The roles may change, but the self that plays them does not.

The same cultural principles underpin the operations of the labor market, as depicted in Tocqueville's discussion of "the relations of servant and master." In a democracy, there are no permanent "classes" of servants and masters, workers and bosses. At least from the perspective of the cultural ideology of individualism, all people are equal. One may occupy the role of a servant or a worker, may sell one's labor to an employer, but such situations are understood to be contractual; one's position in such a contractual relationship does not in any way alter one's fundamental humanity, the fact that one is just as good as anyone else. In a democracy, "not only are servants equal among themselves; one can say that they are in a way the equals of their masters." Indeed, as Tocqueville notes, "at each instant the servant can become a master and aspire to become one," and therefore—note the formulation of the completed thought—"the servant . . . is not another man than the master" (2:549).

Yet, as Tocqueville is at some pains to point out, there is a sense in which this absolute equality is illusory:

> When . . . equality is an old and accepted fact, the public sense, which exceptions never influence, assigns . . . certain limits to the value of man above or below which it is difficult for any man to stay for long.
>
> In vain do wealth and poverty, command and obedience accidentally put great distances between two men; public opinion, which is founded on the ordinary order of things, brings them near to the common level and creates a sort of imaginary equality between them despite the real inequality of their conditions. (2:550)

The wonderful expression "imaginary equality" suggests the deep cultural principle at issue here (as in Anderson's 1983 notion of the "imagined community")—the notion of society as a collection of equal individuals, with their equality a matter of an essential, yet abstract, humanity that all individuals possess but not a matter of the socially particular features that separate them one from another in "real life." Thus the passage anticipates a question that would exercise twentieth-century Marxists: why has there been no working-class revolution in the United States? And Tocqueville answers it, in a chapter called "Why Great Revolutions Will Become Rare" in democracies. Although there are extremes of rich and poor in the United States, its citizens do not form separate classes; rather, even the most disadvantaged share with others the desire to pursue their fortune. As we might say today, most Americans, if not all, believe themselves to be middle class. Moreover, the American economy is a regime of "movable goods" (2:609), and not only are most Americans small property owners (at least), they all aspire to increase their share of the world's goods. "Thus," Tocqueville concludes, "the majority of citizens do not see clearly what they could gain by a revolution, and they feel at each instant . . . what they could lose from one" (2:608). Indeed, Tocqueville notes the apparent contradiction that "society in the United States is at once agitated and monotonous" (2:587). In their restless pursuit of happiness, Americans constantly rearrange the surface details of their lives, just as they ceaselessly strive to discover shortcuts to wealth (2:511). But the fundamental cultural principles of individualism and materialism remain unchanged, and public opinion locks individual minds within a narrow range of imaginative possibilities. No wonder, then, that "the aspect of American society is agitated because men and things change continuously; and it is monotonous because all the changes are similar" (2:587).

The Meaning of Order

As I noted at the outset, Tocqueville's analyses of aristocracy and democracy are at once ideal-typical and historically particular. Certain features of his ideal types may strike us as overdrawn. (For example, even "in theory," could aristocracies be as unchanging, as stable, as "traditional" as his model suggests?) But in his depiction of particular societies (especially of American democracy, his main subject), he is capable of specifying exquisitely complicated patterns of historically unique factors that have shaped them. Still, it seems reasonable to ask whether Tocqueville presupposes a more general model of society. What assumptions about human nature and society underpin, unexamined, his ideal types and his historical analyses?

Tocqueville's most basic assumption, it seems to me, is that "order" is the fundamental problem of human existence. Tocqueville thinks of order in both social and cultural terms (to use a twentieth-century social-scientific dichotomy). For him, order connotes both common action and a meaningful cosmos—both Durkheimian and Weberian integration, we might say.

In his discussion of general ideas and the social sources of moral and intellectual authority, Tocqueville sketches a Durkheimian vision of common belief as a source of common action:

> There is no society that can prosper without such beliefs, or rather there is none that could survive this way; for without common ideas there is no common action, and without common action men still exist, but a social body

does not. Thus in order that there be society, . . . it is necessary that all the minds of the citizens always be brought and held together by some principal ideas. (2:407)

Further, Tocqueville seems to believe that human nature is such that recognizable similarity is the only basis for human empathy: "There is real sympathy only among people who are alike" (2:536). The statement is all the more surprising in that Tocqueville has emphasized that aristocracies are based on social differences. But even in his discussions of aristocracy, Tocqueville imagines homogeneous social groups as the basic building blocks of the society. In other words, he sees aristocracies as ranked, interrelated groups. In such societies, there is little notion of "man" in general, as the members of different groups are defined as different kinds of beings. But Tocqueville often writes as if sociality within the group itself—the caste, class, or guild—depends on similarity, or homogeneity. (He is not consistent in this, as his discussion of the internal differentiation of the aristocratic family [2:559] shows.)

This sort of Durkheimian social solidarity is at odds with what I think is the more powerful strain in *Democracy*, the concern with human meaning-making. Here Tocqueville is at his most subtle, as a careful look at his discussion of material well-being will show. At first glance, it appears that Tocqueville does not relativize material desires as completely as he does individualism, that, indeed, he takes the search for material goods and comforts to be instinctive, the human nature that one finds once culture is stripped away. When he writes that equality isolates individuals and "opens their souls excessively to the love of material enjoyments" (2:419), it is tempting to read the statement in terms of Lockean contract theory. From that perspective, equal individuals in the state of nature all compete, naturally and instinctively, to amass private property.

A closer look, however, shows other theoretical postulates: a mind-body dualism ("traditional" enough in Western thought) with a semiotic twist due, no doubt, to the epistemological speculations of French Enlightenment philosophers:

Beasts have the same senses as we and nearly the same lusts: there are no material passions that are not common to us and them, of which the seed is not as much in a dog as in ourselves.

How, therefore, does it come about that animals know only how to provide for their first and coarsest needs, whereas we vary our enjoyments infinitely and increase them constantly?

What renders us superior to the beasts in this is that we employ our souls in finding the material goods toward which instinct alone leads them. In men, the angel teaches the brute the art of satisfying itself. It is because man is capable of elevating himself above the goods of the body and of scorning even life—of which beasts do not have any idea—that he knows how to multiply these same goods to a degree that they cannot conceive of. (2:521–22)

In humans, then, material needs (and their satisfaction) are not instinctively given, as they are for all other animals. They are, instead, culturally constructed, as anthropologists say—a product of mind rather than body. And different kinds of societies have different philosophies about what sort of material pleasures and progress are appropriate for their members. Thus it is that Tocqueville can imagine an egalitarianism that does not lead to excessive materialism, although such a society would be gloomy, indeed, with its people stuck at a kind of ground-zero of creative thought, all sharing "in the same ignorance and in an equal servitude" (2:430).

Material need, then, is a question of meaning, as is the human need for order itself, which, in the last analysis, is a need for a meaningful universe. As we saw, Tocqueville praises religion because it provides humans with answers to fundamental ontological questions, and he is surprisingly catholic in his willingness to accept the possibility that religions other than Christianity can do this as well as it can: "Metempsychosis is not more reasonable than materialism; however, if a democracy absolutely had to make a choice between the two, I would . . . judge that its citizens risk brutalizing themselves less by thinking that their soul is going to pass into the body of a pig than in believing it is nothing" (2:519–20). And Tocqueville extends this sort of relativism beyond religion to social and cultural formations as such. As he works his way through the comparison of aristocracy and democracy in the second volume of *Democracy*, he claims that he prefers neither: "I have not inquired here whether this new state that I have just described is inferior to the one that preceded it or whether it is only otherwise. It is enough for me that it be regulated and fixed; for what is most important to encounter among men is not one certain order, but order" (2:551).

Nonetheless, Tocqueville's readers continue to speculate about his preference for one or the other, aristocracy or democracy. I suggest, however, that if Tocqueville has a preference at all, it is not for human order but for divine. As I noted earlier, for Tocqueville, God's omniscience contrasts with all human orders of meaning, for the latter depend on the limitations that abstraction provides, whereas God's knowledge is unlimited, infinite. As creatures with souls, humans aspire to transcend their bodily limitations: "Alone among all the beings, man shows a natural disgust for existence and an immense desire to exist; he scorns life and fears nothingness. These different instincts constantly drive his soul toward contemplation of another world" (1:284). To contemplate "the admirable order of all things" is the best "pleasure" that humans can have (2:505). But no human being, and no human society, could create such an order. Aristocracy and democracy can serve as each other's "otherwise," but neither can escape the vices of their virtues.

CHAPTER 2

The Dainty and the Hungry Man

Literature and Anthropology in the
Work of Edward Sapir

"We lived, in a sense, lives in which the arts and the sciences fought uneven battles for pre-eminence." So wrote Margaret Mead of her student days in the early 1920s at Columbia University (1959:xviii). Mead's "we" refers to a community of anthropologists that included Franz Boas, Edward Sapir, and Ruth Benedict. That Boas was privately a pianist and the others more publicly poets is well known; that they developed a science of anthropology centered on the concept of culture and that some of them came to see culture as the art of living—as lifeways at once "satisfactory and gracious" (Mead 1928:12)—is also well understood. But the connection between the practice of art and the development of anthropology has been less thoroughly explored. That connection was crucial in the work of Edward Sapir, Boas's most brilliant student and a key figure in the development of Boasian anthropology. For Sapir, art became a medium in which to work out an approach to questions of culture. What he came to understand in the practice of poetry, music, and criticism became central to his understanding of culture.

Sapir's contribution to Boasian anthropology must be understood in the context of the tensions and ambiguities in Boas's work (Stocking 1966a: 214). On the one hand, Boas saw culture as "an accidental accretion of individual elements." At the same time, he recognized that culture could be understood as an organizing spirit, or "genius," continually assimilating these atomistic elements, integrating them in a "spiritual totality" that must be appreciated as a unique, historical whole. Beneath this seemingly simple opposition lie a host of epistemological difficulties, stemming, at least in part, from Boas's "peculiar position within and between two traditions in German thought," those of "monistic materialism" and "romantic ideal-ism" (Stocking 1974a:8–9; also Stocking 1996:3–5). Thus, for example, Boas recognized the validity of two types of science, the physical and the his-torical, and claimed that each originates in a fundamental disposition of the human mind. Physical science stems from an "aesthetic" impulse that re-quires order, or system; it seeks general laws that transcend individual facts. Historical science depends on an "affective" impulse, "the personal feeling of man towards the world" (Boas 1887:644); it seeks to understand phenom-ena on their own terms rather than as exemplifications of general laws. Boas believed that both types of science aimed for "the eternal truth" (643), but at the same time he feared that the search for true scientific laws meant an imposition of conceptual schemes onto raw facts. On the other hand, Boas understood the objects of historical science (cultural wholes and the *Geisten* that animated them) as "phenomena having a merely subjective con-nection"—that is, as phenomena unified only by "the mind of the observer" (642–43). In this, history was akin to art, for "the way in which the mind is affected by phenomena forms an important branch of the study" (646). Boas also insisted, however, that these subjectively determined phenom-ena be studied inductively, that they were, in fact, "directly and concretely observable and distinguishable" (Stocking 1974a:13). But, again, to observe and distinguish cultural wholes, it was necessary to examine culture ele-ments, which meant that "in practice, Boas' historical methodology was perhaps archetypically exemplified by his quasi-statistical study of the dis-tribution of folk-tale elements" (Stocking 1974a:15).

Without attempting to discuss such issues in any detail, let me rephrase them in terms that more clearly relate to Sapir's concerns. Simply put, then, the contrast between element and whole implies the problem of the onto-logical status of pattern or structure in human affairs. Are social-scientific laws nothing more than analytic impositions, or do they describe entities or aspects of the real world? What is the ontological status of cultural things—do whole cultures exist (either as things or as sets of relations) or are there only culture elements in ever-changing associations? Finally, how can anthropologists apprehend the phenomena of culture? Should anthro-pologists work to construct general laws of human history or ought they to focus "affectively" on the facts themselves? In either case, how are they to go about studying culture, which, whether directly observable or only a product of the observer's subjectivity, nonetheless concerns human subjec-tivity on a grander, collective scale?

Sapir came rather early in his career to differ from Boas with respect to these questions as they were posed in the study of language. Hymes has written that "Sapir, more than any American anthropologist," realized—as "an empirical fact"—"that the persistence of recognizable form . . . is greater in language than in culture" (1970:259). Behind this realization lay a facility for analyzing linguistic form that made Sapir's doctoral dissertation, a grammar of Takelma, "almost a miracle for its time" (Hymes and Fought 1975:918). But though Boas himself recognized Sapir's linguistic brilliance and even deferred to it at the time of the Takelma work, in his own linguistic practice Boas "hesitated to carry the reduction to system too far" (Stocking 1974b). This was equally true of his approach to culture. In general, Boas's anthropology was "pre-structural" (Hymes 1961:90). Caught between element and whole, Boas never developed a consistently holistic or structuralist conception of culture. But the questions he raised were to prove so suggestive that "much of twentieth-century American anthropology may be viewed as the working out in time of various implications in Boas' own position" (Stocking 1974a:17). This "working out" was effected by Boas's students. What Sapir contributed, among other things, was a remarkable, and iconoclastic, theory of culture—a theory that is structuralist in its analysis of formal patterning but transcends structuralism in its concern for individual experience, creativity, and the possibility of change.

At a rather early point in his career, Sapir became interested in apprehending subjectivities rather than developing abstracted overviews of an objective reality. That is, Sapir sought techniques that would allow an observer to portray from the "inside" the realities that other individuals understand. These interests are expressed most completely in his writings on art. At the same time, Sapir elaborated his critique of the "superorganic" concept, arguing that to analyze the social aspects of human behavior did not require the analyst to posit a distinct level of reality ("the social") that transcends human individuals. These insights are combined in the issue that most interested Sapir at this time, the relationship between individual creativity and given cultural forms. Again, this is a theme dominant in the writings on art. Moreover, Sapir's concern with the creative processes of art, as well as his work in linguistics, led him to another realization—the understanding that a cultural pattern, a patterning of values and attitudes, would be something like the formal patterns of art and language (Hymes 1970:260–61). These two sets of insights—concerning the relation of individual and culture, on the one hand, and the nature of formal patterning, on the other—are brought together by the notion of unconscious patterning. The idea that individuals "intuit" pattern and that this intuition allows them to participate in patterned social action without at the same time being coerced by "society"—the intuition allows them, in short, to communicate with others in interaction without thereby surrendering the possibility of creativity—cements a theory of culture that accounts both for given form (culture) and the subjective experience of individuals. And though this idea of unconscious patterning was elaborated with respect to an anthropological conception of culture only in 1927, much of it, too, is present in the earlier writings on art (Fernández Casas 2004:233–73). Hence an examination of Sapir's artistic concerns will deepen our understanding of the origins of his mature theory of culture.

It will also show something of how his thought developed. The question of "how" in cultural processes was an important one for Sapir, touching on issues of form and meaning, individuality and creativity. Hymes has shown that Sapir initially separated questions of "how" and questions of "what"—with linguistic form (how) merely expressing cultural content (what)—whereas in his later thought he brought them together—with form actively shaping content and language creating worldview (1970:258–64). But this is only part of the story, for Sapir's mature formulation of these issues grew out of an artistic praxis and the theorizing associated with it. In addition to the questions of "how" and "what," Sapir posed problems in terms directly reminiscent of Boas's dilemmas in the epistemology of science. Sapir sought in art a way to unite form and feeling, cultural givens and subjective experience—a way to reconcile what Boas had called physical science, with its "aesthetic" search for impersonal laws, and an "affective" understanding of individual human hearts. In brief, in art Sapir attempted to come to terms with both his scientific and his romantic yearnings, to reconcile what he portrayed, in one of his poems, as the dainty man and the hungry man within himself. To contextualize this conflict, which for Sapir was both personal and philosophical, we need to know something of his intellectual biography.

From Anthropology to Art

The bibliography of Sapir's published work suggests that 1916 was a turning point in his intellectual development. That year saw the publication of his famous monograph "Time Perspective in Aboriginal American Culture," his last major work purely in the Boasian mold. The same year also produced a paper on the Australian composer Percy Grainger and an essay on American culture in response to one by John Dewey. In 1917, in addition to technical papers and reviews, we find two reviews of psychoanalytic works, reviews of a series of novels and of a musician's biography, and two essays on literary theory, all published in the *Dial*. From 1918 through 1921, Sapir's output of this latter type of writing approximately equaled that of specifically anthropological papers, and during 1922 the number of literary and general reviews, published in such magazines as the *Dial, Freeman, New Republic*, and *Nation*, far outweighed the number of technical pieces. More important, it is in the nonprofessional writing—and in the brilliant little book on language that he published in 1921 for a general intellectual audience—that we get a sense of inspiration and creativity, as compared to the more routine analyses in linguistics and ethnology. After 1922, Sapir's literary pieces became more and more incidental, with his last literary reviews appearing in 1928. The publication of Sapir's poetry follows the same course. His first published poems and his only volume of poetry (*Dreams and Gibes*) appeared in 1917. From 1918 to 1927, he published a substantial number of poems each year; his last four published poems appeared in 1931. From this "trait analysis" alone, then, we can guess that for Sapir the late teens were a time of shifting interests and even "profound rethinking," as Preston has put it (1980:367). What Sapir rethought were some of the premises of Boasian science and his intellectual commitment to them (Newman 1951:181–82; Darnell 1990:87–170)

Sapir began his graduate training in anthropology under Boas at Columbia University, receiving his doctoral degree in 1909. During his years of graduate study, Sapir did linguistic and ethnological fieldwork among several Native American groups and was affiliated in research and instructional capacities with the University of California and the University of Pennsylvania. After a student career "marked by great phonetic virtuosity, enormous bursts of energy, great hopes" (Voegelin 1952:2), Sapir accepted an appointment in 1910 as chief of the division of anthropology in the Geological Survey of Canada, a position he was to hold until 1925.

The record of Sapir's first years in Ottawa shows that he immediately established a Boasian program in ethnological and linguistic research, as well as in his work with the ethnological collection of the Victoria Memorial Museum (Darnell 1990:44–64). During the first years of his appointment, Sapir carried out this program without much apparent dissatisfaction. His publications from 1910 until 1916 are primarily concerned with his work on

North American languages, as well as ethnological data he had gathered while doing linguistic research. His major theoretical contribution was "Time Perspective" (1916), in which he used techniques developed in historical linguistics to elaborate a methodology for the reconstructive work of ethnology. "Time Perspective" summarized and even exhausted the Boasian paradigm and, when compared to Sapir's later essays in anthropological theory, seems out of character for him. For example, in "Time Perspective," Sapir claimed "historical understanding" as the "properly ethnological goal" and eschewed the study of individuals for that of "generalized events and individualities" (1916:391–92). He echoed Boas in warning against imposing theoretical categories on raw data where knowledge of historical connections is lacking. He repeatedly spoke of culture in terms of "elements" and "complexes" that have come together in elaborate historical processes to form whole cultures. The "structure" of a "culture complex" was of interest because the analyst could use it to recover chronology, since more loosely "associated" elements could be presumed to be more recent (405). Sapir spoke of cultural survivals and origins but made only passing reference to the influence of individuals on culture. Though his application of linguistic techniques to ethnological problems took him beyond Boas in methodological daring, the piece remains fundamentally Boasian in orientation and conception. Because this monograph adheres so closely to Boasian orthodoxy—indeed, giving it its most elegant expression with respect to the problems treated—we should bear in mind how soon after its publication Sapir was to strike out in new directions.

The first strong expressions of intellectual dissatisfaction on the part of Sapir are to be found in his letters of 1916 to Lowie. We might well imagine that as Sapir came out from under the direct supervision of Boas, and as Sapir's comparative analyses of American languages pushed his thinking well beyond what the master would sanction, elements of intellectual rebellion began to crystallize into a new orientation. Preston suggests (1980: 368–69) that Sapir was stimulated in this by his friendship with Radin, and Preston reproduces a long letter that Sapir received in 1914, in which Radin castigated Boas for his methodological timidity and lack of historical imagination. As Radin saw it, Boas was far too concerned with reconstructing chronological accounts of the development of primitive culture, and with "certain general factors, like dissemination, convergent evolution, independent origin, etc." An ethnology exclusively animated by such interests would fail to fulfill its promise; anthropologists should concentrate instead on "sympathetic interpretation" and "intimate" portrayals of daily life (369).

Whatever Sapir's immediate response to Radin's ideas, Sapir began to raise similar doubts in his letters to Lowie. The record of their regular correspondence begins in 1916 (Lowie 1965). According to Lowie, Sapir's position in Canada, "judged purely on its potentialities for scientific research," was "ideal" (2). But Sapir felt isolated from the academic and artistic centers of the American cities and became increasingly dissatisfied with anthropological work. There are indications that he felt himself to have been cast off—presumably by Boas—in his placement in Ottawa. Sapir envied those among his peers who had landed academic jobs in the States and resented Boas's criticisms of his linguistic work. Sapir also suffered difficulties in his personal life with the onset of his wife's physical and mental illness as early as 1913 (Darnell 1990:133–37). Sapir's first nontechnical publications (in 1916 and 1917) show traces of profound moral questioning in addition to social criticism. He was particularly appalled by World War I and expressed his pessimism and sense of horror in his poetry. The war also affected his research program, the public funding for which was drastically reduced as money was diverted to the war effort (Murray 1981a:65). These troubled aspects of Sapir's situation fostered anxiety and resentment, frustration and boredom. He sought an outlet in musical and literary pursuits. In a letter of August 12, 1916, he tells Lowie, "I do practically no anthropology out of office hours, most of my time being taken up with music" (Lowie 1965:20).

This remark must have elicited a query from Lowie, for in the next letter Sapir explains his musical interests in a long passage that is worth reproducing in full:

Why do I engage in music? I suppose I could call it recreation and be done with it, but I do not think it would be quite sincere for me to put off your query like that. Whether or not I have "missed my vocation" is not for me to decide. I feel I can do not only eminently satisfactory linguistic work but also satisfactory ethnological work, as I proved to myself in my two Nootka trips. I have now an enormous amount of linguistic and ethnological data on my hands from various tribes, certainly enough to keep me busy for at least five years of concentrated work. But (and here's the rub and the disappointment) I don't somehow seem to feel as much positive impulse toward disgorging as I should. A certain necessary enthusiasm, particularly towards ethnological data and problems, seems lacking—lacking beyond a mild degree, anyway. I somehow feel in much of my work that I am not true to my inner self, that I have let myself be put off with useful but relatively unimportant trifles at the expense of a development of finer needs and impulses, whatever they are. A chafing of the spirit, the more annoying because there is externally so little excuse for it! I know, as no one else can, that it is this profound feeling of dissatisfaction and disillusionment which hardly ever leaves me, that is mainly (not altogether, for I must waste much time on office routine, but mainly) responsible for my relatively unproductive scientific career up to date. To amass data, to write them up, to discuss "problems"—how easy, but *cui bono*? Do not misunderstand me. My "cui bono" is not grounded in any philosophy of relative values. I have no theoretical quarrel with anthropology. The fault lies with me. Being as I am, for better or for worse, the life of an Americanist does not satisfy my inmost cravings. To be frank, I do not believe this discontent is due chiefly to the unhuman aspect of our discipline, to its narrow range of appeal. I am afraid I may have too much of the "shut-in" personality about me to feel that sort of limitation as keenly as a Smith or perhaps yourself. I find that what I most care for is beauty of form, whether in substance or, perhaps even more keenly, in spirit. A perfect style, a well-balanced system of philosophy, a perfect bit of music, a clearly-conceived linguistic organism, the beauty of mathematical relations—these are some of the things that, in the sphere of the immaterial, have most deeply stirred me. How can the job-lot of necessarily unco-ordinated or badly co-ordinated facts that we amass in our field-work satisfy such longings? Is not the incessant poring over of such facts a punishment to the liberty loving spirit? Does not one most "waste time" when he is most industrious? And yet one always feels relieved and a bit pleased to have done with some bit of "scientific" work. I do not really believe that my temperament is so very unscientific either, for I am surely critical and almost unreasonably analytical. A scientific spirit but an aesthetic will or craving! A sort of at-cross-purposes-with-oneself type of temperament that entails frequent inhibitions, frustrations, anything but a smooth flow of self-satisfied and harmonious effort. Shucks! my self analysis may be all wrong, but the inner dissatisfaction is there. (Lowie 1965:20–21)

A letter is, typically, spontaneously dictated and thus may reveal not carefully thought-out analyses but deeper, more tangled, and even contradictory motives. Here are several apparently simple dichotomies—art and science, harmonious form and a formless assemblage of heterogeneous elements, the inner life and the outer—but they cannot be taken as simple oppositions.

They crosscut one another and, as the letter reveals, Sapir was hard put to choose among them. Certain oppositions seem relatively clear—Sapir chafes at the sacrifice of inner needs to outer trifles, he seeks harmonious form and recoils from formlessness, he feels torn between an aesthetic will and a scientific spirit. But what, we might ask, is art, and what is science? For Sapir, science is ethnology and linguistics, but he is less sure of his ethnological than his linguistic science, the latter being the more technically precise of the two. Science is also data amassed and "written up," but what good are such activities compared to beauty of form? Yet formal beauty must be discoverable by science as well, for who but a scientist can apprehend linguistic and mathematical relations? Reading from another point of view, we might say that Sapir is here expressing frustration that ethnology is not linguistics: what he can accomplish in the latter—the discovery of form—eludes him in the former. But this formulation is immediately crosscut by another, for linguistics and ethnology are taken together as science—it is both linguistic and ethnological data that Sapir has "on his hands," ready to be "disgorged." And these two—combined as "our discipline," the science of anthropology—have an "unhuman aspect." Is, then, the beauty of form characteristic of such human endeavors as music, philosophy, and mathematics unhuman? Is Sapir at once attracted to it and repelled by it? (see Sapir 1924b:159).

At this point, it might be useful to recall Boas's discussion of the two types of science, physical and historical. Physical science depended upon aesthetic impulses, historical science upon affective ones. "Aesthetic" for Boas here meant regularity and generality, whereas the affective approach in history, as in art, sought uniqueness. Perhaps Sapir's dilemma was that he was drawn to aesthetic phenomena (form) in an affective way ("what I most care for"). At any rate, Sapir's crisis was not merely personal: he was struggling with implications that contradict one another within a single scientific discipline. Radin also had been threatened by the horns of the dilemma: he yearned for "a real human science instead of one of bones and dust" (Preston 1980:369). Or consider Mead's recollection of how Boasian anthropology was taught by Boas's students around 1920: on the one hand was Alexander Goldenweiser, "mercurial, excited by ideas about culture, but intolerant of the petty exactions of field work, . . . working on the first book by an American anthropologist which was to present cultures briefly as wholes"; on the other hand, Elsie Clews Parsons, from whom "students learned that anthropology consisted of an enormous mass of little bits of

material, carefully labeled by time, place, and tribe—the fruits, arid and bitter, of long, long hours of labor and devotion" (Mead 1959:8). Among the
Boasians, then, there was the duty to study culture elements and a desire to
discover culture wholes—an inhuman science in place and a human science
on the horizon. Or, perhaps, there was science and there was art, fighting,
as Mead put it, "uneven battles for preeminence." To get a better sense of
how the match stood with Sapir, let us turn to his poetry and literary essays.

The Poet's Dilemma

Sapir's poems are short and of the lyric variety. His essays and reviews
show that he studied the important American and British poets of his day,
but because he experimented continuously with poetic technique, he never
developed a fixed style from which it would be possible to trace strong influences. As for general content, one finds an intriguing blend of emotion,
anthropological insight, social criticism, and a touch of the Orientalism of
the period—though Sapir's poetic exotica are drawn more often from the
"primitive" peoples of ethnology than from the East of classical and Ori-
entalist scholars.

Many of Sapir's poems reflect great personal anguish and doubt. Sometimes such feelings are unmotivated and unexplained:

Silence, silence,
Dearest friend, I pray you
For it is not merry in my soul. (1917a:54)

Other poems imply, or frankly discuss, the reasons for melancholy. There is
a general alienation from the "dismal efficiency-mongering" of the modem,
bureaucratized world (1917a:65) and, related to this, dismay at hypocrisy,
particularly that of religion and patriotism. Several poems express horror
and outrage at the war, and many suggest the personal tragedy associated
with the illness of Sapir's wife. What is of most interest for my purposes
here, however, is a theme that may be summarily described as the gap
between inner and outer human realities.

Dreams and Gibes opens with "The Mislabeled Menagerie" (1917a:9–10):
the poet visits a zoo and finds himself in a "Topsyturvydom" where the
monkey is labeled *Ursus*, the camel ostrich, and so on. His initial suspicion
is that some "fussing pedagogue" has attempted a "new labeling scheme,"
but a zookeeper informs him that the animals have been moved so recently

that there has been no time to change their signs. The poet then realizes that this mislabeling phenomenon, temporary in the zoo, applies permanently in the lives of many people: the grocer is a statesman, the mayor a grocer, the clergyman a simpleton. Because Sapir felt the arrangement of poems in a collection was significant (Mead 1959:172), we may assume that the placement of "The Mislabeled Menagerie" at the beginning of the book announces a major theme in *Dreams and Gibes*. The sixteen poems that follow (there are fifty-three in the collection) speak directly of people who are not what they seem, and most of the others suggest related problems.

Among those people who are not what they seem, whose inner life differs from their "outward shell" (1917a:21), is the poet. Self-doubt and a feeling of being at odds with one's true self are implied in several blunt, sarcastic pieces aimed at academicians. The metaphysician is a dog chasing his tail, the philosopher constructs daily a new system to explain the universe. "Professors in War-Time" chides those who stand aloof, refusing to apply their wisdom and skill "while all the world is soaked in blood and groans with pain" (27). Other poems develop this theme of inner dissatisfaction in more personal ways. "Helpless Revolt" (64) expresses irreducible rebellion against an unyielding reality:

> I have no respect for what is.
> I can not mend and patch,
> I can not bend my soul to the twist
> That will make it fit with the brutal fact,
> That will make it yield to the tyrant world.
> My soul stands firm.
> It would annihilate all in its rage and build anew,
> Rather than bend.
> Therefore it breaks, and the brutal fact remains
> And the tyrant world wags on.

And "Reproof," a beautiful sonnet published a year later in the *Dial*, has the poet mock his own soul for shunning life and light, losing itself in "endless, brooding self-pursuit" (1918a:102).

Beyond the brooding and rebellion of these poems, others go on to suggest personal approaches that enable one to make sense of, or to come to terms with, difficult human realities. "The Dainty and the Hungry Man" portrays two such approaches: that of the aesthete, for whom beauty alone matters, and that of the Hungry Man, who craves "the crassness of life" (1917a:35–37). One might guess that the poet sides with the latter, for in the dialogue (which is the poem) he consistently allows him the last word. But if this poem expresses self-reflection on Sapir's part, as I think it must, one would be nearer the mark to assume that the two characters represent conflicting aspects of the poet's personality.

"I distil from the crassness of life / What matters alone—Beauty. / Take it" (37). Such is the philosophy of the Dainty Man, who is portrayed coldly, critically, as if he were heartless. The preciousness of his taste suggests a Byzantine formalism untouched by human passion. Yet despite the pejorative tone taken toward the Dainty Man, Sapir could not flatly condemn his faith in beauty. As he had written Lowie, "What I most care for is beauty of form" (Lowie 1965:20).

On the other hand, the Hungry Man voices passions and themes that run consistently through Sapir's writing (and not only the literary writing) of this time. The Hungry Man shuns the delicacies offered him by his opposite, seeking instead "the thick of life," the tangle of "crowds in the street" (36). This image of the crowd appears frequently in Sapir's poetry and represents the public face of the urban world. The poet's typical response to this outward spectacle is to ask what hidden passions animate its participants. Such is the credo of the Hungry Man: "And more to me than thoughts serene are the strivings and turmoils of the heart, / And more to me than lovely images is the wayward current of life" (37). We might summarize his attitude by saying that the Hungry Man seeks to experience the apparently disorganized, meaningless assemblage of detail and event that constitutes the surface of human life yet at the same time to understand the inner truths of the heart. But the accomplishment of both aims can be achieved only through a correct appreciation of that which the Dainty Man worships yet misunderstands: beauty of form. Or, put another way, to understand formal beauty ought not to be an end in itself but should lead to a better understanding of human existence. The Dainty Man and the Hungry Man must be merged to become the artist, the creator who works with formal beauty to communicate the truths of the heart.

Cultural Form and Individual Expression

Sapir's literary essays of this period explore these same issues of outer and inner realities and their connection to aesthetic form. In this, they prefigure his treatment of such problems in more purely anthropological terms in the later essays on culture theory. In 1917, the year that *Dreams and Gibes* was published, Sapir published two essays on literary theory, "The Twilight of Rhyme" and "Realism in Prose Fiction." The former counters the preciousness of the Dainty Man, while the latter addresses the problems of the Hungry Man. That is, the first essay discusses the relationship of aesthetic form to self-expression and thus justifies beauty and art in humanly significant terms. The second proposes a method for achieving both an understanding of human hearts and an objective grasp of the outer surfaces of life.

Sapir's antagonists in "The Twilight of Rhyme" might seem at first to differ from the Dainty Man, for the imperialist orator (who ruins fiery oratory with hackneyed rhyming poetry) and Max Eastman (who campaigns against "Lazy Verse") have passion on their side. But their passion is strangled by the outmoded forms chosen to express it. According to Sapir, Eastman is correct to argue that the "technical limitations" of an artistic medium have "disciplinary value which is of direct aesthetic benefit" (1917b:99). He errs, however, in valuing a particular technique (rhyme), appropriate in certain cultural contexts but by no means universally, instead of the general principle of the necessity of technical limitations. Sapir then outlines his theory of the relationship between individual creativity and traditional formal means. He argues that a delicate balance must be maintained between tradition and innovation, inherited forms and creativity. Otherwise, formalism and externality overcome sincerity and self-expression:

> Just as soon as an external and purely formal aesthetic device ceases to be felt as inherently essential to sincerity of expression, it ceases to remain merely a condition of the battling for self-expression and becomes a tyrannous burden, a perfectly useless fetter. . . . Perfection of form is always essential, but the definition of what constitutes such perfection cannot, must not, be fixed once for all. The age, the individual artist, must solve the problem ever anew, must impose self created conditions, perhaps only dimly realized, of the battle to be fought in attaining self-expression. It would be no paradox to say that it is the blind acceptance of a form imposed from without that is, in the deepest sense, "lazy," for such acceptance dodges the true formal problem of the artist—the arrival, in travail and groping, at that mode of expression that is best suited to the unique conception of the artist. (99–100)

This argument, a cornerstone in Sapir's theory of art, will become central to his theory of culture as well. It brings together two seemingly contradictory forces—cultural form and individual expression—and makes each the condition of the other: given forms are necessary to self-expression, but when the individual works with form instead of merely yielding to it, he changes it. As Sapir says, in true art the formal problem must be solved "ever anew." Thus the pursuit of beauty becomes an attempt to achieve self-expression through creation of form rather than the merely static admiration of beauty espoused by the Dainty Man. That Sapir guided his artistic practice by his theory is evident in his critical judgments and in the curious fact that most of his poetry before the publication of "The Twilight of Rhyme" is unrhymed, whereas after 1917 he experiments, not only with rhyme but with such classical devices as the sonnet form (see Murray 1981a:67).

The second essay in literary theory of 1917 is "Realism in Prose Fiction." Sapir begins with the claim that "prose fiction is the vehicle *par excellence* for a realistic ideal." He distinguishes two aspects of this ideal, "outer and inner realism," or, in words nearer to those of the Hungry Man, "the flow and depth of life." He then asserts the primacy of the second aspect. The secret of "realistic illusion" lies in the ease with which a given literary form enables its audience to identify with the characters portrayed—"to live through," from the inside, their experiences. In conventional prose fiction, the narrator enters the minds of any and all of his characters. In other words, he "claims an unconditional omniscience" that "goes by the name of objectivity" (1917c:503). Yet this apparently objective technique threatens the realistic illusion, for it strains the reader's capacity for identification with the characters.

In response to this tension, a newer form of fiction, animated by "a subtler understanding of reality," has emerged. In this technique, the author confines his vision to the psyche of one character, leaving the presentation of other characters as a function of this dominant vantage point. This narrative stance involves a trade-off in truth value: what the reader can learn of secondary characters is more frequently erroneous than true. This is because the "inner experiences" of secondary characters "can only be inferred, sometimes truly (that is, in a manner roughly coinciding with the viewpoints of their own selves), more often mistakenly." Yet in spite of this, or perhaps because of it, the technique just described is truer to our experience as we know it and is thus more realistic than that of the omniscient narrator. It follows that the objective and the subjective are reversed—an apparently difficult position that Sapir is prepared to defend:

At this point the reader may object that while this method pretends to be sweepingly realistic, to aim to grasp a bit of life and imprison it in narrative form, it yet is the merest subjectivism, an egoist's dream in which everything is hopelessly out of plumb, in which the valid relations of the objective world are badly muddled. Nor would he be altogether wrong. And yet, what is life, as we really and individually know it, but precisely "an egoist's dream in which the valid relations of the objective world are badly muddled"? Objectivity, one might say, is romance. But he would need to add that we crave and demand this romantic objectivity, this mad seeing of things "as they really are," and that the literary artist has therefore a perfect right to choose between rigorous realism, the method that is frankly subjective, and objective realism, the romance of reality. (1917c:504)

Thus these two techniques, rigorous and objective realism, reveal different truths. Objective realism—which is "romance"—aims for the truth of an overview that tries somehow to account, in an orderly way, for the lives of many people. Rigorous realism—"frankly subjective"—aims at an inner truth, an accurate portrayal of the way one person might see the world. Yet Sapir is not content merely to juxtapose the two. Impelled, perhaps, by his scientific spirit, he offers a third technique for prose fiction that would make possible "a profound and all-embracing realistic art." He proposes that a given tale be told from the point of view of several characters but each time completely. By being subjective in several ways, the narrator could at last be truly objective: "For may not objectivity be defined as the composite picture gained by laying a number of subjectivities on top of one another?" According to Sapir, such a technique corresponds to an inductive process that guarantees "a steadily growing comprehension of the meaning of the whole" (1917c:505). Thus it satisfies the two desires of the Hungry Man, for it brings knowledge both of individual hearts and the collective life. And it speaks to the epistemological dilemmas of Boasian science, for it allows an observer to study subjective phenomena inductively. As such, it suggests something of the "science of interpersonal relations" that Sapir was to envision in his last essays (1939:579).

In the same year that he published the essays on rhyme (taking up the question of form and creativity) and realism (with its concern for understanding human interaction from multiple inner points of view), Sapir published his famous critique of Kroeber's "superorganic," which gives us a third element in the nascent culture theory. "Do We Need a 'Superorganic'?"

is written for a professional audience, but Sapir's concern for artistic creativity, and for "striking and influential personalities" (1917d:443), would seem
to motivate the argument. Rejecting Kroeber's claim for the existence of a
distinctive, social level of reality (see the discussion in chapter 3), Sapir
argues that individual and social behavior can be distinguished only ana-
lytically, for all behavior is the behavior of individuals. Whether a particular item of behavior is taken to be social or individual depends upon the
interests of the analyst, whose choice is thus "arbitrary" with respect to the
behavior in question (442). It follows that there can be no such thing as a
superorganic level of reality that coerces individuals and nullifies their creative possibilities: human beings can always change the course of history,
can always adapt given forms to their own ends. Thus this essay addresses,
from the anthropological side, the issues of culture and creativity that interested Sapir the artist.

In literary reviews and essays of the next several years, Sapir continues
to work with these issues. Again and again, he speaks of true art as subjective truth externalized in unique form, a formula that unites the themes
of 1917. In his critical analyses, he sharpens his sense of what this means
by examining the degrees to which these elements of art are present or
absent in the work of a particular artist or technique. Thus, for example,
Sapir says that the "later work" of Edgar Lee Masters lacks the technical
means necessary to give expression to feeling. According to Sapir, the poet
forgot that "an unembodied conception is, in art, no conception at all"
(1922a:334). On the other hand, there are works that are purely technical,
that express neither thought nor emotion, and these, too, are destined for
oblivion: "Craftsmanship, no matter how pleasing or ingenious, cannot
secure a musical composition immortality; it is inevitably put in the shade
by the technique of a later age" (1918b:491). In general, Sapir seems to have
won—perhaps in the writing of his own poems—a greater commitment to
the notion that technical discipline is necessary for self-expression: "Perhaps it is precisely the passionate temperament cutting into itself with the
cold steel of the intellect that is best adapted to the heuristic employment
of rhyme. The temperament and the triumphant harnessing of form belong,
both of them, to the psychology of sublimation following inhibition" (1920a:
498). If we remember that Sapir had previously championed the cause of
unrhymed verse, and that he had since begun to use rhyme, it is difficult
not to imagine these lines as a bit of self-analysis. They give us a picture of
Sapir working out a theory of art, and of culture, as he tried to understand,

through introspective analysis, his own artistic praxis. He goes on to call for a new science of aesthetics that will "get down to the very arduous business of studying the concrete processes of artistic production and appreciation" (499).

Sapir's discussions of aesthetic principles were complemented by analyses of particular artistic products, and in these he could develop his technical understanding of formal patterning. It is difficult to tell what effect his previous experience in analyzing linguistic patterning had on his analysis of artistic techniques. The theory of unconscious patterning—which he sketched in *Language* (1921a:55–58) and elaborated in a groundbreaking paper four years later (1925a)—occupied Sapir as a problem in poetry as early as 1918 (Sapir 1919a; 1921b:213; see Murray 1981b:10; Modjeska 1968). It is worked out in some detail in a remarkable paper on poetic form, "The Musical Foundations of Verse," published in 1921. This paper contains, first, a sophisticated structural analysis of poetic "sectioning," showing how various rhythmic elements, defined by mutual opposition, create the "appreciable psychological pulses" of a "rhythmic contour" (1921b:220–21). Second, it relates these rhythmic oppositions to the ability of the listener to perceive them, if only intuitively or subconsciously. "Not all that looks alike to the eye is psychologically comparable," Sapir tells us, and thus "the same passage is both prose and verse according to the rhythmic receptivity of the reader or hearer" (215–16, 226). Here, then, we have the combination of a structural analysis of formal patterning with a concern for the subjective perception of pattern in the minds of those who use it—the essence, in short, of Sapir's phonemic theory and an important component in his anthropological theory of culture. Thus, by 1921, the major elements of Sapir's mature theory of culture are present in his writings on art.

From Art to Anthropology

How did Sapir work into his more narrowly anthropological writing the ideas and insights that he developed in his writings on art? I begin with Sapir's two reviews of Lowie's *Primitive Society*, for these show both the degree to which Sapir remained a Boasian and the degree to which he was reworking Boasian themes to fit his emergent approach. Sapir praises Lowie's book for presenting the "American school" of anthropology to the public. This school is defined by inductive historical research, which it opposes to evolutionary speculation and psychological reductionism: "We learn to see a given primitive society . . . as a complex of historical processes that is only to be unraveled, and then in insignificant degree, through a minute weighing of the concrete, interacting features of that society and through the patient following out of the numerous threads that inevitably bind it to its geographical neighbors" (1920b:378). Though this recalls Boas's distributional studies of folklore traits, or Parsons's "careful assemblage and analysis of details" (Mead 1959:8), Sapir also implies that the historical process is human rather than superorganic: "No one that has watched the gradual, tortuous emergence of a social institution from the warp and woof of circumstance can feel it in his heart to say that he is but beholding the determinate unfolding of . . . whatever psychological concept be accepted for guidance" (1920b:378). The unstated counterpart to this historical critique of various reductionisms would be the role of the individual in the creation of culture. Sapir defines culture itself as "the fine art of living" (1920c:332). And in his approach to culture, the anthropologist must maintain, as Lowie has done, that "humanness of attitude" that "is simply a reflection of his human contacts with primitive folk" (1920b:377).

The implications of such an attitude are more fully spelled out in Sapir's review of *American Indian Life*, edited by Parsons. Sapir praises this group of fictional sketches of individual Native Americans precisely because they attempt to portray an exotic way of life from the point of view of the individual who lives it, rather than in an objective overview of the culture. The latter method highlights the traits of a way of life and, in so doing, obscures the reality of that life as those who live it might understand it. Sapir had earlier denigrated such an approach as "item-listing" (1917e:424), and here he spells out what is wrong with it: "It is precisely because the exotic is easily mistaken for subject, where it should be worked as texture, that much agreeable writing on glamorous quarters of the globe so readily surfeits a reader who possesses not merely an eye, but what used to be called a soul" (1922b:570). Writers tend to concentrate on the surface of an alien way of life because palpable exotic externality commands their attention as the proper object of discourse. But stopping there, they fail to explore the "individual consciousness" of those who experience that life, though this is "the only true concern of literary art." The review thus shows how thoroughly Sapir had assimilated the problem of ethnological description to that of "realism in prose fiction." As he himself asks, "can the conscious knowledge of the ethnologist be fused with the intuitions of the artist?" (570).

These sympathetic reviews of works by Boasian anthropologists should be compared to the "Time Perspective" essay to gain a fuller appreciation

of the development of Sapir's thought between 1916 and 1922. One other
paper of this period should be considered as well, his famous essay "Culture, Genuine and Spurious." By 1918, Sapir had almost certainly completed
it (Lowie 1965:27, 30, 34), though it did not appear in final form until 1924.
Written for a general audience, it is Sapir's first attempt to present a theory of culture. The essay contains the first rigorous definition of the Boasian
conception of culture as the genius of a people, seen in terms of the patterning of values. At the same time, it goes beyond a merely scientific, or
anthropological, definition of culture to include aesthetic and moral con-
siderations. In the discussion of these latter issues, Sapir sketches his vision
of cultural harmony, thus presenting the first explicit statement concerning what came commonly to be known as "cultural integration."[1]

Sapir begins by considering three common understandings of the meaning of the word "culture." First, he distinguishes a technical usage in which
"culture" refers to "any socially inherited element in the life of man, material or spiritual" (1924a:309). To avoid confusion, Sapir rejects the label
"culture" for this Tylorian assemblage and speaks instead of "civilization."
Second, he examines (and finds wanting) the popular notion of culture as
individual refinement based on selected acquisitions of intellect and manner. Sapir next goes to some length to spell out a third definition—perhaps
because, as he says, "those who use it are so seldom able to give us a per-
fectly clear idea of just what they themselves mean by culture" (310). This
third usage—that of the Boasians?—takes from the technical conception
its emphasis on the group, and from the popular notion the idea of a selection of those elements that are "more significant in a spiritual sense than
the rest" (310). Spiritual significance is not, however, dependent upon art,
science, and religion—as adherents to the second definition might assume—
but upon preeminent attitudes and values, drawn from whatever domain:

> We may perhaps come nearest the mark by saying that the cultural conception
> we are now trying to grasp aims to embrace in a single term those general
> attitudes, views of life, and specific manifestations of civilization that give a

---

1. I base this claim for the originality of Sapir's formulations on Kroeber and Kluckhohn's study (1952) of the culture concept. The claim of absolute priority is relatively
insignificant, for these were ideas in the air at the time. Sapir's contribution to their
elaboration is incontestable, as is his influence on colleagues who were working on the
same problems.

particular people its distinctive place in the world. Emphasis is put not so much on what is done and believed by a people as on how what is done and believed functions in the whole life of that people, on what significance it has for them. . . . Large groups of people everywhere tend to think and to act in accordance with established and all but instinctive forms, which are in large measure peculiar to it. (311–12)

Here, then, we have the idea that a culture is a patterning of values that gives significance to the lives of those who hold them and, furthermore, that people's participation in the pattern is "instinctive"—in other words, unconscious. But Sapir does not stop there, for even this third definition is merely "preliminary" (312). What interests him is the "genuine" culture, which he defines in terms of features drawn directly from his work in poetics and literary theory. First, in the genuine culture, the patterning of values is aesthetically harmonious. In other words, like a work of art, the genuine culture is formally perfected, or, in a later terminology, "integrated": "The genuine culture is not of necessity either high or low; it is merely inherently harmonious, balanced, self-satisfactory. It is the expression of a richly varied and yet somehow unified and consistent attitude toward life" (314–15). Second, this perfection of form is "expressive"—it is the embodiment of living thought, of values that people practice: "If it [the genuine culture] builds itself magnificent houses of worship, it is because of the necessity it feels to symbolize in beautiful stone a religious impulse that is deep and vital; if it is ready to discard institutionalized religion, it is prepared also to dispense with the homes of institutionalized religion" (315).

There is a significant comparison to be drawn here to a key idea in Boas's work—that of the secondary rationalization of unconscious formal patterns (Boas 1911b:67). In his discussions of form and function, Sapir follows Boas in this, arguing that actors' appeals to function—or to ultimate truth—are often mere rationalizations for actions whose origins are purely formal. Yet the argument is expanded here to coincide with Sapir's theory of art. What is rationalized, and clung to, is "the dry rot of social habit, devitalized" (1924a:315)—in other words, empty shells of formal patterning that no longer express living values. Just as the genuine poet would discard a formal device once it "ceases to be felt as inherently essential to sincerity of expression" (1917b:100), so the genuine culture discards institutional forms once they have lost their expressive function. Thus it is that the genuine culture "is not of necessity either high or low." As in art, what matters is the embodiment of thought in form, not the sophistication of formal technique as such (see 1918b).

Finally, the genuine culture is expressive in another sense. It is "internal." As Sapir says, "It works from the individual to ends." In other words, its ultimate values are built "out of the central interests and desires of its bearers," rather than imposed externally, from history and tradition down to the passive individual (1924a:316). For Sapir, this internal quality of a genuine culture manifests itself in the relationship of individual creativity and cultural form. Here the similarity to his arguments on poetic rhyme is apparent. "Creation," he argues, "is a bending of form to one's will, not a manufacture of form *ex nihilo*" (321). A genuine culture provides the context of traditional forms that nourishes each individual. At the same time, it allows the individual to "swing free," to express his inner self through the creation of new forms (322). By contrast, the external or spurious culture suffers either from "surfeit" or from "barrenness." In the first case, it overwhelms the individual with devitalized forms, which, like trite rhyme in poetry, inhibit self-expression; in the second, it does not provide the support and stimulation necessary for the realization of the individual will in acts of creativity. The spurious culture is thus a land of tinkers, for it can neither nourish nor tolerate "the iconoclasms and visions" of true artists.

Like the monograph "Time Perspective," "Culture, Genuine and Spurious" is in some respects uncharacteristic when compared to Sapir's later essays on culture theory. The romantic formulation of the idea of cultural harmony or integration would give way to the epistemological doubts expressed in his argument against the superorganic. Sapir came to insist that cultural wholes are analytic constructions, not real objects. When anthropologists speak of "a culture," they refer to a pattern or system that they themselves have constructed in the analysis of their data. Culture in this sense is a model abstracted from human interaction. But most anthropologists take a further step by reifying this model, treating it as a real-world existent and then using it to explain the very interactional data from which it has been abstracted. Sapir calls this "a fatal fallacy with regard to the objective reality of social and cultural patterns defined impersonally" (1938a:576). This fallacy allows theorists to oppose the entities of "culture" and "individual" and then to imagine that the former controls the latter— that is, that cultural norms constrain individuals, forcing them to behave in socially accepted ways (see Preston 1966).

In contrast to this position, Sapir was to argue not that culture does not matter, as Benedict interpreted him (Mead 1959:201), but that "the true locus of culture is in the interactions of specific individuals and, on the subjective side, in the world of meanings which each one of these individuals may unconsciously abstract for himself from his participation in these interactions" (1932:515). From this, it follows that culture "varies infinitely" (518), since each person can interpret any element of patterned interaction in a way that will be psychologically satisfactory to her. Furthermore, because every individual can convince others as to the validity of his interpretation, any such interpretation has, "from the very beginning, the essential possibility of culturalized behavior" (1938a:572). It is thus misleading to speak of individuals "adjusting" to culture, for what they in fact do is to bend cultural givens to their own ends, using them for creative self-expression and constructing culture anew in the process.

However abbreviated this summary of Sapir's later work may be, it should suffice to show the relationship between his art and his anthropology. In both, Sapir's first goal is to understand subjective realities and experiential truths as individuals know them. In both, he concludes that an excessive concern with outer realism—on the part of the omniscient narrator or the anthropologist who reifies culture—produces a distorted view of reality, however much it pretends to objectivity. In both, he favors instead a focus on the interaction of subjectivities, on multiple inner points of view. Finally, in both his art and his anthropology, Sapir treats formal givens—artistic conventions or cultural values—as means to self-expression rather than constraints upon individual freedom.

To argue that in the practice of art Sapir worked out ideas that later became central to his anthropological theory of culture raises the larger issues of intellectual influence and personal experience in the trajectory of a career. What, precisely, does it mean to say that Sapir worked out ideas in the practice of art? Did the ideas originate in the praxis, or were they present already, if merely latently, in his mind, accessible through some combinations of experience? How are we to understand Sapir's poetic endeavors in the context of a larger biography? Does his poetry represent a detour, motivated by frustrations and personal anxieties, from an otherwise normal career, or ought Sapir's art to be seen as part of his anthropology?

When I became acquainted with Sapir's poetry, I noticed first the thematic evidence of anthropological influence on poetic content. But the more I read, the more I decided that it makes as much sense to seek the influence of Sapir's poetry on his anthropology as to expect to find things the other way around. Only retrospectively can it be claimed that Sapir's poetry was merely a diversion: in actuality, art and anthropology were united in the life and mind of one man, and that life was lived in a particular intellectual milieu, at a time when certain questions and ideas were in the air. In practice, it is rarely possible to construct the history—as a unilinear series of influences and events—of a mind, a life, a milieu. The associations are too complex.

Take, for example, the question of intellectual influence, of the "origin" of Sapir's ideas. In addition to Boas, whose influence on Sapir can hardly be overestimated, who were the other thinkers that Sapir responded to? One can, of course, cite Freud and Jung on the basis of Sapir's sympathetic reviews of some of their works. But Sapir rarely acknowledged intellectual debts. Thus it is all the more remarkable that he should explicitly avow a debt to Croce in his book *Language*: "Among contemporary writers of influence on liberal thought Croce is one of the very few who have gained an understanding of the fundamental significance of language. He has pointed out its close relation to the problem of art. I am deeply indebted to him for this insight" (1921a:iii). Both Modjeska (1968:346–47) and Hymes (1969; 1970:261, 264) have reasonably suggested that Croce's influence might have been important in Sapir's intellectual development. Yet Hall has argued that Sapir could not have been significantly influenced by Croce—that Sapir merely read into Croce more than was actually there—interpreting him "in the light of his own much . . . deeper knowledge of linguistic structures" (1969:499). But, however useful such an argument is to preserve Sapir's reputation for brilliance, it fails to account for the enthusiasm of his explicit acknowledgment. I would suggest that the problem vanishes when we understand that influences are rarely specific causal connections. Even in the case of Sapir's debt to Boas, the question is not so much one of where a person's ideas originated but, rather, of why he chose to develop those ideas and not others, and how—under what circumstances and in what directions—he developed them. It is in response to the question of "how" that Sapir's art becomes relevant. He once wrote to Benedict that poetic technique "comes to its own only after great experience in handling words and forms" (Mead 1959:163). That his understanding of linguistic form was intuitive is perhaps true, but the development of his linguistic theory must have depended at least as much on long experience in working with particular languages as on native ability (see Pike 1967:65). The same may be said of his theory of culture. He had at hand the prototheory of Boas, his developing understanding of language, and inspiration from people like Croce, Rickert, Freud, and Jung. But it was in the practice of art, where Sapir could experience the living force of the relationship between feeling and form, that he was stimulated to forge ideas—some borrowed, some reformulated, some original—into his own theory of culture.

In light of this argument, we are led to reconsider the relationship between Sapir's art and his anthropology. There is a surface plausibility to the claim that his poetry was a temporary response to the difficulties of a particular phase of his life. But poetry was not merely an outlet, an activity utterly separated from his "serious" work. Several commentators have pointed out that Sapir's poetry influenced the style of his anthropological writing (Newman 1951:182–83; Voegelin 1952:2). In addition to this stylistic influence, we should, I have argued, recognize the influence of Sapir's artistic endeavors on the substance of his theory. This is, after all, what we would expect if we take seriously his theory of culture: just as the form of a language or culture cannot be separated from the content or thought that it embodies, so a self-conscious creative praxis, as in music and poetry, must inevitably shape any deliberate reflections on human creativity, as in a theory of culture.

CHAPTER 3

Antiromantic Romanticism

Sapir's Critique of American Individualism

In the memorable final paragraph of "The Grammarian and His Language," Edward Sapir proclaimed his allegiance, and the allegiance of linguistics, the discipline for which he was speaking, to what he called the "classical spirit." Drawing on a conventional dichotomy, Sapir contrasted the classical "freedom in restraint" of disciplines such as linguistics, mathematics, and music to the "romanticism," with its "frenetic desire," that he found "rampant in America today" (1924b:159). Sapir's defense of linguistics was published in the first issue of H. L. Mencken's *American Mercury,* certainly a forum for what, even in Sapir's time, was called "cultural criticism."[1] In his essay, Sapir not only defended linguistics from the philistines, he suggested something of why a "romantic" American culture was ill prepared to appreciate it.

An expressed preference for the classical over the romantic, for "freedom in restraint" over "frenetic desire," runs through Sapir's work of three decades. Yet there is another strain to Sapir's thought, an "antiromantic

---

1. The term "cultural criticism" became fashionable in anthropology in the 1980s, partly because of the influence of George Marcus and Michael Fischer's *Anthropology as Cultural Critique* (1986), which advocates a "repatriated" anthropology focused on the critical analysis of modern Western societies, an anthropology that Marcus and Fischer see as continuous with that of Ruth Benedict and Margaret Mead. I find the term "cultural criticism" in Waldo Frank's *The Re-Discovery of America,* a book that Sapir (1929a) reviewed. Frank (1929:313–27) used the term to refer to a discourse about American culture that he dated to 1909, a discourse that Sapir knew and contributed to.

romanticism," that is central both to his science and to his cultural criticism. Antiromantic romanticism permeates Sapir's essay "Culture, Genuine and Spurious" (1924a). It also marks his later critique of American culture and its "spurious" individualism. Indeed, the antiromantic romanticism of Sapir's cultural criticism derives ultimately from the "cosmographical" orientation to science that Sapir, more than any of Boas's students, pursued and elaborated.

To begin, I should note the relatively uncomplicated sense of "romanticism" and "romantic" that Sapir most often employed. In this usage, the term was opposed not so much to classicism as to practical realism: to be romantic is to orient oneself to a dreamworld, a romance, rather than reality. This sense of the term is developed at length in Wyndham Lewis's *Time and Western Man* (1927), a book that Sapir admired (Sapir 1929b). Lewis tried to capture the meaning that "romantic" had for his contemporaries in the following terms:

> We say "romantic" when we wish to define something too emotionalized . . . , something opposed to the actual or real: a self-indulgent habit of mind or a tendency to shut the eyes to what is unpleasant, in favour of things arbitrarily chosen for their flattering pleasantness. Or else we apply it to the effects of an egoism that bathes in the self-feeling to the exclusion of contradictory realities, including the Not-self; achieving what we see to be a false unity and optimism. (1927:10)

Lewis's discussion comes close to Sapir's use of the term "romantic" when he is writing in an antiromantic vein. Yet Sapir's characteristic intellectual attitude, directed as it was to the dialectical interaction of individual experience and cultural form, may well strike us as profoundly romantic, if we understand that term as it has been defined by literary historians and critics. Thus M. L. Abrams's groundbreaking *The Mirror and the Lamp* (1953) discusses romanticism as an aesthetic revolution in which self-expression rather than mimesis or moralism came to be seen as the proper goal of literature. Self-expression, creativity, sincerity, spontaneity, the foundational rather than merely decorative role of metaphor, technique as personal discovery rather than traditional canon: these themes that Abrams (1953:100–103) finds at the heart of romanticism are central to Sapir's aesthetic theory and are prominent as well in his anthropology and linguistics.

Sapir's aesthetics and literary criticism are inextricably tied to his cultural criticism, as "Culture, Genuine and Spurious" shows. The essay suggests a romanticism that characterizes much of cultural anthropology: the romance of the individuated, organic cultural whole. This romantic strain has obvious connections to Herder and the German romantic tradition, and it came to modern American anthropology by way of Franz Boas. Yet the romance of organic culture was for the most part foreign to Sapir's work. Its appearance in "Culture, Genuine and Spurious" seems due to the fact that the essay was written not for an audience of professional anthropologists but as a piece of cultural criticism directed to a long-standing debate about the existence and value of an American national culture. As such, its romanticism owes as much to Matthew Arnold as to Boas, and its hopeful vision of an organically integrated, or genuine, American culture derives from a temporary flush of cultural optimism that vanished from Sapir's work, and from the work of many of his contemporaries, after the world war.

That optimism gave way, in Sapir's cultural criticism, to increasing distress concerning what he saw as the spurious—and romantic, in Lewis's sense—individualism of modern American culture. Sapir's criticism of American individualism depends heavily on another trend of nineteenth-century thought that literary historians have taken as central to romanticism: "anti-self-consciousness." According to Geoffrey Hartman (1970), the romantics' cultivation of anti-self-consciousness was undertaken as an antidote to the triumph of Enlightenment reason, those analytic habits of mind that "murder to dissect," in Wordsworth's famous phrase. Sapir, too, came to believe that the misuse of science and an overly sophisticated self-consciousness were at the heart of the modern malady that barred the way, in his view, to the achievement of a genuine American culture. And the critique of spurious individualism has its obverse in Sapir's theoretical writings on culture and personality, which call for an anthropological science capable of accounting for cultural forms without discounting the experience and creativity of the individuals who enact them.

Matthew Arnold, Randolph Bourne, and the Quest for Genuine Culture

Sir: Long before I had met Randolph Bourne I seemed to divine from the tenor of his writing that he was one of those extraordinarily fine-grained men that one meets but rarely in a lifetime and that it is always an exceptional privilege to know. It required only a little sympathetic insight to feel that his occasional "bitterness" was in reality but the keen edge of a remorseless sincerity and that he would have been as eager to cut and change his own soul with it as anyone else's. His extraordinary combination of the will to see things as they are with a warmth of idealism (not the phrase-making kind) still haunts me as something particularly inspiring. What I most liked, however, about Bourne was his exquisite sensibility to the esthetic in literature, to the nuances of thought and feeling and expression. One knew instinctively that if anything passed by him with his approval or sympathy, it was indeed something genuine. His own style was well-nigh perfect. Often clever, he was too sensitive ever to be merely clever. I imagine him shrinking from vulgarity of any kind as one shrinks from a disgusting bug. (Sapir 1919b:45)

Today resuscitated as a "forgotten prophet" and "cultural radical" (Clayton 1984; Vaughan 1997; also see Blake 1990), Randolph Bourne was "the nearly official voice of the Rebellion" of a new generation of American intellectuals against the "custodians" of Victorian culture symbolized (at least for Bourne) by Matthew Arnold (May 1959:297). Sapir's elegiac letter for Bourne was published in the *Dial* shortly after the latter's death, at thirty-two, on December 22, 1918. Revealing a personal acquaintance between the two men as well as the intensity of Sapir's admiration for Bourne, this letter aids us in placing Sapir's cultural values, as formulated in "Culture, Genuine and Spurious," on the intellectual landscape of the late teens and early twenties. Sapir's praise of "remorseless sincerity," "the will to see things as they are"(1919b:45), and aesthetic "sensibility," combined with his marked distaste for "vulgarity," remind us that his philosophy of culture was rooted in sources beyond the narrowly anthropological.

In *The End of American Innocence*, Henry May argues that a "belief in culture" was an important value in the United States at the turn of the twentieth century (1959:30; also see Hegeman 1999; Manganaro 2002). The culture championed by American patricians and intellectuals, and aspired to by the middle classes, was elitist, evolutionary, unitary, and European. It was culture as defined by Matthew Arnold—or as his critics claimed he had defined it—and at first glance it seems the antithesis of the relativistic culture that Boasian anthropology was conceptualizing during the same period. Yet, as Stocking has suggested (1963:89), concern for integration and holism made Arnold's notion of culture closer in some respects to the modern anthropological notion than was that of Arnold's contemporary,

E. B. Tylor. Moreover, the rejection of Matthew Arnold by Bourne's generation was linked to a nationalistic quest for an American culture distinct
from European culture. The uniqueness and vitality of American industry
and democracy meant, according to some nationalist intellectuals, that
American culture had to develop apart from European civilization, which,
in any case, could be seen as crumbling in World War I. Thus, in addition to conventional elitist notions of cultural standards, discussions of
culture in the teens and twenties could draw on a nationalistic (and ultimately romantic) conception of cultural plurality, if not on anthropological relativism.

In *Culture and Anarchy*, Matthew Arnold had drawn a sharp distinction
between culture and civilization. For him, England's development represented civilization, not culture, and Arnold defined English civilization as
external and mechanical, suffering from a spiritual aridity that only culture could remedy. (Tylor, by contrast, equated civilization and culture and
assumed, with some hesitation [1871, vol. 1:24–28], that England's advanced
industrial state was matched by an equally advanced moral and intellectual
development.) Arnold defined culture as the "pursuit of our total perfection by means of getting to know . . . the best which has been thought and
said in the world; and through this knowledge, turning a stream of fresh
and free thought upon our stock notions and habits, which we now follow
staunchly but mechanically" (1868:6).

So reads Arnold's basic definition, but we must note three further aspects
of his cultural philosophy. First, culture for Matthew Arnold was an
"inward operation" (7), that is, it concerned the intellectual and spiritual
aspects of human nature, "as distinguished from our animality" (47). Second, the perfection of culture was, as Arnold put it, "harmonious" (11, 49,
151), by which he meant that it entailed the development of all the spiritual faculties of human beings. Arnold insisted on this because he saw one
of the chief obstacles to culture in England to be Puritan religiosity, which
he found stifling and narrow. When Arnold spoke of harmonious perfection, he wished to include "art, science, poetry, philosophy, history, as well
as . . . religion" within the realm of culture (47). Third, Arnold thought that
culture ought to be "general," or democratically available to all social classes
(11, 48). In sum, for Arnold, "culture, which is the study of perfection, leads
us . . . to conceive of true human perfection as a *harmonious* perfection,
developing all sides of our humanity; and as a *general* perfection, developing all parts of our society" (11; emphasis in original).

Though American acceptance of Arnold's cultural outlook was not as uncontested as Bourne portrayed it (Raleigh 1957), Arnold exerted a strong and lasting influence in the United States, perhaps more so than in his native England. As Bourne's writings attest, Matthew Arnold stimulated both those who followed his gospel and those who rebelled against it. Among the rebels, Bourne took on Arnold and the standards that he represented in essays that Bourne published in the *New Republic*, *Atlantic Monthly*, *Dial*, and other periodicals that Sapir read. For example, in "Our Cultural Humility," Bourne pointed to an uncritical reception of Arnold's message as a central feature of the American cultural landscape: "It was Matthew Arnold, read and reverenced by the generation immediately preceding our own, who set to our eyes a definition and a goal of culture which has become the common property of all our world. To know the best that had been thought and said . . . was a clear ideal which dissolved the mists in which the vaguenesses of culture had been lost" (1914:31).

According to Bourne, Arnold's culture appealed with particular force to Americans because it was both "quantitative" and "democratic"—since "culture was a matter of acquisition," everyone could aspire to it (31). Bourne depicted Americans of several classes flocking to Europe and American millionaires carrying away cultural samples to fill American museums and private mansions; all were motivated by "the idea that somehow culture could be imbibed, that from the contact with the treasures of Europe there would be rubbed off on us a little of that grace which had made the art" (33). Bourne contrasted this American "cultural humility"—which, he claimed, was in itself "humiliating" for a "genuinely patriotic American" (36)—to what he saw as the living culture of at least some Europeans. American tourists "astonished" the cultured European who, according to Bourne, was "more interested in contemporaneous literature and art and music than in his worthies of the olden time," and whose "attitude towards . . . culture . . . is one of daily appreciation and intimacy, not that attitude of reverence with which we Americans approach alien art" (34–35). Above all, Bourne objected to Americans' acquisitive quest for culture because he thought it would "prevent forever any genuine culture." Culture, he wrote, "is not an acquired familiarity with things outside, but an inner and constantly operating taste, . . . the insistent judging of everything that comes to our minds and senses. . . . By fixing our eyes humbly on the ages that are past, and on foreign countries, we effectually protect ourselves from that inner taste which is the only sincere 'culture'" (37–39).

In another essay, "The Cult of the Best," Bourne developed similar ideas with reference to art education. Here "the Best" was, once again, "what Matthew Arnold has stamped as right" (1917a:196). As Bourne saw it, "Artistic appreciation in this country has been understood chiefly as the acquiring of a familiarity with 'good works of art,' . . . rather than as the cultivating of spontaneous taste" (193). Contending that the spontaneous taste of individuals varies as temperaments vary, he argued that an art education that forces everyone to conform to the same taste, that is, to appreciate the classics, leads either to exclusion—those for whom the classics are uncongenial simply lose interest in art—or to spuriousness—people who pretend to like what has been sanctified by the Matthew Arnolds. As Bourne put it, "You get as a result hypocrites or 'lowbrows,' with culture reserved only for a few" (194). And then the nationalistic note: attributing "our failure to develop . . . [an] indigenous art spirit" to this slavish imitation of the best in place of the "vital," he called for art education focusing "on what you do like, not on what you ought to like" (194–95).

The similarity of Bourne's arguments and rhetoric to Sapir's "Culture, Genuine and Spurious" is striking. Sapir's letters to Lowie suggest that his essay was completed in 1918, at a time when Sapir would regularly have read Bourne. To his chagrin, Sapir had trouble publishing "Culture, Genuine and Spurious" in its entirety (Lowie 1965:27, 30, 34). Parts of it appeared in the *Dial* in 1919 and in *Dalhousie Review* in 1922. A complete version was published in 1924 in the *American Journal of Sociology*, but most readers today will find it in Mandelbaum's 1949 collection of Sapir's essays. There it appears as one of a number of general or theoretical papers on culture. Yet, as Lowie remarked (1956:126), albeit disparagingly, the essay "explicitly sets aside the technical meaning of 'culture,' thus dealing with something beyond the sphere of the science [of anthropology] altogether."

As I have shown, in "Culture, Genuine and Spurious," Sapir defined not just culture but "genuine" culture. He began by reviewing three commonplace uses of the term: the ethnological (culture as the totality of "socially inherited" human achievements), the elitist (culture as art and refinement), and the romantic (culture as the *Geist* of a people) (1924a:309–11). Drawing on the second and third senses of the term but going well beyond them, Sapir proceeded to define the genuine culture. According to Sapir, the genuine culture is, first, spiritually harmonious: a "unified and consistent attitude toward life" (315), one in which all aspects of life are "bound together into a significant whole" (318). Second, genuine culture has nothing to do with functional efficiency or technological progress. Cultural harmony or the lack of it can coincide with any degree of material civilization: "Civilization, as a whole, moves on; culture comes and goes" (317). Third, in a genuine culture individuals are never sacrificed to efficiency. Even where the division of labor is elaborate and people's tasks highly specialized, "a genuine culture refuses to consider the individual as a mere cog" (315). As Sapir put it, "The genuine culture is internal, it works from the individual to ends" (316). In other words, cultural goals or ends are not to be mechanically imposed upon the members of a culture; rather, individuals should experience cultural goals as their own goals and contribute to defining them. Finally, in the genuine culture there is a dialectical interaction between individual personalities and cultural forms: a genuine culture provides individuals with the social and aesthetic resources they need to become creators; they in turn can renew and alter their culture through their creativity. Thus Sapir saw art as central to culture—not because it represents the "refinement" that high-culture elitists seek but because it is, above all, through art that individuals, starting with traditional forms, can express their personalities.

It is impossible to know if Sapir took the term "genuine culture" from Bourne (who, as we saw, used it [1914] before Sapir), nor can we tell the exact nature of Bourne's influence on Sapir. It seems likely that the two men were thinking along the same lines and that Bourne's writings spurred Sapir to formulate his own developing ideas about culture and the individual. Like Bourne's discussions of culture, "Culture, Genuine and Spurious" emphasizes artistic creativity and aesthetic values. Also similar to Bourne, and appropriate to the audience for whom both were writing, is the mild optimism concerning the future of a genuine American culture with which Sapir's essay ends (328–31). Above all, Sapir followed or agreed with Bourne in stressing the individual's aesthetic sensibilities at the expense of externally imposed cultural standards. And the spurious culture that Sapir described— "It is not uncommon to find in America individuals who have had engrafted on a barren . . . culture a cultural tradition that apes a grace already embalmed" (323)—is American culture as depicted by Bourne, overburdened with the European past recommended by Matthew Arnold.

But Randolph Bourne is only part of the story: equally suggestive are the similarities between "Culture, Genuine and Spurious" and *Culture and Anarchy*. Indeed, it is possible to read a passage from the opening of the former as a playful allusion to the latter. Arnold had written, "I propose now to try and enquire . . . what culture really is, what good it can do, what is our own special need of it" (1868:41). Sapir wrote: "Whatever culture is, we know that it is, or is considered to be, a good thing. I propose to give my idea of what kind of a good thing culture is" (1924a:308).

Whether Sapir's wording contains an allusion to Arnold or not, the substantive similarities between the two discussions of culture are not insignificant. Both Sapir and Arnold considered genuine or true culture to be internal, and though they use the word somewhat differently, for both it concerned the spiritual accomplishments of humanity. Moreover, both opposed culture to civilization, which they saw as external and mechanical. Arnold criticized his compatriots for considering as "precious ends in themselves" such externals as coal, railroads, population growth, and religious organization (50), that is, all the things by which Victorian progressives measured the greatness of their civilization. Similarly, Sapir ridiculed the American fetishism of technological prowess: "Perched on the heights of an office building twenty or more stories taller than our fathers ever dreamed of, we feel that we are getting up in the world. Hurling our bodies through space with an ever accelerating velocity, we feel that we are getting on" (317). And he explicitly rejected the idea that technological or material progress, to which he, too, applied the term "civilization" (309), had any necessary connection with genuine culture.

A second similarity is the insistence of both Arnold and Sapir on the importance of culture as a stimulus to creativity and a challenge to unthinking routine. Both were sensitive to the inertia of habit, people's willingness to accept their social heritage passively, even clinging to it as an end in itself rather than as the means to further development. Arnold's bête noire in this respect was the Protestant ethic, whereas Sapir's was high-cultural snobbishness. Still, when Arnold speaks of using "fresh and free thought" to criticize mechanically followed "stock notions and habits" (6), we are reminded of Sapir's aesthetic theory, in which personal creativity is seen as the transcendence of inherited forms.

A third similarity between Arnold and Sapir is to be found in the notion of harmonious development. For Arnold, harmony indicated an elitist well-roundedness encompassing all the domains of traditional high culture: art, science, philosophy, and so on. By contrast, Sapir's well-roundedness was sociological: all domains of social life, not merely those associated with high culture, must be interrelated rather than functionally fragmented. But Sapir also argued that genuine culture in an advanced civilization, that is, in one having a complex division of labor, had to rest upon high-cultural activities. Since individuals could no longer be expected to achieve mastery in the interdependent economic and political domains, they had to be able to find compensation in a realm of spiritual activity that is nothing other than Arnold's "culture."

There are, of course, differences in Sapir's and Arnold's approaches to culture. Arnold's culture is high culture; it is an evaluative concept that singles out one and only one tradition as "culture." Arnold's culture is "the best which has been thought and said in the world" (6), and there is no question but that his "best" refers to the Western tradition, classical, Christian, and humanist. As Stocking, making the comparison to Tylor, notes (1963: 87), "Arnold could never have called a work *Primitive Culture*: the very idea would have been to him a contradiction in terms." By contrast, Sapir was a Boasian relativist for whom all peoples are cultured or, at least, have the potential to develop genuine culture.

Moreover, Arnold wrote in a nineteenth-century idiom in which the term "character" was positively valued and allied to duty, as opposed to the negatively valued "personality," linked to an irresponsible freedom (Susman 1984:275). For Arnold, the fact that culture was absolute and inextricably linked to the Christian tradition meant that individuals were morally bound to pursue it. Moreover, "sincerity" was, above all, a moral quality, allied with "discipline," not freedom: "To walk staunchly by the best light one has, to be strict and sincere with oneself, not to be of the number who say and do not, to be in earnest,—this is the discipline by which alone man is enabled to rescue his life from thralldom to the passing moment and to his bodily senses, to ennoble it, and to make it eternal" (37). At the same time, Arnold used the term "personality" pejoratively, when he criticized English individualism as "our hatred of all limits to the unrestrained swing of the individual's personality" (49). By contrast, Sapir understood "sincerity" in relation to the expression of personality, and sincere self-expression, though it depended on discipline, led to that freedom in creativity which only genuine cultures made possible: "The creative spirit gains sustenance and vigor for its own unfolding and, if it is strong enough, it may swing free . . . with a poise hardly dreamed of by the timid iconoclasts of unformed cultures" (322).

Yet these differences should not lead us to overlook the fact that Sapir, Bourne, and Arnold participated in a shared discourse heavily influenced by romantic thought. Like the romantics in general, all three sought a way to recover genuine culture in the post-Enlightenment world of rationality, antitradition, and industrial democracy. Moreover, for all three, genuine culture had a personal as well as a collective dimension. Arnold's reliance on tradition coexisted alongside a concern for personal development, "the conscious effort of each man to come to the realization of his complete humanity," as Trilling summarizes Matthew Arnold's position (1939:252). Conversely, the emphasis that Sapir and Bourne placed on personal creativity was, in their more optimistic moments, linked to their belief that a genuine collective culture would develop in the United States. As Sapir phrased it in "Culture, Genuine and Spurious": "In time . . . a genuine culture— better yet, a series of linked autonomous cultures—will grace our lives" (331). Yet the closing sentences of his essay represent the high point of Sapir's hopes for American culture. The war and its aftermath discouraged Sapir, Bourne, and most of the cultural critics of their generation, as the twenties ushered in not culture but jazz, the cult of business efficiency, and emancipated sex.

Spurious Culture: The Critique of American Individualism

The rebellion of American cultural critics against Victorian society and culture was profoundly affected by the war. Before the United States entered the hostilities, it had been possible for intellectuals and artists to foresee social reform and cultural flowering as the issue of their efforts. Some even saw the outbreak of war as potentially beneficial: it would hasten the death of the old cultural order, thereby making room for a renewal of civilization. As Harriet Monroe, writing in *Poetry* magazine, put it: "At first [war] seems merely a murderous violator, hideously interrupting all the good works of the world. . . . And yet war is a builder. Out of the ruins of eras it tumbles together foundation-stones for new ones" (1917:142–43). Despite such naive optimism, the costs of American participation in a war that came to seem more and more irrationally destructive, followed by the complexities, vindictiveness, and ultimate futility of the peace-making process, ended the optimism of many liberal and radical reformers. As Sapir himself wrote, discussing the "peace terms" in a May 1919 letter to Lowie, "more and more one realizes the hopelessness of getting anywhere through the accepted legal channels. It's all a most laughably vicious circle" (Lowie 1965:34–35).

Once again, Randolph Bourne appears in retrospect as a leader for the intellectuals of his generation. As May (1959:394–95) puts it, "the precise moment of change," from "belief in progress" to "conservatism" or "despair

. . . can be seen in one famous case, the wartime metamorphosis of Randolph Bourne" (1959:394–95). When John Dewey announced in a series of *New Republic* articles his support for American participation in the war, Bourne broke with his mentor and responded with an essay entitled "Twilight of Idols." Prefiguring the critique of efficiency that would become increasingly common in critical discourse in the twenties, Bourne decried what he saw as a purely instrumental pragmatism unconnected to higher ideals:

> One has a sense of having come to a sudden, short stop at the end of an intellectual era. In the [war] crisis, this philosophy of intelligent control just does not measure up to our needs. What is the root of this inadequacy that is felt so keenly by our restless minds? . . . Is there something in these realistic attitudes that works actually against poetic vision, against concern for the quality of life as above the machinery of life? Apparently there is. The war has revealed a younger intelligentsia, trained up in the pragmatic dispensation, immensely ready for the executive ordering of events, pitifully unprepared for the intellectual interpretation or the idealistic focusing of ends. . . . It is true, Dewey calls for a more attentive formulation of war-purposes and ideas, but he calls largely to deaf ears. His disciples have learned all too literally the instrumental attitude toward life, and . . . they are making themselves efficient instruments of the war-technique, accepting with little question the ends as announced from above. (1917b:342–43)

The cult of efficiency unlinked to higher values would become a specific focus of Sapir's cultural criticism, as would the naive faith in social engineering also suggested in Bourne's remarks. In addition, when Bourne spoke of values "announced from above"—the "formulation of opinion . . . left largely in the hands of professional patriots, sensational editors, archaic radicals" (343)—he put his finger on another problem that would increasingly inspire pessimism among cultural critics in the twenties: the relationship of intellectual elites to mass society and culture. Once again, we find Bourne and Sapir closer to Matthew Arnold than to the spirit of cultural revolution of the prewar years. "Vulgarity" is a key word with respect to this issue (recall Sapir's strong praise for Bourne's avoidance of vulgarity). Bourne railed against the movies, in a 1915 tirade about "lowbrow snobbery" and "the stale culture of the masses." For Sapir, the vulgarity and untrustworthiness of mass taste were epitomized by the success of jazz.

Finally, as I will show in chapter 4, during the twenties, Sapir became critical of changing sexual mores and the trend toward more "freedom" in personal life, a freedom justified by the popularization of the work of such thinkers as Dewey and Freud (Crunden 1972:29–75).[2]

On several counts, then, intellectuals like Bourne and Sapir became disillusioned by the war and increasingly pessimistic about American culture during the twenties. Describing his reaction to the movies, Bourne (1915) had written, "I begin to feel like an esoteric little bubble on a great stream of the common life." Twelve years later, in September 1927, Sapir described a related sentiment in a letter to Ruth Benedict: "The age and I don't seem to be on very intimate speaking terms" (Mead 1959:185). Bourne, and then Sapir, came to see themselves as isolated not only from the masses but from much of the intelligentsia as well. The dominant view of American civilization during the twenties was an optimistic one, based on a belief in technological progress and social engineering. This view was fostered by the business and social-scientific communities and agreed to more generally by many intellectuals (May 1956:406–7). Dissenters like Sapir felt themselves in the minority (see Stocking 1976:32–33).

Sapir's alienation both from mass society and from the popular intelligentsia is expressed first in his literary criticism and later in essays on social issues and cultural trends. As I have suggested, his literary and cultural criticism is shaped by an antiromantic romanticism that relies on the notion of sincere yet unself-conscious self-expression while rejecting the undisciplined, self-indulgent romanticism sketched at the outset of this chapter.

2. Sapir was prepared to find aesthetic value in Negro spirituals but not in jazz, a common attitude during the twenties (see M. Berger 1947). Reviewing a collection of spirituals, Sapir noted their combination of "nobility" and "a delicately toying spirit" but added: "This spirit never degenerates into the vulgarity of jazz" (1928a:174). Four years earlier, he had written a poem entitled "On Hearing Plaintive Jazz by Radio," in which he imitated the (to him) nervous syncopation of the music:

Not joy's fly-off, but desiccated, quick quick
Clap-trap, rumble and run of inanity,
Hilarious clatter of sticks semi-military,
Xylophone tumble, sad saxophone sweetly sick;

Not joy on the wing, but sprightly heart gone dying,
Experimental joy, grotesqueried
Chow-chow of emotional hints, the liveried
Wee tatters of the soul gone dragon-flying. (SUP:6/15/1924)

As I have noted, Sapir praised Bourne for his "remorseless sincerity." Writing to Monroe in March 1925 about Benedict's poetry, Sapir's highest praise was for its sincerity: "Above all, every line of her work is sincere" (PMP: 3/23/1925). And a year later he chided Benedict herself for writing poetry under a pseudonym: "Pen names are an abomination. You know how I feel about even toying with the idea of dissociation of personality. I hate it" (Mead 1959:182). Pen names, of course, make sincerity impossible.[3]

Closely allied to sincerity is unself-consciousness. Sapir thought that sincerity could "win through" (1925b:99) only at those moments when the self was not consciously taking stock of itself. Increasingly disenchanted with the new American poetry, he repeatedly observed that American poets were too concerned with self-analysis and with other self-conscious intellectual exercises to be able to express themselves in genuine art. Explaining to Benedict in September 1927 why he felt out of tune with "the age," he described "intelligence and its vanity" as the "arch disease of the time and the reason for its choking vulgarity and its flimsiness" (Mead 1959:186). In the same letter, he criticized the poetry of Hart Crane for its "nervous excitement" and elsewhere (1922c) spoke of "the too clever smoothness that has been made fashionable by Mr. T. S. Eliot." By contrast, he always found in those poets that he praised—Edwin Arlington Robinson, "H. D." [Hilda Doolittle], Emily Dickinson, Gerard Manley Hopkins, Leonie Adams— sincerity allied to, and made possible by, unself-consciousness. Commenting on how thought and expression coincided in the work of Robinson (perhaps his favorite contemporary poet), Sapir concluded that "in this man thought is not far from feeling, that what we behold is the genuinely artistic record of a rigorous personality. Mr. Robinson has not merely asked himself to think and feel thus and so: he has taken his sophisticated bitter soul for granted" (1922d:141).

A remarkable review of Emily Dickinson's work sets out Sapir's critique of his compatriots' poetry in some detail. Sapir noted Dickinson's technical deficiencies (she had not been nourished in the "soil" of a genuine culture [1924a:322]) as well as her poetic failures but found not "the slightest alloy of sham" (1925b:98–99), from which, he thought, she had been protected

3. Indeed, Sapir's insistence on sincerity at a time when literary artists wished to be "hard," impersonal, and invisible tended to date him (Langbaum 1957:30). As Trilling noted, "To praise a work of literature by calling it sincere is now at best a way of saying that although it need be given no aesthetic or intellectual admiration, it was at least conceived in innocence of heart" (1971:6).

by her isolation from the intellectual trends of her time. In particular, he noted that "she was somehow unaware of the fact that we are living in a material age" and was thus delivered from the necessity of an intellectualized revolt against it (100). Sapir saw Dickinson as "a primitive" (101) utterly without doctrine. Not sustained by God, by love, by intellectual revolt, "she asks nothing further of the soul than that it be itself" (104). But such, precisely, was the quality that Sapir thought lacking in most modern poetry:

> Poetry has become externalized, and the intuitive hunger of the soul for the beautiful moulding of experience actually felt, not fiddled with or stared at, is not often stilled. The bulk of contemporary verse, with its terrifyingly high average of excellence, gives us everything but the ecstasy that is the language of unhampered intuitive living. We have shrewd observation, fantasy, the vivid life of the senses, pensive grace, eloquence, subtle explorations of the intellect . . . but curiously little spiritual life. Very few poets seem willing, or able, to take their true selves seriously without either indulging in irrelevant biography or fleeing into the remoter chambers of some ivory tower. (100)

Flight to the ivory tower concerned Sapir not a little, and here his criticism bore not only on poetry but also on the misuses of science that he found increasingly prevalent in the 1920s. His quarrel was not with the disciplined, classical practice of science that he invoked at the end of "The Grammarian and His Language." Indeed, he thought pure science to be ahead of its time, as the following remarks to Monroe indicate:

> I believe I know something about the imaginative, even mystical, tendency in contemporary scientific thought. It interests me more than a little. Nevertheless the age as a whole is still . . . "material" in its general philosophy, particularly in America. . . . It is one of the most interesting ironies of cultural history that hard-headed scientific thinking (for example, in Mendelian heredity with its chromosomes and genes; in atomic structure; in conceptions of space, time, motion, and matter) is forcing a sort of mathematical mysticism which leaves official philosophy and humanism behind as more crassly material in thought than the spirit they thought they were combating as material. (PMP:5/6/1925)

What bothered Sapir particularly was the "romantic" misuse of science to provide easy and apparently authoritative answers to difficult questions.

For example, Sapir contributed "Let Race Alone" to a series of articles published in the *Nation* during 1925, a time when heightened racism and xenophobia had stimulated liberal thinkers to publicize a critique of such "scientific" doctrines as those propounded by the eugenicists. Sapir's essay should be compared to an essay by Boas, which preceded it. Boas (1925) had confined himself to a sober scientific refutation of the presuppositions of eugenicist doctrine. Sapir, too, debunked racist assumptions, but he was equally concerned to present a critique of the culture that readily believed them. Thus he framed his argument against the "romantic race-mongers" (1925c:213) with a telling analysis of the American religion of science: "We live in an age not so much of science as of scientific application. We are not so much possessed of a philosophic criticism that may be supposed to be born of scientific research as we are urged on by a restless faith in the pronouncements of science. We have made it a religion" (211). Sapir went on to point out that Americans had no patience with the tempered, even "dim" and "cryptic" results of scientific research; rather, Americans sought easy answers, "systematically" using science to rationalize their prejudices. Thus Sapir found scientistic racism to be "as good an example as we could wish of heated desire subdued to the becoming coolness of a technical vocabulary" (211).

Sapir made similar arguments in reviews of works by Boas and Bertrand Russell. Deeply ambivalent about his teacher Boas, Sapir portrayed him as poetically repressed, his scientific thinking "incomplete in expression" and "prevented by a certain fierce delicacy from ever declaring more than it manifestly must." Yet Sapir much preferred Boas's caution to the misuses of science at the hands of "our fashionable romantic biologists" and, more generally, by "an age that prizes lazy comfort in thought and . . . rigor only in dehumanized action" (1929c:278). Sapir thought that Russell, unlike Boas, was at home in this romantic age. Sapir found the philosopher's rational solutions to social and existential problems to be idle dreaming about "a high Polynesia . . . built on the unshakeable coral reef of science," a world in which "the jaded intellectual faculty" could "do or have anything" (1929b).

Thus, in the spurious American culture, Sapir found that most people gave way to undisciplined desire; at the same time, because they were enamored of efficiency, they pretended to be "cool" and "rigorous," even though they lacked the means to practice such an approach to life. Sapir stated this argument most fully (and in terms that directly recall "The Grammarian and His Language") at the end of his review of Thurman Arnold's *The Folklore of Capitalism*. Arnold (1937) had tried to demystify the rhetoric of American capitalism and democracy, arguing that adherence to an outmoded mythology of individual freedom was being used to obstruct social reforms that could be accomplished only through large-scale government organization. While sympathetic to Thurman Arnold's debunking,[4] Sapir was critical of his naive faith in efficiency as an end in itself. To Sapir, Arnold represented an American culture that was

> pervaded by an almost morbid fear of formal analysis of any kind. Its urge is the manipulative urge of organization, engineering efficiency is its one great value. . . . This attitude wills "realism" and hence protects itself with a skepticism that is anti-intellectualist but that is not proof against all manner of incursions from unacknowledged realms of wishful thinking. "Hard-boiled" is the ideal, "romantic" is the deed. (1938b:147)

Like Alexis de Tocqueville, Matthew Arnold, and Max Weber, Sapir understood that the American religion of efficiency, which brought together "our efficiency-experts and Methodist deacons," as he once put it (1922e), was an unintended consequence of the secularization of Protestant individualism. In a review of James Truslow Adams's *Our Business Civilization*, Sapir sketched a critique of efficiency and its relationship to personality, genuine and spurious (1930a). Years before, Bourne had published an essay called "The Puritan's Will to Power," in which he had denounced the "cult of efficiency" as being "far more coercive than the most sumptuary of laws," a "new Puritanism" that will not "let personality be the chief value in life" (1917c:301–2). In a similar vein, Sapir agreed with Adams's criticism of the American "shibboleth of overt success at whatever cost" but went on to attribute it, not to the excesses of the pioneering spirit, as Adams had, but to the secularization of Protestantism: "For there does seem to be an austere religiosity about the contemporary cult of reckless success which justifies a suspicion that it is both historically and psychologically connected with the zealous avoidance of sin which animated an earlier generation" (1930a:427).

4. Kenneth Burke (1938) also reviewed Thurman Arnold's book. Like Sapir, Burke debunked the debunker, exposing the presuppositions underlying Arnold's rhetoric of demystification.

Sapir also took the theme of the shallowness of American character, which Adams had discussed in terms of the American contempt for the cultural graces championed by Matthew Arnold, and transformed it into a suggestive discussion of the individual in mass society. Like Tocqueville, Sapir pointed out that obsessive individualism led to "anonymity," since the egalitarianism that is inseparable from it means that each person desires only to be like all others: "To be a 'regular fellow' . . . is not important because it expresses the individual, it is important because it does not express him." Sapir mourned not "the decay of good speech and good manners," as Adams did, but "their dissociation from the inner core of personality" (428).

Like Matthew Arnold, Sapir was troubled by the secularization of Protestant individualism. Going beyond Arnold, Sapir saw that the rationalization of unlimited economic growth was accompanied by an emphasis on self-development that was ultimately self-defeating. Sapir's critique of the culture of self-development grew out of his conception of the genuine culture as one endowed with rich aesthetic resources, unconsciously anchored in the personalities of those who participated in it by creatively changing it. His diagnosis of the American cultural malady was simple enough: "the combined immaturity and decay of an uprooted culture" (1924a:322) could not nourish individual growth and creativity. That general proposition led Sapir to find a particular paradox in the American case, for American culture, grounded in Protestant individualism, had made of self-development a consciously valued end, or shibboleth, to use his term. Yet the highly self-conscious individualism of the spurious American culture was, in Sapir's opinion, doomed to sterility, for it made impossible the intuitive spontaneity that alone could give rise to creative individuality.

Sapir repeatedly presented his critique of American culture in terms of a distinction that he drew between "romanticism" and the "classical spirit." He praised the classical "freedom in restraint" (1924b:159) of the genuine culture, where the discipline of convention stimulates creativity. But he believed that the "frenetic desire" of American romanticism led to abortive art, to misapplications of science, and to formlessness and vulgarity in the wider culture. According to Sapir, Americans were without the moral discipline and bedrock of accepted values necessary to creative self-development: "An individual can create true personal values only on the basis of those accepted by his society, but when nothing is accepted, he has no room for the growth of any values that are more than empty formulae" (1928b:523).

Lacking genuine culture, Americans were, in Sapir's view, willing to use any technique or method to rationalize their prejudices or to create the illusion of individual freedom.

The Anthropology of Experience

Sapir's analysis of the anonymity of modern individualism may have seemed either cranky or elitist to his contemporaries (and even to himself), but it places him, as my references to Tocqueville, Matthew Arnold, and Weber were meant to suggest, among a small group of critical thinkers who (fore)-saw only too well the ironies of mass democracies. In anthropology, the counterpart to Sapir's critique of spurious individualism is his well-known insistence that a developing science of humans must proceed by focusing on individual experience, or the "personality-in-culture" (Preston 1980), rather than culture patterns abstracted from human interaction and reified as real-world entities (Sapir once called such social-scientific entities "spurious" [1924b:157]). And that position seemed cranky, flippant, or unworkable to Sapir's colleagues, particularly to Kroeber (1952:108, 147) and Benedict (Mead 1959:325), who were eager to defend the autonomy of culture and the discipline that claimed it (as I will show in chapter 4). Moreover, Stephen Murray (1986:262) has argued that "Sapir was quite ready to reify . . . 'the personality,' while critical of reifying 'the culture.'" Thus the question arises: Does the study of personality-in-culture that Sapir envisioned merely substitute a reified personality for a reified culture—one romanticized object for another?

One can read Sapir's literary and cultural criticism as focused on a reified personality or "soul," an irreducible romanticized entity whose task is but to be itself. But it is also possible to see Sapir as placing the emphasis on the soul's making, as it were, its ongoing efforts to shape self-expression in its struggles with artistic media and techniques. For example, in his review of Emily Dickinson, Sapir speaks of "the intuitive hunger of the soul for the beautiful moulding of experience actually felt," of "unhampered intuitive living" (1925b:100). And, as I showed in chapter 2, in his paper on rhyme, he argued that, while "perfection of form is always essential," every culture and every artist "must solve the problem [of form] ever anew" (1917b:100). In both essays, Sapir speaks in terms of the artist's soul and individuality, but in both he also stresses the artist's experience transmuted into art through an active and ongoing engagement of individual creativity and traditional aesthetic forms.

Turning from aesthetics to anthropology, we must place Sapir's work in the Boasian context out of which it developed. In an influential early paper, "The Study of Geography" (1887), Boas had outlined the distinction between natural science, aimed at general laws, and historical science, or cosmography, focused on particulars (Stocking 1974a:8–12; Silverstein 1986:68–70). Boas wrote, in a romantic vein, that cosmography "holds to the phenomenon . . . and lovingly tries to penetrate into its secrets until every feature is plain and clear" (1887:645). And he went on to quote Goethe as a champion of the cosmographical attitude: "A single action or event is interesting, not because it is explainable, but because it is true" (644). "Truth" from this cosmographical perspective meant a complete account of the particular phenomenon studied, that is, its history as well as a description of its current state of being.

At this point, it is worth noting that the romantics, taking their cue from Blake, Goethe, and Wordsworth, were critical of the reductionism that they discerned in the conceptual abstractions of Enlightenment science; as Robert Langbaum explains it:

> Locke . . . says that the world of our ordinary perception is largely illusory, that the only objective reality consists of particles of matter moving in space. He gives us a world without aesthetic, moral or spiritual significance. Against such a world-view, the romanticist protests by appealing not to tradition but to his own concrete experience of nature. . . . It is matter which is the abstraction . . . whereas "the life of things" is what we perceive at the moment when experience is immediate and unanalysed. (1957:22)

The attempt to understand the "life of things," each as a unique individual or occurrence, each as it is grasped in the mind of a particular human observer, is fundamental to the German historicist tradition that Boas brought to American anthropology (Bunzl 2004). And Boas's attack on evolutionary theorizing can be understood as a critique of scientific abstractions that led, in his opinion, away from the historic experience, hence the truth, of individual cultures and the values that each had elaborated.

Boas's first generation of students wholeheartedly accepted, as the consequence of their teacher's work, that "cultural anthropology is . . . rapidly getting to realize itself as a strictly historical science," as Sapir put it in "Time Perspective" (1916:391). In the first decades of the twentieth century, Sapir, Kroeber, Lowie, Goldenweiser, and Boas himself continued the attack on evolutionary concepts and the racism that often accompanied them. But there was never any ultimate agreement as to the definition of the "historical science" that was to replace evolutionary theorizing. Thus when Kroeber, in the service of an attack on social evolutionism, began to elaborate a theory of history focused on the distinctiveness of what he called the "superorganic" dimension of nature, Sapir felt compelled to respond, in July 1917, with his own interpretation of the proper reading of the German historicist tradition (Lowie 1965:25).

In "The Superorganic," Kroeber argued that the social evolutionists operated by means of a misleading analogy that equated organic heredity with social inheritance. He was particularly concerned, as he explained in a retrospective account of the essay (1952:22), to counter the confusion of "race" and "civilization" (or culture) that social evolutionism had peddled to "the intelligent man on the street" (see Golla 1984:246). To do so, he posited a break between the social and the organic that was as dramatic, he claimed, as that between the organic and inorganic realms of nature; Kroeber placed both the "physical" and the "mental" constitution of human individuals within the realm of the organic (1917:39). The task of biology and psychology was to study human individuals as individuals, and such study included the effects of heredity on individual abilities and pathologies. But individuals as such were not, according to Kroeber, the proper object of study for a historical science like anthropology, which focused on civilizational patterns that existed on the superorganic level, quite independently of the human individuals who formed the raw material that carried those patterns: "For the historian—him who wishes to understand any sort of social phenomena—it is an unavoidable necessity . . . to disregard the organic [i.e., physical and mental] as such and to deal only with the social. . . . Civilization and heredity are two things that operate in separate ways" (35).

Kroeber's argument struck Sapir as "abstractionist fetishism," and he wrote Lowie that he planned to critique Kroeber "on two points: His . . . undervaluation of the individual in history and his interpretation of social phenomena as involving a new 'force' of non-organic character" (Lowie 1965:25). These two points are underpinned by a single epistemological argument, as I suggested in chapter 2. According to Sapir, the distinctions between the individual and history, and between the "psychic" (Kroeber's "organic") and the social, depended not on an ontological break between separate realms of nature but upon the interests of the observer. With respect to the first point, Sapir granted Kroeber that most individuals shrink to insignificance when viewed against the panorama of history, but Sapir went on to protest that "it is always the individual that really thinks and acts and dreams and revolts" (1917d:442). In reality, all of history grows out of the experience of individuals. The individual appears insignificant only to an observer who chooses to privilege the panoramic view: "The threshold of the social (or historical) versus the individual shifts according to the philosophy of the . . . interpreter. I find it utterly inconceivable to draw a sharp . . . line between them" (442).

With respect to the superorganic as a new force or level of nature, Sapir argued that the "irresolvability" of the social into the psychic or organic "is not, as Dr. Kroeber seems to imply, a conceptual one. It is an experiential one" (445). To explain himself, Sapir reverted to the science of geography, the topic of Boas's 1887 essay: geography is conceptual (or of the physical sciences) to the degree that it deals "with abstract masses and forces," historical "in so far as it deals with particular features of the earth's surface" (445). To deal, historically, with particulars, the analyst engages himself, by means of his experience or subjectivity, with social and historical phenomena: "These must be directly experienced and . . . selected from the endless mass of human phenomena according to a principle of values" (446). And Sapir went on to argue that the individual entities of historical study are constructed by the observer: "'Individual' . . . mean[s] any directly experienced entity or group of entities . . . [e.g.,] the Iroquois Indians, some specific Iroquois clan, all Iroquois clans, all American Indian clans, all clans of primitive peoples" (446).

In a footnote, Sapir proclaimed himself "greatly indebted" to the philosopher Rickert "for a penetrating analysis of the fundamental distinction between historical and natural science" (447). But whatever Sapir's debt to idealist philosophers such as Rickert and Croce, the teaching of Boas would seem to have been decisive. Perhaps Sapir's work under Boas interacted with his undergraduate training in Germanics and his emergent (in 1917) interests in poetry and aesthetics; in any case, "Do We Need a 'Superorganic'?" contains in embryo some of the major themes of Sapir's culture theory as he was to work it out over the next two decades in essays on phonemics, cultural patterning, and culture-and-personality. These themes include Sapir's critique of reified conceptions of culture, his understanding of the role of the analyst in constituting the object of study in the historical sciences, and his insistence on the primacy of individual experience.

Sapir's critique of cultural reification is well known, but his arguments are worth examining for the light that they shed on the epistemological status of his conception of the individual: did he, as Murray claims, reify it? When Sapir wrote that "every individual is . . . a representative of at least one sub-culture," he added that "frequently . . . he is a representative of more than one" (1932:515). That qualification directs attention away from individuals understood as self-contained monads and toward individuals multiply defined, as it were, in terms of their participation in a range of varying social relations. Moreover, Sapir's focus in this passage is on culture located in "the interactions of specific individuals," a phrase that suggests ongoing experience as the object of the anthropologist's study. On the other hand, Sapir tended to treat personality as "a reactive system which is in some sense stable or typologically defined for a long period of time, perhaps for life" (1934a:560). When he challenged the "givenness" of culture by urging study of "the culture-acquiring child," he attributed, at least by implication, a fixity to "personality definitions and potentials"—present "from the very beginning" of the child's life—that he explicitly denied to culture (1934b:596).

In the last analysis, then, the locus of individual experience, and the quality of the self to which it is to be attributed, were issues that Sapir did not tackle. But in Sapir's work, alongside the romantic's "personality" and the historian's "individual experience," there is a wealth of classical, "formal analysis" of linguistic and cultural patterns. To return to the terms of "The Grammarian and His Language," which I quoted at the beginning of this chapter: Sapir's critique of American romanticism, and his dissection of the epistemology of an increasingly taken-for-granted culture theory, were more perceptive and classical than the work of many of his contemporaries and successors who devoted themselves efficiently and professionally to cultural criticism.

CHAPTER 4

Vigorous Male
and Aspiring Female

Poetry, Personality, and Culture in Edward Sapir
and Ruth Benedict

Edward Sapir and Ruth Benedict have been placed together in the history of American anthropology—as theorists of cultural patterning, as ancestors of the culture and personality movement, as humanists and poets. Yet neither Sapir nor Benedict agreed or felt comfortable with the ideas that the other held concerning cultural "integrity" and the relationship of individuals to cultures. For Sapir, Benedict's conception of culture as personality writ large was but another example of the reification he had first criticized in his 1917 comment on Kroeber's notion of the superorganic. Thus, in April 1937, in his Yale seminar called the "Psychology of Culture," he mentioned Benedict's *Patterns of Culture* as typical of what he called "the as-if psychology." "A culture," he remarked, "cannot be paranoid," and he criticized both Benedict and Margaret Mead for their "failure to distinguish between the as-if psychology and the actual psychology of the people participating in the culture." "In itself," he concluded, "culture has no psychology" (Irvine 1994:593). For her part, Benedict was troubled by certain implications of Sapir's notion of a "genuine culture" (Sapir 1924a). As she was writing *Patterns of Culture*, she formulated her critique in an October 1932 letter to Mead:

> I understood him to say that centrifugal cultures (ones with many uncoordinated elements) were spurious, and centripetal ones (well-coordinated) genuine. Then he remarks that genuine cultures are poised, satisfactory, etc., etc., spurious ones muddled, unsatisfactory, etc. Therefore I remarked that homogeneous cultures could be built on basic ideas far from gracious . . . and

that the fact that a society indulged in pretentiousness and hypocrisy might be because it had a most well-coordinated culture which expressed itself in that form. (Mead 1959:325)

There is more here than mutual conceptual discomfort. Sapir's and Benedict's differing orientations to culture theory grew out of many years of intense discussions not only of anthropology but of poetry and, especially, the aesthetic philosophy of the "new" poets of the teens and twenties. A central value in the culture of the new poets was "hardness," a metaphor Ezra Pound used to convey his theory of the relationship between self-expression and poetic form—or, one might say, between personality and culture-writ-small. The poetic aspirations of Sapir and Benedict—their striving for hard personality and genuine culture—reflected the broader experiences from which their anthropological discourse emerged. Moreover, "hardness" has obvious sexual implications, and, as I will show, questions about sexuality and gender roles became major sources of disagreement between Sapir and Benedict, both personally and professionally. It is tempting, therefore, to suggest that their contrasting theories of culture and personality—Sapir's concern for genuine culture, Benedict's for cultural tolerance—mirror their profoundly different approaches to what Sapir called, in the title of a 1928 essay, "the sex problem in America."

Hardness: Passion and Intellect

Historians like T. J. Jackson Lears and Warren Susman have written persuasively on what Susman has called "the transition . . . from a culture of character to a culture of personality" that occurred at the turn of the twentieth century (1984:275). The argument goes back at least to Weber, who pointed out that the worldly success of ascetic Protestants often led to moral laxity among their descendants, who found themselves possessed of great wealth but lacking in spiritual fortitude (1905:155–76). In Lears's version (1981; 1983), the modernization of American society—involving the replacement of Puritan morality and a frontier economy oriented to production by a liberalized Protestantism and an urbanizing, mass-market consumer economy—led to a "crisis of cultural authority," the symptoms of which, among the bourgeoisie, were feelings of "weightlessness" and "unreality" leading to "neurasthenic" mental breakdowns. Lears argues that the demise of Puritanism left a secular culture still obsessed with an individualistic work ethic but without the transcendental referent that had earlier validated the suffering and striving of individuals. In such a cultural void, the hard work to which people were driven came to seem meaningless, and people's lives, weightless and unreal. The cultural response was a new "therapeutic" morality of personal health and self-development, in which the secular self became an ultimate value, an end in itself that people systematically cultivated in order to achieve fuller lives and truer experiences. As Susman puts it, the earlier concern with "building character" gave way to the desire to "develop personality."

Much of Lears's analysis concerns the "anti-modernistic" reaction against weightlessness, including people's search for "reality" and "real experience" in the past, the primitive, the natural, and the exotic. And it is here that these historians' interpretations help us to place the yearnings of Sapir, Benedict, and the poets of their generation—for the characteristic quest of the new poets was for the real, the authentic, vital, and genuine. "I go about this London hunting for the real"—so wrote Ezra Pound to Harriet Monroe in October 1912, the early days of *Poetry* magazine, when Pound, as Monroe's foreign correspondent, had taken on the task of purveying real poetry, "the good work . . . obscured, hidden in the bad" (Pound 1971:12). Pound's equation of the real with the artistically valid is characteristic, and he came to formulate that equation in the aesthetic of what he called hardness, an aesthetic that tempted both Sapir and Benedict.

For Pound and the imagist poets, hardness pertained first of all to style, both personal and poetic—or, better, the personal in the poetic. The crucial notion was that sincere self-expression—considered the essence of art— depended (in poetry) upon an absolutely original use of language, because the individual's unique experience could not be conveyed through conventional language, encumbered as it is with dead metaphors and cliché. Thus Pound included among his "principles" of imagism such dicta as: "1. Direct treatment of the 'thing' whether subjective or objective," and "2. To use absolutely no word that does not contribute to the presentation" (1918:3). This is not a prescription for realism: the "thing" can be "subjective or objective"—"of external nature, or of emotion" (11). In other words, the "thing" is any experience of the poet, whose task is to translate that unique experience "directly," through an absolutely original use of language. T. E. Hulme, advocating "dry, hard, classical verse," put the matter in these terms:

> The great aim is accurate, precise and definite description. The first thing is to recognise how extraordinarily difficult this is. It is no mere matter of carefulness; you have to use language, and language is by its very nature a

communal thing; that is, it expresses never the exact thing but a compro-
mise—that which is common to you, me and everybody. But each man sees
a little differently, and to get out clearly and exactly what he does see, he
must have a terrific struggle with language. (1924:132–33)

Since "communal" language is inadequate to express individual experience,
the poet is enjoined to create his own language by avoiding past usages, dead
metaphors—all "decorations and trappings," "flaccid" styles, or "slither"—
that do not and cannot contribute to the presentation because they belong
to the language of past, of someone else's, experience (Pound 1914a:217;
1918:3, 12).

This emphasis on the poet's experience—on the direct intuition of reality, as Croce phrased it (1902:30)—suggests the significance of another key
element in the aesthetics of the new poetry: sincerity. In Pound's view,
conventional language meant conventional thought, impersonal, unorigi-
nal, insincere: "Most men think only husks and shells of the thoughts that
have been already lived over by others" (1914b:371). By contrast, the poet sees
in an original fashion—"intuits reality directly"—and expresses what he
sees originally; the poet is "sincere." This was explained to readers of *Poetry*
by the imagist poet Richard Aldington, translating and quoting Edouard
Dujardin, a symbolist poet and critic: "'An artist's first problem is sincerity
. . . the bad writer . . . is the man who is not "sincere." ' . . . All artists believe
they say what they think; in reality they only repeat and re-arrange what
others have thought before them. Result: an approximation, insufficient,
factitious and generally false expression'" (1920:166–67). When writers fall
back on convention, they abandon the attempt to intuit reality directly,
adopting instead the experiences, thoughts, and expressions of others; in
other words, their experiences and their poetry become "unreal." And the
lure of convention plays at all levels of poetic language: metaphor, diction,
rhyme, meter. Thus, for example, the vers-librists battled to escape conventional metric schemes that, they thought, corrupted poets by extracting
loyalty to traditional form at the expense of personal intuition. The temp-
tation when using traditional forms was, as Pound phrased it, to "put in
what you want to say and then fill up the remaining vacuums with slush."
For Pound, "technique" was "the test of a man's sincerity" (1918:7, 9).

Hardness, then, in the aesthetics of the new poetry, referred both to technique and to the artist's vision; it suggested that real art depended on the
discovery of a personal reality, a reality penetrated, understood, embraced,
and expressed by the self, standing alone. Such a conception accorded well

with the mystique of the artist in the wider culture, preoccupied as it was with the search for real experience; it also helps to explain the spate of would-be poets who emerged during and after World War I as poetry became, unbelievably, "popular." Ever the elitist, Pound inveighed against "my *bete noire*—the charlatans," those "turning out shams" instead of real art: "I know there are a lovely lot who want to express their own personalities. . . . Only they mostly won't take the trouble to find out what is their own personality" (Monroe 1938:263; see Sapir 1925b:100). Pound also complained about the "many habile poseurs . . . who only want to be 'prominent'" (1971:15). Similarly, Monroe wrote a *Poetry* editorial called "Those We Refuse," in which she pictured the magazine's office as flooded with "intimate self revelations" expressed in "comically-pathetically bad verse," though she admitted that "even the editors, hardened as they are, sometimes 'fall for it' . . . [for] some poem whose softness makes our readers marvel" (1920a:322).

Like other contributors to *Poetry*, Sapir and Benedict found the aesthetic of hardness compelling as a model for the artist's personality and work. For both, hardness combined passion and intellect—represented, that is, an emotional, personal commitment to aesthetic craftsmanship and intellectual striving. Sapir analyzed such issues in his theoretical and critical writings on literature, music, and culture, where he examined the relationship between technique and vision—the artist's creative appropriation of traditional forms to express a personal conception. As we have seen, "Culture, Genuine and Spurious" presented these ideas in their broadest application, as a theory of culture; there Sapir defined the "genuine" culture as one sufficiently rich in aesthetic resources to stimulate (rather than hinder) creative personalities to express themselves and, thereby, to develop the cultural tradition still further. In his essays on poetry, Sapir explicitly formulated these ideas in terms of the aesthetic of hardness (recall his essay on rhyme, in which he spoke of "the passionate temperament cutting into itself with the cold steel of the intellect" [1920a:498]). And he also expressed such ideas, in more obviously self-referential fashion, in his poetry:

Blue Flame and Yellow

I strove for a blue flame
That would rise like a point of steel,
Cleaving the vast night
Up to the starry wheel.

I burned with a yellow flame,
I was edged with a curl of smoke,
I went out under the stars,
Leaves of the world oak. (SUP:3/15/1919)

Images of flame and steel were congenial to Benedict, too, who aspired, in diary entries rather than critical essays, to a hardness combining passion and intellect. On October 25, 1912, she wrote of her "aspirations" and "longing" for "understanding," "expression," "service," and "friendship," a list that runs from intellect to passion (Mead 1959:122). In January 1917 Benedict listed the "big things of life" as "love, friendship, beauty, clear thinking, honest personality;" and on August 15, 1919, she praised "hard thinking" as well as "art values" (Mead 1959:139–40, 143). But she turned to Walter Pater for a philosophy that captured these disparate goals in one image. In December 1915, she relived her discovery of Pater's philosophy of art for art's sake, a discovery she dated to her freshman winter at Vassar in 1906:

And it is Pater's message that comes back to me as the cry of my deepest necessity: "to burn [always] with this hard gemlike flame"—to gain from experience "this fruit of a quickened, multiplied consciousness," to summon "the services of philosophy[,] of religion, of culture as well, to startle us into a sharp and eager observation." (Mead 1959:135)

Benedict quoted accurately (though not word for word) from the conclusion to *The Renaissance.* There Pater adumbrated what Hugh Kenner has called "an aesthetic of glimpses" (1971:69). Pater wrote of a once-unified reality that was dissolving under the pressure of "modern thought," with the result that "what is real in our life fines itself down" to a succession of fleeting, disconnected, private experiences. In the face of such chaos and isolation, Pater urged his readers to a passionate, aesthetic savoring of each momentary experience: "How may we see in them all that is to be seen in them by the finest senses? How shall we pass most swiftly from point to point, and be present always at the focus where the greatest number of vital forces unite in their purest energy?" (1873:194–95).

To succeed in the endeavor was "to burn always with this hard, gemlike flame." And, he continued, "our failure is to form habits," in other words, to surrender to conventional interpretations of experience, to become insincere. Like Pater, Benedict feared insincerity and, much worse, a loss or absence of selfhood. Again and again in her diaries, she echoes Pater as she urges herself on to a "superb enthusiasm for life," an "enthusiasm for one's own personality," or, attributing to Mary Wollstonecraft what she felt to be lacking in herself, "a passionately intellectual attitude toward living" (Mead 1959:123, 491).

Vigorous Male and Aspiring Female

Personality imagined as a hard, gemlike flame is the self standing alone, creating and mastering reality with its passion, intelligence, and art. But in a culture that associates hardness with masculinity and softness with femininity, to conceive the essence of human personality in terms of hardness poses a particular problem to women: the generically human attribute belongs preeminently to the other sex. The problem was implicit in the new poetry, which, in rejecting the softness of Victorian art, also rejected a conception of culture as a feminine domain, the domain of "sweetness and light," as Matthew Arnold termed it in *Culture and Anarchy*. Monroe broached the issue in a comment entitled "Men or Women?" in which she responded to a Philadelphia newspaper editorial lamenting a perceived demise of "the vigorous male note" in poetry. Monroe remarked that the magazine received some three thousand "real or alleged poems" each month, adding, "*Poetry* receives more publishable verse, and less hopelessly bad verse, from the 'vigorous male' than from the aspiring female." And she concluded by encouraging female aspirations in the arts, calling for a "feminine note . . . as authentic . . . as vigorous and beautiful, as the masculine" (1920b:148).

Monroe's pairing of masculine vigor and feminine aspiration reminds us that Sapir and Benedict were differently situated as each undertook the quest for poetry, personality, and culture. In their private lives, each had to confront "the sex problem in America," a problem that included not only sexuality but marriage, family, and gender roles. Sapir faced such issues with a professional identity at least minimally secured; as his poetry and letters show, his dilemma was to make room for other aspects of life—familial, romantic, artistic—during the course of the productive scientific career that he expected of himself. By contrast, Benedict, without a secure identity during much of her early adulthood, was torn between "feminine" and "masculine" aspirations: marriage and motherhood, on the one hand, and the desire for work and for intellectual and moral purpose, on the other.

The "sex problem," then, was posed more sharply for Benedict than for Sapir: his dilemma was one of accommodation; hers involved a fundamental

choice. We can read this contrast in their literary endeavors, and it is reflected as well in their approaches to the study of culture and personality.
To begin with an analysis of their poetry, we can ask: why did they write
poetry, and what did they write about?

Though both Sapir and Benedict were skeptical of the value of their own
poetry, both very much desired to publish it, and that desire is different
from other (though not incompatible) reasons for writing poetry. Among
the latter, we must recognize self-expression as a response to loneliness, as
well as the cultural definition of poetry as an appropriate medium in which
to discuss the personal agonies associated with love, sex, death, and fate. For
Sapir, as I have shown, writing poetry also provided an alternative method
to work out his developing culture theory, with its concern for the dialectic
between traditional discipline and individual creativity. Modell has made a
similar point about Benedict: "Absorption in anthropology . . . led her back
to poetry. Ruth Benedict entered a discipline just developing a concern for
individual creativeness within cultural constraints. . . . She was encouraged
at once to learn scientific procedures and to have confidence in her own
voice" (1983:129). Yet one might turn to poetry without attaching importance to publication. What, then, is the cultural significance of publication?

An answer is suggested by Arthur Symons's account of the symbolist
Mallarmé, an account that was influential when Sapir and Benedict were
writing poetry. According to Symons, Mallarmé considered "publication
. . . unnecessary, a mere way of convincing the public that one exists"
(1919:193). The remark recalls Pound's irate dismissal of the "lovely lot who
want to express their own personalities . . . [without taking] the trouble to
find out what is their own personality." Beyond Pound is the critique of
egalitarian mass societies that begins with Tocqueville and goes through
Riesman (1950) to Lears (1983)—the idea that anonymous and indistin-
guishable individuals must struggle to raise themselves above the crowd, to
forge a personal identity, yet must construct their "unique" identity out of
symbols readily comprehensible to the mass public. The result, as Pound's
remark suggests, is that people seek personality in and of itself rather than
develop, in the pursuit of other goals, personal qualities that, after the fact,
might constitute personality.

Certainly for Benedict, publication (whether of poetry or of prose) was
a way of convincing the public, and herself, that she existed (see Modell
1983:107–9). In her earliest journal entry, written when she was twenty-five,
Benedict tells of an identity crisis that suggests Susman's transition from

"character" to "personality": "I tried, oh very hard, to believe that our own characters are the justification of it all. . . . But the boredom had gone too deep; I had no flicker of interest in my character. What was my character anyway! My real *me* was a creature I dared not look upon" (Mead 1959:119). Thereafter, the quest for personality was a major theme of her journals, as it was of her biography of Mary Wollstonecraft, who, as Benedict saw it, "never flinched before the hazard of shaping forth a personality" (Mead 1959:494). Benedict prodded herself to "self development" by means of a "culture of . . . aspirations," seeking the "me . . . of untold worth" that she found in poets like Whitman, and promising to "manage" herself and avoid "floundering" (122–23, 128). She described her "striving toward the dignity of rich personality" as a "consummate duty" (134)—an attitude that suggests Lears's interpretation of the "therapeutic world view" of modern culture, that is, the Puritan concern with personal salvation transmuted into a purely secular, though religiously obsessive, pursuit of self cultivation, guided by therapists instead of clerics (1981:52–58). Sapir remarked on this aspect of Benedict's quest for personality. Commenting on a poem entitled "Our Task Is Laughter," he saw her "banking a little too heavily on the philosophy of prescription and therapeutic protest. . . . It seems hard to have to say, 'Our *task* is laughter'" (Mead 1959:166; emphasis in original).

Seeking personality, Benedict had to work her way through the issues raised by feminism. She never renounced love, marriage, or the desire for children as high ideals for women but came to reject the social arrangements that made it impossible for women to fulfill those ideals without sacrificing the "achievement of a four-square personality" (Mead 1959:147). Shortly after her marriage, she told herself, "It is wisdom in motherhood as in wifehood to have one's own individual world of effort and creation" (136). And she rejected such conventionally feminine efforts as teaching and social work, remarking that "the world has need of my vision as well as of Charity Committees" (135)—a comment that recalls Pound's equation of committees (for awarding prizes to artists) with "mediocrity" and "the least common denominator," that is, with the abandonment of creative personality (1914a:223; see Banner 2003:129–36).

All of which brought Benedict to writing. As a child, she had received familial encouragement for her writing, and, later, during her struggle for personality, she could tell herself, "my best, my thing 'that in all my years I tend to do' is surely writing" (Mead 1959: 144). But writing without recognition was not sufficient: "More and more I know that I want publication" (135). Writing became a duty for her in her therapeutic quest for personality: she chided herself to "work at writing with sufficient slavishness" and longed "to prove myself by writing" (136, 142). At first, she worked at her biographies of famous women (a project rejected by Houghton Mifflin in 1919) and, later, at poetry and anthropological writing.

Benedict was a careful writer who revised her work extensively (Modell 1983:18, 76–77). In a 1929 letter to Mead, Benedict described "the process of verse" in terms of "incubation, gestation" (Mead 1959:94), metaphors that suggest composition over extended lengths of time, and it is clear that she expected to work meticulously at poetry. Since her poetry expressed a private self that she feared showing to others, the quest for recognition through publication aroused no little anxiety—a dilemma solved by writing poetry under a pseudonym. By the time Benedict felt enough confidence in her voice and the self that it represented to abandon her pseudonym, she had begun to achieve success as an anthropologist (Stassinos 1998). According to Mead, after *Patterns of Culture*, Benedict was unwilling "to trade on her success in one field to bolster up a much more minor success in another" (1959:93). One publicly validated professional identity was enough for her, and she gave up poetry.

For Sapir, by contrast, public recognition as a poet seems to have been a sign of intellectual vigor, of Renaissance virtuosity. He began writing poetry in 1917 (Mead 1959:185), at a time when American intellectuals were engaged in a search for "a real national culture," as Mead put it in a 1924 letter to Benedict (285). As I have shown, "Culture, Genuine and Spurious" was intended as a contribution to that search, and Sapir's poetry and literary criticism represented further modes of participation. Moreover, the practice of art was congenial to Sapir—a "cosmographical" scientist for whom the human realities studied by anthropologists were, above all, aesthetic phenomena (see Silverstein 1986).

Beyond Sapir's desire to participate in the general intellectual culture of his time lay the possibility of another career. He flirted with the idea of leaving anthropology for music, but he knew that his music was not of professional quality—so also, his poetry (Lowie 1965:21). Despite Sapir's refusal to delude himself, however, the publication of poetry and criticism gave him, one feels, a sense of alternative career possibilities at a time when he felt frustrated by his inability to land a university position. The other intellectually dominant figure among the prewar generation of Boas's students, A. L. Kroeber, was later to explain Sapir's personalistic theory of culture as "wish-fulfilment expression set against the backdrop of a partly regretted career" (1952:148), but the remark more justly applied to Sapir's poetic aspirations. From the security of his professorship at the University of California, Kroeber lectured Sapir about building a professional reputation: "If I had half your philological wits I'd have five times your place and influence in the philological world" (Golla 1984:245). For his part, Sapir sometimes expressed a sense of guilt in the face of his inability to live up to his own expectations for scholarly productivity: "[Paul] Radin may have sinned in starting too many things and leaving them unfinished, but I have sinned so much more that I am inclined to be charitable" (Golla 1984:281). Poetry must have served at once as an escape from such anxieties and, when practiced in place of scientific work, as a stimulus to them.

Whatever the relationship between Sapir's professional ambivalence and his poetic aspirations, he wrote more than five hundred poems, and he wrote them quickly. Seeing his work in print excited him with the "feeling of being a poet" (Mead 1959:179, 185), but he habitually submitted what he called "half-baked stuff" for publication (Golla 1984:296). As he admitted to Monroe, "Yes, you are right about my not working hard enough at my verses. I do let things go before I should" (PMP:10/28/1918). Perhaps Sapir expected the same degree of virtuosity in poetry that he possessed in linguistics. Lacking it, he accepted Monroe's sometimes drastic editing in exchange for the possibility of publication: "I think it would be well to omit stanza 3 of 'Charon.' I am not quite so certain of both stanzas 4 and 5 of 'She went to sleep below,' but am inclined to think stanza 4 should come out. Stanza 5 seems somehow to place the sun image that follows, but if you feel that it too should come out, please remove it" (PMP: 3/7/1925). It is hard to imagine Sapir's brooking such interference in his linguistic work. When Boas suggested that Sapir send him a preliminary outline of his Paiute grammar, Sapir reacted indignantly:

> The precise method that you suggest for the preparation of the manuscript by July 1st is in the highest degree irksome to me.... My own habit is always, in both scientific and literary attempts, to prepare the ground thoroughly beforehand and write out the final manuscript once and for all. In fact, I think that I have never in the course of my whole life written a second or revised version of anything. (ANMM:3/28/1917)

It is equally hard to imagine Benedict's reacting in such obstinate fashion to editorial criticism. Daring and vigorous, Sapir expected to be able to "dash off" publishable writings in half a dozen genres (Mead 1959:171). Benedict's aspirations were more modest: she was contented with the possession of but one voice, coherent and publicly acclaimed.

As to what Sapir and Benedict wrote about, Modell has described Benedict's poetry as combining "an English metaphysical tradition" with biblical and Greek mythology and "her own perceptions of landscape" in an "eccentric yoking of image to abstraction" (1983:135–37). Sapir, too, saw Benedict's poetic originality as lying in the seriousness of her themes and the relationship of her work to English religious poetry. "Your great merit," he wrote her in late 1924, "is that you are finely in the tradition, even Puritan tradition, but with a notable access of modernity" (Mead 1959:166). Or, as he told Monroe, "I know of no one who has anything like her high and passionate seriousness. She knows how to use difficult words well, her imagery is bold, and her thought is never banal" (PMP: 3/23/1925).

Religious imagery is central in Benedict's poetry, but she used it without religious conviction. As she explained in an autobiographical fragment written for Mead, Benedict's religion was a culture, not a faith: "I was brought up in the midst of the church. . . . Nevertheless my religious life had nothing to do with institutional Christianity nor with church creeds. . . . For me, the gospels described a way of life" (Mead 1959:107). Thus her poetry used religious imagery to speak of the impossibility of belief, the hollowness of high ideals, or the futility of striving. Only rarely did Benedict write of the believability of ideals and dreams, and even then her attitude was ambivalent. In "Sight," for example, she mocked those who would confine their "dreaming" within "four walls" yet equated dreaming with "tortured promises" (Mead:170). Such imagery accords well with Benedict's quest for personality and career, for something "real" to believe in.

Aside from metaphysical despair, the dominant theme of Benedict's poetry is passion—suppressed or uncontrollable, sated or unfulfilled, but, above all, passion confined to the self, passion without reply. As Modell has pointed out, Benedict wrote most of her poetry while she was withdrawing from a sexually barren and failing marriage yet before she had secured the professional identity that would sustain her after 1930: "In the guise of Anne Singleton, Ruth Benedict expressed a self that included 'ripeness' and 'ecstasy' along with high moral purpose, a self that Stanley

Benedict no longer recognized and Edward Sapir would be permitted to know" (1983:129). To express that private, passionate self, Benedict used religious and naturalistic imagery, as, for example, in "She Speaks to the Sea" (Mead 1959:487):

> For I am smitten to my knees with longing,
> Desolate utterly, scourged by your surface-touch,
> Of white-lipped wave and unquiet azure hands.

In other poems Benedict wrote of the autumnal beauty of barrenness, and the deathlike quiescence following the consummation of passion.

According to Modell, "Benedict's poetry reveals a repetitiveness in concept and vocabulary" (1983:140). It is also stylistically narrow, most of it written in the sonnet or similar lyric forms. In 1925, Sapir urged Benedict to experiment with other forms: "Have you ever thought of dramatizing your theme and treating it in . . . narrative blank verse? . . . I am very eager to see you get away for a while from the sonnet form, for I want an ampler field for your spirit" (Mead 1959:171). Yet Benedict had not gained enough control of her voice to distance herself from it, to allow herself to experiment outside the narrow range of techniques that she found intuitively congenial. In Benedict's confessional poetry, there is little to separate the poet's persona from the poet herself. As Modell puts it, "At its best the poetry of Anne Singleton displayed a classical purity and disciplined cadence," but at its worst "confession lay close to the surface and control tightened into hysteria" (1983:140).

It is with respect to stylistic and technical choices that Sapir's poetry can be most usefully compared with Benedict's. Sapir not only wrote theoretical papers on the relationship between technique and conception (1917b; 1920a), he actively experimented with a wide range of poetic forms. His poetry includes sonnets and other short rhymed forms, blank verse, free verse, and dramatic and narrative verse; he wrote short poems of two lines as well as longer pieces of several pages. More important, Sapir tried on different voices in his poetry, characteristically distancing himself from his subject, writing *about* personalities and states of mind rather than expressing them as the immediate product of his own soul. If Benedict's poetry is confessional, Sapir's is observational—though he himself is often the object observed.

Sapir's penchant for psychological observation was mentioned by Kroeber, who reminisced about Sapir's "intense interest in people and seeing what made their wheels go around." According to Kroeber, Sapir "was likely to take a close friend and watch him, dissect him, try to draw him out . . . just from sheer interest in individuals, in personalities" (1959:136). That attitude suggests why Sapir was particularly drawn to the poetry of Edwin Arlington Robinson. Sapir wrote Monroe, "I am left with an impression of overwhelming mastery, a strength at once fine and careless, in Edwin Arlington Robinson. He has the real stuff—for psychology" (PMP:9/20/1918). Elsewhere, Sapir analyzed Robinson's "real stuff" in some detail: "One of the most striking features in his poems is the use of 'Skeleton Plots.' It is as though he had a specific plot in mind, made vivid the psychology, then rubbed out the plot and kept the psychology, giving the reader the opportunity to build up one of several possible explanations" (SN:28–29).

Like Benedict, Sapir used poetry to talk about love and passion. Sapir wrote most of his poetry between 1917 and 1925, when he was preoccupied with the tragedy of his first wife's physical and mental collapse, leading to her death in 1924. Sapir's poems explore the sentiments and experiences shared "Twixt a Man and a Wife," as the title of an unpublished poem puts it, projecting and analyzing feelings that run "from love to kindred hate" (SUP:9/30/1918). In these poems, Sapir rehearses the romantic relationship backward and forward, reminiscing about first love, imagining the death of love or unsuccessful love, creating heartbroken characters who indulge in their own reminiscences, and occasionally narrating psychological confrontations in the manner of Robinson. Though some of Sapir's poems seem to be direct expressions of immediate feeling, he more frequently uses poetry to stand aside, even from his closest relationships:

She Has Gone Out

She has gone out for a walk in the twilight snow
With our little daughter by her side,
And she will have sweet, prattling words, I know,
To hear in the dusk till eventide.

But they have left me sitting by the fire
To think of how they both are dear,
Of how another love than first desire
Is flaming softly down the year. (SUP:12/28/1919)

Elsewhere he wrote, "The fruits of marriage are disillusionment and children" (SN:25)—a remark that, when contrasted to poems like "She Has
Gone Out," suggests the complexity of Sapir's private world.

Sapir did not confine himself to poems about his personal life but wrote
on a variety of topics, from social satire to philosophical speculation. He
self-consciously attempted to portray his poetic personality in several
lights. After Monroe had accepted several of his poems for publication, he
complained jokingly that her choices "misrepresent me as an extremely sad
fellow with a horrible case of Weltschmerz!"—and he demanded "the
opportunity later on to qualify this dismal impression with a set of lighter,
cynical-frivolous shots (I have a bunch of them for you)" (PMP:5/14/1920).
A year later, on June 30, 1921, he sent a new batch, characterizing each poem
for Monroe with terms such as "nostalgic," "facile-pretty," "old-fashioned
eroticism," and "impertinent." In a letter dated October 28, 1918, he described poems ranging from "mordant or hopeless" to "thumbnail symbolic
things" to "the regular sentimental things," though with regard to the last
he wrote: "I hope I have avoided treacle."

Yet with his penchant for the facile-pretty, the nostalgic, and the sentimental, Sapir had difficulty avoiding treacle. Monroe criticized his poems
for their lack of "hardness," as did Kroeber:

> I see no evidence of anything abnormal or tortured or warped in your work.
> It rather comes out clean and neat. All I don't see is the drive behind that
> makes the product compact and hard and arresting. . . . You evidently have
> great sensitiveness toward images. They run away with you over two and
> three pages. But the intensity of emotion that cuts them out and burns them
> in isn't there. (Golla 1984:294)

Sapir was appreciative of Kroeber's reading, but he defended himself to
Monroe, going so far as to advocate softness in a critique of her editorial
biases: "Why not look for hardness in the soft-textured stuff (better, soft-
surfaced) too? Such a lot of bluff around these days!" (PMP:5/14/1920).

Sapir's poetic voice tended to be soft and sentimental, on the one hand,
or aloof and distanced, on the other. In any case, it lacked the intensity and
"hardness" that were in demand but that he equated with "bluff." As I will
show, "bluff" for Sapir was symptomatic of spurious personality, epitomized in the distorted sexuality of women who aspired to hardness.

The Sex Problem in America

Both Sapir and Benedict used poetry to express the agony of marriages un-
raveling. Benedict, who said that her husband rejected her sexually (Modell
1983:131–32), wrote poems that are cries of passion frustrated:

> Weep but for this; that we are blind
> With passion who have been clear-eyed
> As planets after rain: and know
> No longer any grief, who go
> Just to see love crucified. (Mead 1959:70–71)

Or, reverting to the imagery of cutting flame, she wrote in an undated journal entry: "There is only one problem in life: that fire upon our flesh shall
burn as a knife that cuts to the bone, and joy strip us like a naked blade"
(Mead 1959:154). Sapir, too, wrote of dying love and frustrated passion, but
he also explored the happier aspects of romance. In contrast to Benedict's
poems, Sapir's tend to objectify his situation, allowing him to stand apart
from it and analyze its various emotional and psychological components.

As Mead and Modell have noted, during these difficult years of their
lives, Benedict and Sapir turned to each other, using poetry—which both
aspired to publish—to communicate what could not be easily discussed in
less stylized modes. When Benedict "initiated" their friendship by send-
ing Sapir a draft of her doctoral dissertation (1923), she must already have
been aware of his poetic interests, since he commented, as if in answer to
her query: "No, I have not written any poems lately." Responding at length
to her still somewhat conventionally Boasian thesis, Sapir urged that "the
problem of the individual and group psychology [be] boldly handled, not
ignored, by some one who fully understands culture as a historical entity"—
confiding also that he felt "damnably alone" on the "long and technical . . .
road I must travel in linguistic work" (Mead 1959:49–53). Although Benedict's diary entries over the next few years suggest an infatuation with Sapir,
he kept his emotional distance, preferring to coach her professional development in both anthropology and poetry. He dedicated "Zuni" to "R.F.B.,"
urging her to "keep the flowing / Of your spirit, in many branching ways"
(Mead 1959:88). On the day that he wrote "Zuni," he composed "Acheron,"
in which he mourned his wife in images of water that would flow no more:

Come, I have brought you here by the dim shores of water,
By the faint lapping of scarce moving water. . . .
And you will sink into the ghostly midst without sound,
In the middle of great widening ripples round. (SUP:8/26/1924)

Two poems written on the same day, to two women, one living, one dead: Sapir must have seen, in Benedict, unstifled feminine aspiration, that of a woman with a hopeful future. And, as Perry (1982:243–49) has suggested, Sapir must have felt a terrible sense of guilt at his wife's death. Florence Delson had left Radcliffe before graduation to go with Sapir to Ottawa, where she had borne three children in little more than three years (Darnell 1990:45–49, 133–37). Sapir was undoubtedly a loving husband and father, but he was also devoted to scholarship. Perry says, "He seems to have been so immersed in his work that he sometimes tended to resent the intrusion of the children on his studies" (245). This is perhaps exaggerated, but, on the other hand, it is not incompatible with the observational aloofness toward family life that one finds in some of his poems. According to Perry, when Sapir first met Harry Stack Sullivan, in the fall of 1926, they talked for about ten hours, as Sapir spoke of the responsibility he felt for his wife's death. She had, after all, abandoned her studies to become a wife in a setting where "isolation and loneliness had . . . shattered . . . her mind and body" (249). Benedict, with Sapir's encouragement, sought to avoid a similar trap as she moved from marriage to anthropology and poetry.

But Sapir and Benedict grew apart and by the end of the decade were quarreling, as their letters show (Mead 1959:95, 192–95, 307, 325). They disagreed profoundly about the issues that Sapir raised in a 1928 essay, "Observations on the Sex Problem in America." In that essay, Sapir attacked an emergent sexual freedom that, as he saw it, unnaturally separated romantic and sexual love. He also denounced the therapeutic quest for personally enriching sexual experiences. And he singled out "the modern woman" as especially guilty in both regards (1928b:528).

Sapir began his essay with the admission that "there is little herein set forth which is not a rationalization of personal bias" (519). In all societies, he argued, the satisfaction of basic needs such as hunger and sex involve "the attempt of human beings to reconcile their needs with cultural forms that are both friendly and resistant to these needs" (520). Sapir thought that his contemporaries, in their revolt against Puritan repressions, had treated sex as "a 'good' in itself" to be pursued without regard for conventional regulations, and that this had led to an "artificial divorce . . . between the sex impulse and love" (521) and to a romantic glorification of sex as "primitive" and "natural":

> What has happened is that the odious epithet of sin has been removed from sex, but sex itself has not been left a morally indifferent concept. The usual process of over-correction has invested sex with a factitious value as a romantic and glorious thing in itself. The virus of sin has passed into love, and the imaginative radiance of love, squeezed into the cramped quarters formerly occupied by sin, has transfigured lust and made it into a new and phosphorescent holiness. (512)

Such an attitude was psychologically unnatural, for "the emotion of love . . . is one of the oldest and most persistent of human feelings" (525). Human culture has everywhere linked sex to love in such a way that sexual love "takes the ego out of itself" and becomes the prototype for "all non-egoistic identifications" (527). Anthropologists, Sapir felt, had helped to obscure this truth, with their "excited books about pleasure-loving Samoans and Trobriand Islanders" (523); the reading public, for its part, was all too prone to mistake the absence of Western-style taboos for "primitive freedom" and, at the same time, to overlook the coercive presence of culturally unfamiliar sex regulations.

Equating the pursuit of sex in itself with "narcissism" (529), Sapir sketched a critique of the therapeutic quest for self-development: "The plausible terminologies of 'freedom,' of 'cumulative richness of experience,' of 'self-realization' . . . lead to an even more profound unhappiness than the normal subordination of impulse to social convention" (528). In other words, the pursuit of sexual experience and personality, as ends in themselves, unlinked to cultural values that transcend the self, was doomed to failure—because "sex as-self-realization unconsciously destroys its own object" which, in the "natural" case where love is valued, is to "take the ego out of itself" (529).

Sapir went on to suggest the harmful consequences of such attitudes, focusing his critique on women. Women who justly sought economic emancipation (see Sapir 1930b:146–48) erred by linking it to sexual freedom, with unhappy results: "Every psychiatrist must have met essentially frigid women of today who have used sex freedom as a mere weapon to feed the ego" (1928b:528). At the same time, the devaluation of "passion between the sexes leads to compensation in the form of homosexuality," a form that Sapir found "unnatural" (529). He dismissed the "smart and trivial analysis of sex by intellectuals," who justify promiscuity and homosexuality, and rationalize their attacks on such phenomena as jealousy and prostitution by linking them to the economic underpinnings of romance and marriage (525). For Sapir, it was "an insult to the true lover to interpret his fidelity and expectation of fidelity as possessiveness and to translate the maddening grief of jealousy into the paltry terminology of resentment at the infringement of property rights" (531). Similarly, prostitutes "despise their own bodies," not simply on account of the social sanctions they suffer but because their behavior violates "a natural scale of values," and their shame is shared by "many of the protagonists of sex freedom" (532):

> The "free" woman . . . , whether poetess or saleslady, has a hard job escaping from the uncomfortable feeling that she is really a safe, and therefore a dishonest, prostitute. . . . The battle shows in the hard, slightly unfocused, glitter of the eye and in the hollow laugh, and one can watch the gradual deterioration of personality that seems to set in in many of our young women with premature adoption of sophisticated standards. (533)

Such, then, was the fate of women aspiring to hardness.

Although Benedict read the paper as a personal attack, Sapir vigorously denied this: "You were never once in my thoughts when I wrote the paper on sex, which I did . . . rather reluctantly at the request of Harry Stack Sullivan" (Mead 1959:195). It seems likely that the "personal bias" that Sapir was rationalizing focused on another aspiring female—Margaret Mead, who had a brief affair with Sapir but refused to "be mama" to his three motherless children, scheming instead to "have him reject her" before she went off to do fieldwork in Samoa (Howard 1984:52, 60; Silverstein 2004: 145–53). And while Sapir's paper endorses the distinction between love and lust that Sullivan drew so sharply (Perry 1982:90–92), Sapir's thinking along those lines had developed well before he knew Sullivan, Benedict, or Mead, as the following poem shows:

The Jackal

When the heart is broken and dream is out,
A glimmer crushed by night,

The jackal's footsteps patter the sand,
The jackal's eyes bring a light. . . .

When the heart is dead and dream is lost,
The jackal devours the flesh;
The passion of the heart and the passion of the dream—
They live in his lust afresh. (SUP:7/11/1919)

"The Jackal" was published in 1923 in *Queen's Quarterly,* but Sapir had previously sent it to Monroe. "Of course, you know who the jackals are," he told her, his indirection suggesting that the poem is about prostitutes (PMP: 7/12/1919). If so, it should be compared to Sapir's reaction to Robinson's poem, "Veteran Sirens" (1916), which one Robinson scholar, a contemporary of Sapir, describes as "an expression of pity for old prostitutes" (Winters 1946:33). By contrast, Sapir read the poem as "a most caustic sketch of the vanity of oldmaidishness" (SN:43)—as if this normally sympathetic interpreter of Robinson were unable to share the poet's pity for prostitutes or old maids.

Benedict was in a better position to sympathize with old maids, having worked with several during her years as a teacher (1911–14). "They are doing their best," she wrote in her journal, "to trump up a reason for living" (Mead 1959:121), but Banner (2003:127) says Benedict found these women "dreary" and "unpleasant." She also speculated about prostitution, which she saw as rooted in the economic and sexual subordination of women in an acquisitive society (Mead 1959: 146–49). For Benedict, Sapir's discussion of the "natural" shame felt by prostitutes, and his claim that the "free" woman "is really a safe . . . prostitute," must have seemed both insensitive and farfetched. As Benedict herself had turned sexually toward women— among them the bisexual Mead (see M. C. Bateson 1984:115–27; also Lapsley 1999; Banner 2003:129–35)—Benedict must have felt equally discomfited by his attitude toward homosexuality. In *Patterns of Culture,* she explicitly linked jealousy in American culture to capitalistic acquisitiveness: "Without the clue that in our civilization . . . man's paramount aim is to amass private possessions . . . , the modern position of the wife and the modern emotions of jealousy are alike unintelligible" (1934a:245). Elsewhere in the book, she chose homosexuality as an example of a trait stigmatized in our society but not necessarily everywhere (262–65). It is difficult not to read Benedict's arguments as direct responses to Sapir. Their profoundly different approaches to "the sex problem" epitomized the differences in their theories of culture and personality.

The Spurious and the Intolerant

The central element of Sapir's approach to culture and personality is an epistemological critique of the reification inherent in the term "culture." As I have shown, Sapir's argument is that culture is not a "thing," monolithic and equally "shared" by all those included within its boundaries. Rather, every person has a unique culture, because, first, one's personal history brings one into contact with a unique configuration of influences, and, second, one must interpret or respond to those cultural influences in a manner consistent with the unique organization of one's personality. True, many people respond to cultural forces in ways so similar as to be nearly identical—much culture does appear to be shared—but there is always the possibility of an idiosyncratic response, a reinterpretation or rejection. Moreover, cultural rebels can persuade others of the validity of their responses, hence the importance of the statement that Sapir remembered (1938a:569) from an ethnography of the Omaha Indians: "Two Crows denies this" (Dorsey 1884:297). For Sapir, the personal visions or contrarian opinions of any "Two Crows" could be "culturalized" (1938a:572). In other words, culture is not fixed and static but open-ended; it is not thinglike, but exists only as it is continually reinterpreted by creative personalities. Here are the grounds for Sapir's remarks about Benedict's "as-if psychology," which, from his perspective, reified culture in personalistic terms. Or, as Sapir phrases the criticism more generally, "It is not the concept of culture that is subtly misleading but the metaphysical locus to which culture is generally assigned" (1932:516).

For Sapir, then, culture—located not "above" people but "between" them—does not overwhelm individuals in oppressive or deterministic fashion. Rather, the relationship between individuals and culture is dialectical: culture provides individuals with the traditional givens—linguistic, aesthetic, social—out of which they will construct their lives, and individuals, as creative personalities, can bend those cultural givens to their own purposes, reshaping culture in the process. As Silverstein (1986) has shown, Sapir's earliest linguistic work is grounded in this dialectical understanding of cultural phenomena—which suggests that Sapir's epistemology of social science precedes the period of his absorption in poetry and music. But, as I have argued in the last two chapters, Sapir worked out the consequences of his position in his aesthetic endeavors, where he experienced and analyzed the relationship between given form and personal creativity.

Moreover, familiarity with Sapir's aesthetic and poetic concerns can help us to understand some apparent contradictions in his writing on culture and personality. On the one hand is his paean to personality, his stress on individual uniqueness at the expense of culture: "Every individual is . . . a representative of at least one sub-culture" (1932:515). On the other hand, Sapir well understood the force of tradition and sometimes spoke, as did most of his colleagues, of individuals caught in its grasp. For example, in an encyclopedia essay, "Custom," Sapir wrote:

> Custom is generally referred to as a constraining force. The conflict of individual will and social compulsion is familiar, but even the most forceful and self-assertive individual needs to yield to custom at most points in order that he may gain leverage . . . for the imposition of his personal will on society. . . . The freedom gained by the denial of custom is essentially a subjective freedom of escape rather than an effective freedom of conquest. (1931a:370)

In another encyclopedia essay, "Fashion," Sapir portrays individuals torn between the desire to be creative and the desire to conform: "Human beings do not wish to be modest; they want to be as expressive—that is, as immodest—as fear allows; fashion helps them solve their paradoxical problem" (1931b:380).

Thus there are two poles in Sapir's theory: individual creativity and cultural constraint. On the one hand, Sapir's theory of culture and personality privileges the possibility of individual creativity while rejecting notions of reified culture. On the other hand, Sapir recognized the importance of cultural tradition—the "genuine" culture, rich enough to stimulate rather than hinder creative personalities. And he argued (as did Tocqueville) that in most situations, most people surrender to tradition rather than act innovatively. There is an implicit elitism in the argument: "genuine artists" (1921b:222) are urged to create, but less is expected of ordinary people, who succumb too easily to spuriousness, either by abandoning any pretense of creative effort, or by adopting the guise of "high" culture without practicing the "self-discipline" necessary for true creativity. This imitative or spurious approach to culture "too often degenerates into a pleasurable servitude, into a facile abnegation of one's own individuality, the more insidious that it has the approval of current judgment" (1924a:323–24).

In Sapir's theory of culture and personality, spuriousness is seen as the greatest danger. And he found spuriousness rampant in the therapeutic culture of self-realization, where, in his judgment, the pursuit of personality as an end in itself was inherently self-defeating. As I have shown, sexual liberation came to epitomize for Sapir the cult of spurious personality. A freedom romantically admired as "primitive" was, in Sapir's opinion, nothing but "spiritual sloth" (1929c:278). No wonder he retitled "Observations on the Sex Problem in America" as "The Discipline of Sex" (1929d). For him, free love was spurious love, undisciplined, hence unrealizable: "The 'enrichment of personality' by way of multiple 'experiences' proves to be little more than a weary accumulation of poverties" (1928b:523). And the aspiring woman was particularly vulnerable to such traps.

Benedict's understanding of the relationship between the individual and culture differed from Sapir's approach in several ways. First, she never accepted (indeed, like most anthropologists, never understood) Sapir's critique of reification. Like Kroeber (1952:148), she dismissed it as an idiosyncratic expression of personal hostility; consider the following remarks, from a letter to Mead describing a paper given by Sapir at a 1932 professional meeting:

> Edward's got a new way to free himself from the necessity of admitting the role of culture. He analyzed his reactions to football, and he drew the moral that every phase of culture—in all cultures—is all things to all people, and that this concept dissolves Function, i.e. it outlaws Radcliffe-Brown's contentions. Well! All I got out of it was that Edward had satisfactorily phrased his quarrel with the universe again. (Mead 1959:325)

It is tempting to speculate that Benedict, like Kroeber, tended to reify culture because both were more concerned than Sapir to guard the conceptual boundaries of the profession that guaranteed their public identity. In any case, Benedict's theory of culture and personality stressed not creativity but correspondence: the degree to which cultures might be seen as personality writ large and, consequently, the ways in which cultures might glorify or suppress basic personality traits. Though she recognized (1934a: 251–54) the kind of dialectical interaction between individuals and culture that Sapir stressed, she glided over it to focus not on culture in relation to unique individuals but on cultural patterns in relation to personality types: "We have seen that any society selects some segment of the arc of possible human behaviour, and . . . its institutions tend to further the expression of its selected segment and to inhibit opposite expressions. But these opposite expressions are the congenial responses, nevertheless, of a certain proportion of the carriers of that culture" (254).

Benedict argued that most individuals are malleable or "plastic": "The vast majority of the individuals in any group are shaped to the fashion of that culture" (1934b:278). Here is the reifying rhetoric of culture and conformity, and she extends it even to the cases of those individuals whose "congenial responses" are so far from what is culturally valued that they cannot be "shaped" to the cultural norm. Ungovernable, they will nonetheless find their lives largely determined by culture: they become abnormals and deviants, "exposed to all the conflicts to which aberrants are always exposed" (1934a:265).

This brings us to the second difference between Sapir and Benedict. In Benedict's view of culture and personality, intolerance replaces spuriousness as the gravest of cultural ills. The deviant's tragedy stems not from inherent unfitness but from the accident of birth into a culture that happens not to value the behavior congenial to those of his or her personality type. Benedict believed that anthropology could teach people to become "culture-conscious," that is, to avoid believing that local culture traits are natural and inevitable. Without the justification of a presumed inevitability, institutions could be rationally examined "in terms of the less desirable behaviour traits they stimulate, and in terms of human suffering and frustration." Those aspects of culture found to be too costly might be reformed, and, at the same time, the treatment of deviance made more humane: "The inculcation of tolerance and appreciation in any society toward its less usual types is fundamentally important in successful mental hygiene. The complement of this tolerance, on the patient's side, is an education in self-reliance and honesty with himself" (1934a:245–48). In the end, Benedict hoped that tolerance on the part of the majority would enable deviants "to achieve a more independent and less tortured attitude" (1934b:278–79).

Erudition and Engineering

Benedict's notion of self-conscious and rational cultural criticism led her to aspire to "what may some day come to be a true social engineering" (1934b: 280), and here we find the final difference between her and Sapir. As I have shown, Sapir did not expect creativity of anyone but the genuine artist, and he made a similar argument with respect to cultural self-consciousness.

For the most part, according to Sapir, "we act all the more securely for our unawareness of the patterns that control us" (1927:549). Moreover, as a passage quoted earlier suggests, even the creator, the "forceful and self-assertive individual" who manages to "conquer" a particular cultural pattern, must rely upon cultural patterns in all the other domains of life that have not been chosen as the focus of creative reinterpretation (1931a:370). The argument is central to Sapir's hermeneutic: one can never control thought with total, self-conscious rationality, for thought is by its very nature grounded in unconscious cultural categories; these, when brought to consciousness, are more often rationalized than rationally analyzed, precisely because any rational analysis of them must itself be based upon unconscious categories. As Sapir puts it in a critique of "orthodox psychology": "Introspection may be a dangerously elusive method, for the moment of consciousness that we set out to describe can not be strictly synchronous with the moment of observation" (1922f:619). All of which leads to the stringent final paragraph of "The Unconscious Patterning of Behavior in Society," where, we are told, "It can be laid down as a principle of far-reaching application that in the normal business of life it is useless and even mischievous for the individual to carry the conscious analysis of his cultural patterns around with him." There may be occasions, Sapir says, when the "student" of culture can use his analysis as "the medicine of society," but for the most part, "we must learn to take joy in the larger freedom of loyalty to thousands of subtle patterns . . . that we can never hope to understand in explicit terms" (1927:558–59).

Sapir's conclusion must be contrasted to the scientific and practical optimism that Benedict admired in both Boas and Mead (Banner 2003:194). Mead's indefatigable pursuit of fieldwork inspired Benedict with visions of scientific progress based on the constant accumulation of new evidence: "When I think of all the material you'll be able to control by the time you come back this next time, I think we needn't limit any of our problems" (Mead 1959:324–25). For her part, Mead self-consciously used her published studies to sketch possible solutions to American social problems. Such pragmatic speculation reached an early high point in *Sex and Temperament in Three Primitive Societies*, where Mead attacked a problem central in Benedict's life as well as her own, that of sex roles and deviance. Mead argued that societies that arbitrarily defined sex roles (we would today say "gender roles") in terms of narrow temperamental types condemned to deviant status those whose natural temperament did not match their biological sex.

To remedy that problem, Mead proposed "a groundplan for building a society that would substitute real differences for arbitrary ones," a society that would "permit the development of many contrasting temperamental gifts in each sex" (1935:217).

Though more cautious than Mead, Benedict, too, was drawn to the role of the expert, offering answers to current problems. In both *Patterns of Culture* and *The Chrysanthemum and the Sword*, Benedict was concerned to enlighten a broad public that was facing, during the depression and the Second World War, the task of constructing a more rational and humane social order: "Social thinking at the present time has no more important task before it than that of taking adequate account of cultural relativity. . . . The implications are fundamental, and modern thought about contacts of peoples and about our changing standards is greatly in need of sane and scientific direction" (1934a:278). Thus despite her earlier aspiration to escape women's committees and the associated social services that they offered, she never renounced "service" as an important responsibility. Now, however, woman's duty had been replaced by that of the scientist (see Modell 1983:247–49).

The search for a meaningful reality led poets and intellectuals in Sapir's and Benedict's generation to pursue genuine culture and hard personality. Sapir and Benedict sought both in poetry, but neither could achieve it there. In his letters to Kroeber and Lowie before 1920, Sapir expressed cautious enthusiasm for his poetry, but his correspondence of the mid-twenties with Benedict reveals that enthusiasm projected, ambivalently, onto her poems and a corresponding sense of failure with respect to his own: "I'm beginning to feel the best thing I can do with poetry is to let it strictly alone. After all, one ought not to write verse when he hasn't the stuff" (Mead 1959:183). At the same time, he criticized the poetry of his contemporaries for being either too soft or too hard. For example, he attributed Monroe's editorial rejection of some of Benedict's poems "to her [Monroe's] inveterate softness or sentimentality. Difficult or in any way intellectual verse gets past her only with difficulty" (179). But he himself criticized the work of another poet, whom Benedict had praised, because it "sounded more like keen cerebration in verse form than poetry. And I'm utterly sick of intelligence and its vanity" (186). Realizing that his own poetry was unsuccessful, Sapir retreated to erudition: "Poetry I neither read nor write. . . . I really think I shall end life's prelude by descending into the fastnesses of a purely technical linguistic erudition. . . . I can understand better than ever before what content there may be in pure mathematics" (180). This echoes the closing sentences of "The Grammarian and His Language," where Sapir claimed for linguistics "the same classical spirit" that he attributed to "mathematics and music at their purest" but found lacking in the spurious culture of his contemporaries (1924b:159). Thus for Sapir, linguistics remained the supreme art to which he could always return.

Benedict, too, retreated from poetry, but her search led in a different direction, to a science that would "contribute . . . toward the saving of humanity," as Sapir put it, contrasting her scholarly engagement to his own erudite withdrawal (Mead 1959:180). Benedict's mature anthropology focused on culture and personality but looked beyond purely theoretical speculation to social engineering. She discovered her convincing sense of selfhood not simply in anthropology as scholarship but in the role of the technical expert, the scientific creator who puts her individual talents at the service of the collectivity. One could play such a role cautiously (Benedict) or boldly (Mead), but in either case it guaranteed a genuine self and at least the promise of a genuine culture—one in which hardness and softness would no longer matter.

CHAPTER 5

Ruth Benedict
and the Modernist Sensibility

The opposition, within Boasian anthropology, of a culture theory emphasizing individual creativity and one privileging cultural holism reflects a wider tension in the literary, artistic, and social "modernism" of the early twentieth century. Critics Michael Levenson (1984) and Kathryne Lindberg (1987) have charted the tension within literary modernism between the quest for self-expression and the desire to recover a viable tradition. Both scholars, in strikingly different ways, have presented the dialogue and debate between Ezra Pound and T. S. Eliot (among others) as emblematic of the larger opposition of individuality and tradition, or deconstructive originality and cultural constraint. Using Levenson and Lindberg to construe the contrast between the literary and anthropological writings of Edward Sapir and those of Ruth Benedict, I could offer the following formula: Pound is to Eliot as Sapir is to Benedict. Put less cryptically, the contrast between Pound's iconoclasm and Eliot's Catholicism is similar to that between Sapir's emphasis on the individual and Benedict's championing of culture. As I have shown, Sapir focused on the individual as a crucial locus of cultural action, and for the most part refused to reify culture, whereas Benedict emphasized cultural integration and the determination of individuals by culture.

This theoretical opposition between individual and culture can be located in the work of separate scholars (Sapir versus Benedict), but it can also be traced as a tension in the writings of both. In this chapter I trace the interaction of the quests for individuality and tradition in the writings of Ruth Benedict. Although her developed theoretical position within anthropology places her among the champions of culture, an examination of her emergence as a professional scholar suggests that her personal quest for self-expression led her to that position. This biographical argument must be linked to a Tocquevillian understanding of modern culture, for Benedict's case shows that self-expression and cultural holism require each other in any formulation of the modernist sensibility.

Benedict's journals, diaries, and letters of 1912–1934, edited and published by Mead (1959) and exhaustively reviewed in biographies of Benedict (Modell 1983; Caffrey 1989; Lapsley 1999; Banner 2003), document a long period of personal struggle. Graduated from Vassar in 1909 with a major in English literature, Benedict traveled extensively in Europe, worked as a teacher and social worker, married and then watched her childless marriage disintegrate, tried her hand at writing both prose and poetry, and found her way to anthropology. Beginning her studies at the New School for Social Research in 1919, Benedict earned her doctoral degree from Columbia University in 1923. Her early years in anthropology were marked by continuing self-doubt, but she seems to have crossed a threshold to professional maturity during summer field trips among Pueblo Indians in 1924 and 1925. The publication of her first book, *Patterns of Culture*, in 1934 (the last year in which she published a poem [Mead 1959:563]) can be taken to mark the end, and fulfillment, of Benedict's quest for personality and achievement (Modell 1983:213).[1]

Benedict's journals and diaries evidence the almost obsessive concern with self-realization and self-expression that is a hallmark of modernism. I take as characteristic of twentieth-century thought (of which modernism is one variety) the emergence of a fully secularized individualism. In this ethos, still prevalent today, one's highest duty is self-realization, or the fullest possible development of one's personality (Lears 1983). True to its Puritan origins, the modern personality proves its existence through work, or, phrased slightly differently, one expresses oneself through one's achievements. In the literary and scientific circles to which Benedict was drawn, work and self-expression meant the production of aesthetic objects, whether poems or scientific studies. The self—"hard," inviolable, unique, authentic—observed the world, experienced the world, mastered the world, and proved itself as a locus of ultimate reality against the world. And from its observations and experiences, the self constructed intricate, original,

---

1. Benedict published professional monographs in 1923 and 1931, but *Patterns of Culture* was the first work she placed with a trade publisher, aimed at a general audience and, most important, that she herself considered to be a book.

beautifully patterned expressions. The successful products of self-expression could then be consumed by other, lesser selves—the vast public—who were also engaged in the business of self-realization but vicariously, through contact with the productions of artists whose lives had been deemed "authentic" (Trilling 1971:99–100).

It is possible to trace Benedict's progress toward a mature anthropological vision, as represented in *Patterns of Culture*, in her private writings. But there are some suppressed or subordinated aspects of Benedict's culture theory, which come into focus by examining some of the anthropological articles that she published before *Patterns of Culture*. "A Brief Sketch of Serrano Culture" (1924) is a derivative piece representing Boasian anthropology as Benedict had learned it but before she had contributed to reshaping it. By contrast, not only are "Psychological Types in the Cultures of the Southwest" (1930) and "Configurations of Culture in North America" (1932) preliminary versions of portions of *Patterns of Culture*, they are more innovative in terms of culture theory than the more cleanly modernist model presented in her first masterwork. As I will show, the authorial persona of *Patterns of Culture*, like that of her second great book, *The Chrysanthemum and the Sword* (1946), is a solution to the modernist problem of the relationship of personality and culture, the artist and tradition.

Experience without Pattern

In a diary entry for December 1915, Benedict describes what she calls the "passionate blank despair" she felt when, as a freshman at Vassar in the winter of 1906, she puzzled over the purpose of life. In that mood, she read the conclusion to Walter Pater's *The Renaissance*. As I showed in chapter 4, his injunction "to burn always with this hard, gemlike flame" (Pater 1873:195) thrilled Benedict: "The book fell shut in my hands at the end," she recalled, "and it was as if my soul had been given back to me" (Mead 1959:135).

Benedict's attraction to Pater epitomizes an enduring theme in her private writings: the desire to live intensely, to "have experiences" of an outer reality that prove to oneself the reality of one's personality. As she put it in another journal entry, perhaps from 1915: "Anything to live! To have done with this numbness that will not let me feel" (Mead 1959:136). The passage concerning Pater, in which she recalls an apparently intense experience of communion with an intensity that matches the initial experience, suggests how early and how profoundly Benedict was committed to—or ensnared by—the modernist sensibility. The desire for experience, as formulated by

Pater, leads in two contradictory directions: toward egoism or the cult of
personality, and toward a reaction to the meaninglessness or incoherence
of a reality defined solely in terms of fragmented personal experiences. In
Levenson's genealogy of modernism, mid-Victorians such as Matthew
Arnold attempted to ground Christian belief in personal experience instead
of dogmatic assertion. But after Arnold, Pater "recognized . . . that to
redefine traditional values as phases of the self was to weaken traditional
sanctions. . . . Subjectivity was a double-edged sword. In the hands of
Pater, it was used not only to cut away the metaphysical, but also the
traditionally moral, the traditionally religious, the objective and the permanent" (Levenson 1984:18–19).

The follower of Pater, then, was left alone with the self. Benedict wanted
to "realize" or develop that self, but she craved also a source of stability or
order beyond the self. On the one hand, her private writings are replete
with admonishments to believe in her own personality:

> I have been reading Walt Whitman, and Jeffries' [Jefferies] *Story of My Heart.*
> They are alike in their superb enthusiasm for life[,] . . . their unwavering,
> ringing belief that the *Me* within them is of untold worth and importance. I
> read in wonder and admiration—in painful humility. Does this sense of per-
> sonal worth, this enthusiasm for one's own personality, belong only to great
> self-expressive souls? or to a mature period of life I have not yet attained?
> (Mead 1959:123)

On the other hand, Benedict describes herself as unfulfilled by episodic
epiphanies unconnected to larger patterns of significance: "The trouble is
not that we are never happy—it is that happiness is so episodical. . . . I
cannot see what holds it all together" (Mead 1959:121).

Benedict knew, however, what could *not* hold it all together: conventional culture. In 1912, she described her "real me" as hidden behind the
"mask" she had donned in choosing the role of schoolteacher (Mead 1959:
119). Later, she described as "distractions" the customary rituals, such as
funerals and weddings, that anthropology would teach her to examine
more respectfully: "All our ceremonies, our observances, are for the weak
who are cowards before the bare thrust of feeling" (Mead 1959:136). And
elsewhere she spoke with mild contempt of the conformity of the masses,
"lost and astray unless the tune has been set for them, . . . the spring of
their own personalities touched from the outside" (Mead 1959:144).

Benedict was also dissatisfied with unconventional answers to her existential dilemmas, even those formulated by the great creative personalities of history:

> The trouble with life isn't that there is no answer, it's that there are so many answers. There's the answer of Christ and of Buddha, of Thomas a Kempis and of Elbert Hubbard, of Browning, Keats and of Spinoza, of Thoreau and of Walt Whitman, of Kant and of Theodore Roosevelt. By turns their answers fit my needs. And yet, because I am I and not any one of them, they can none of them be completely mine.

Here an "answer," a believable and believed-in moral system, seems of less moment than the need of the personality to appropriate such an answer as "mine." As Benedict's meditation continued, she admitted that moral questions are never solved. "What we call 'answers' are, rather, attitudes taken by different temperaments toward certain characteristic problems—even the interrogation may be an 'answer'" (Mead 1959:126). The phrasing is egocentric ("attitudes," "temperaments") and relativistic—a striking prefiguring of the position developed later in *Patterns of Culture*, where she portrays authentic cultures not as answers but as existential attitudes in terms of which both answers and questions are constructed.

In addition to the quest for personality and the rejection of convention—quintessentially modernist themes—Benedict's private writings reveal a painfully explicit consciousness of the dilemmas that the task of self-realization posed for women. She wavered between a belief that woman's "instinctive" vocation is domestic and a reluctance to sacrifice apparently masculine aspirations to the domestic role. "Nature lays a compelling and very distressing hand upon woman," she wrote in 1913. Women could deny "that the one gift in our treasure house is love," but their quests for fulfillment—"in social work, in laboratories, in schools," with marriage considered merely "a possible factor in our lives"—would end in failure (Mead 1959:131, 133). At other times, however, Benedict sensed that the sacrifice of self and self-development to domestic duties could not but lead to frustration, bitterness, and waste. After a year of marriage, she felt that she needed a career or mission beyond her marriage (Mead 1959:136). Four years later, she wrote that woman's sacrifice of self to family was both socially wasteful and psychologically harmful. Whatever natural differences there might be between the sexes—another question to be settled by anthropological inquiry!—both men and women had to take responsibility for their own personal development. Yet disparities in culturally constructed gender roles made the pursuit of self-development more problematic for women than for men: "The issue . . . is fine free living in the spirit world of socialized spiritual values—for men as for women. But owing to artificial actual conditions their problems are strikingly different" (Mead 1959: 146–47). Small wonder that the first anthropology course in which Benedict enrolled was "Sex in Ethnology," taught by Elsie Clews Parsons (Deacon 1997:235; the course title appears in the *New School Bulletin*, but Banner [2003:146] found a different course title, "Women and the Social Order," in Parsons's papers).

As Benedict struggled to find her way, she sensed that fulfillment was most readily accessible to her in literary endeavor. Her problem was to find an appropriate voice and genre. Her first major effort was biography, as she planned a book charting the lives of three famous women. She wrote at least six drafts of an essay on Mary Wollstonecraft but was unable to finish the project after it was rejected for publication in 1919. As Modell has suggested, Benedict sought in biography a way to see life whole, to discover her own personal integrity by constructing storied, hence coherent, accounts of women whose lives had been judged by their contemporaries to be out of control. But the biographer could not achieve a satisfactory distance from her subjects: their lives and problems seemed too much her own (Modell 1983:105–6). We can say the same thing of Benedict's poetry, which she wrote on and off for years: in her poems, she could not achieve the "hard," polished self that she desired. Rather, her poems tended to express an unhappy and fragmented self, at times almost hysterically out of control (see Modell 1983:140).

Benedict's search for a literary voice is linked to still another recurrent theme in her private writings, summarized by what she called "detachment." Coupled antithetically to her desire to experience the world with the intensity that Pater advocated is her fear of that intensity. "I dread intense awareness," she wrote in her diary on March 8, 1923, the day that she completed the writing of her doctoral thesis. Yet, having admitted the fear, she went on to express fear of its opposite: "And then it seems to me terrible that life is passing, that my program is to fill the twenty-four hours each day with obliviousness" (Mead 1959, 67). By contrast, "detachment" seems to have represented a transcendence of both fears:

I divide the riches of the mind into two kingdoms: the kingdom of knowledge, where the reason gives understanding, and the kingdom of wisdom,
where detachment gives understanding. This detachment is the life of the
spirit, and its fruit is wisdom. That would cover it fairly well—the life of the
artist and the life of the mystic. Its essence is its immediacy—without the
distractions of belief or anxiety. It has no dogmas, it has no duties. It is a final
synthesis of knowledge, and it is also a laying aside of knowledge. (Mead
1959, 136–37)

Here Benedict envisions an almost utopian solution to the modernist quest.
It couples Pater's immediacy to a coherence of perspective that transcends
the purely personal. Moreover, transpersonal coherence is not bought at
the expense of personal integrity. There will be, Benedict tells us, no "distractions of belief or anxiety," no "dogmas" or "duties." It is almost as if she
sought the vision, the voice, the perspective of a god, or of an omniscient
narrator.

Drawing together these fragments of Benedict's private writings, we find
a neat model of the modernist sensibility. Benedict sought to realize an
authentic personality in an individually chosen career or lifework. Although
tempted by conventional roles, including domestic duties and female pro-
fessions, she found herself unable to settle for them. Coupled with her
quest for self-realization was the desire to discover an authentic moral order,
but such an order had to be acceptable to her personality and temperament.
Thus writing, through which one might create order in a fragmented world,
came to represent a solution to her. Anthropology would give her the institutional framework within which to forge an alternative genre.

Mastering Pattern

When Ruth Benedict came to anthropology, the Boasian school was beginning a transition from the study of the distribution of isolated culture "traits"
to the study of cultural wholes and the processes whereby traits are assembled to form such wholes (Stocking 1974a, 1976). Boas had spent several
decades attacking nineteenth-century evolutionary anthropology. He argued
that evolutionary schemes of universal history were based upon ethnocen-
tric and unreliable categories, and he demonstrated their improbability when
confronted with empirical studies of the diffusion and distribution of culture traits. But the ethnographic research that permitted Boas and his students to trace the empirical (as opposed to speculative) origins of culture

traits raised new questions. How did such traits come to be amalgamated into living cultures, and what was the nature of the integrative force that held amalgamated traits together? To the latter question, Ruth Benedict's work would provide an important answer.

Like many of Boas's students, Benedict wrote a library dissertation treating not culture wholes but the diffusion of culture traits. (It was entitled *The Concept of the Guardian Spirit in North America*.) The summer before she completed her dissertation, she traveled to Southern California to do "salvage ethnography" on an apparently disappearing Amerindian group, the Serrano. It is unclear whether Benedict lived among the Serrano for any length of time or stayed mainly with her mother and sister in Los Angeles. Her work consisted of interviewing aging informants about past customs (Modell 1983:169–71; Caffrey 1989:104–5, 365–66). In any case, not until her trip to Zuni in the summer of 1924 did Benedict experience what she considered to be her professional initiation, doing fieldwork in a living culture. She returned to the pueblos the next summer and made further field trips to the Southwest in 1927 and 1931 (Modell 1983:171–77; Caffrey 1989:108).

According to Mead, "Anthropology made the first 'sense' that any ordered approach to life had ever made to Ruth Benedict." She arrived at Columbia when "Boas was still interested in diffusion and in having his students laboriously trace a trait or a theme from culture to culture" (Mead 1959:8, 11). Benedict's dissertation on the guardian spirit was just such a tracing, and apparently the work of poring over the technical literature on Indian cultures did not discourage her: "A good day at relationship [that is, kinship] systems—not Mohave however," is a typical diary entry from the months that she was finishing her thesis (Mead 1959:59). Her field trips to the pueblos seem to have marked a personal turning point for Benedict. Writing to Mead in 1925 from the Peña Blanca Pueblo, Benedict described her newly won confidence: "Three years ago it [a month's isolation] would have been enough to fill me with terror. I was always afraid of depressions getting too much for me. . . . But that's ancient history now" (Mead 1959:295).

"A Brief Sketch of Serrano Culture" (1924) was Benedict's first publication based on her own field materials (she had already published her dissertation and an article based on it). Modell (1983:170) points out that Benedict "had trouble writing" about the Serrano, "partly because data were scant and partly because she did not see a design in the disparate remaining elements of Serrano culture." The article is organized in terms of standard ethnological categories, with major sections entitled "Social Organization," "Ceremonial Observances," "Shamanism," and "Material Culture." Benedict announces at the outset that she will do little more than report information that "is almost entirely exoteric," for "a great deal of the old meaning . . . is undoubtedly lost." From her perspective, the Serrano, like the anthropologist herself, faced the dilemma of a meaningless existence: "It is largely by guess-work that they can give the meaning of any of the ceremonial songs; and any religious connotation in such practices as rock-painting, for instance, is now unknown" (Benedict 1924:366, 368). (It is, of course, possible that the anthropologist's quest for authenticity generated questions that consultants either did not understand or declined to answer, thereby leading Benedict to perceive their situation as meaningless.)

Benedict's Serrano article is little more than a listing of traits. Significantly, items that Benedict would bring together in later publications as elements of an internally meaningful ceremonial complex are here reported under different headings (for example, information on the use of hallucinogenics [375, 377, 383]). Also significant is the absence in this early work of holistic comparisons, for the placing of whole cultures side by side would become a cornerstone of her later narrative and epistemological method. By contrast, in the Serrano essay, cross-cultural comparison is confined to traits, as it typically is in the work of both evolutionists and diffusionists. For example, Benedict points out that Serrano joking relationships seem congruent with a form of moiety organization well known in the literature but that kinship and joking status do not coincide as they should in the standard moiety system (373). Benedict's discussion here demonstrates deference to the authority of a technical jargon, but it lacks conviction. The article ends, abruptly and almost surrealistically, with a section on food. Describing Serrano methods for harvesting and preparing mesquite, nuts, and deer, Benedict tells us in the final sentence of the essay, "The bones were pounded in mortars while fresh, and eaten in a sort of paste" (392).

In the four years between the Serrano article and the first of the papers that resulted from the pueblo field trips, Benedict reformulated Boasian anthropology into her own approach, in which, as Modell (1983:171) puts it, "culture wholeness became her disciplinary idea." Other American anthropologists were moving in the direction that Benedict took; particularly important was Sapir's essay on genuine culture. Benedict was also influenced by Jung and by the Gestalt psychologists, as well as by her reading of German philosophers of history such as Spengler and Dilthey (Stocking

1976:16). In 1928, she presented a paper called "Psychological Types in the Cultures of the Southwest" (published in 1930) and in 1932 published "Configurations of Culture in North America." These papers, and a third entitled "Anthropology and the Abnormal," published in 1934, together contain most of the central arguments of *Patterns of Culture*.

Benedict's key idea was that cultures are configured or integrated around one or a few dominant drives, themes, or patterns. The obverse of the ongoing diffusion of culture traits is the absorption of borrowed traits into a preexistent culture whole. Benedict argued (in almost unavoidably personifying terms) that each culture selects from material available to be borrowed, as well as from the creative productions of its own members, and reinterprets the materials that it "chooses" to incorporate. Such selection and reinterpretation are to be accounted for by the existence of a "fundamental psychological set" or "configuration" that can be taken to characterize and permeate the culture as a whole.

In the 1928 paper, "Psychological Types," Benedict confines herself to these points, exemplified in a contrast she draws between the Pueblos and other Native American cultures of the Southwest. She begins where the diffusionists leave off, pointing out that the most striking feature of Pueblo culture—its ceremonialism—hardly distinguishes it from other Indian cultures, since most also show "high ritualistic development." The difference, according to Benedict, lies in the spirit of Pueblo ceremonialism: the two groups of cultures differ in their "fundamental psychological sets," which she labels with terms taken from Nietzsche: "Apollonian" and "Dionysian." The Apollonian pueblos share with their neighbors such religious and ceremonial traits as hallucinogenics, fasting, and the vision quest. But the pueblos have purged from these traits all traces of Dionysian ecstasy. Whereas diffusionists were content to plot the distribution of traits and trait complexes, Benedict sought to portray whole cultures by interpreting the inner spirit that knits traits together into a way of life that is meaningful and coherent to those who live it. As she concludes, "It is not only that the understanding of this psychological set is necessary for a descriptive statement of this culture; without it the cultural dynamics of this region are unintelligible" (1930:261).

A more sophisticated version of these arguments is found in the 1932 essay on North American culture configurations. There, Benedict draws on the interpretive philosophies of history of Dilthey and Spengler to develop her notion of a culture's psychological set. She does not abandon psychologistic concepts but enlarges her notion of culture so that her arguments can no longer be dismissed as psychological reductionism. Moreover, Benedict's comparative hermeneutics of culture is now developed in stunning fashion, setting up a paradoxical resolution to the modernist quest for holism.

Benedict begins by reviewing the "anecdotal" status of most of the ethnological data compiled in the past. These data, she claims, have been presented as "detached objects" with no attention to "their setting or function in the culture from which they came." She then praises Boas's field studies and Malinowski's functionalism as representative of a new anthropology that has begun to study cultures in holistic fashion. But Malinowski's functionalism is inadequate, she argues, because once it has shown that "each trait functions in the total cultural complex," it stops—without considering "in what sort of a whole these traits are functioning" (1932:1–2). In other words, analysis of a functioning whole differs from that of a meaningful whole, a distinction basic to Boasian anthropology, the roots of which lay deep in German historicism. As Sapir had put it in his essay on genuine culture, "A magical ritual, for instance, which, when considered psychologically, seems to liberate and give form to powerful emotional aesthetic elements of our nature, is nearly always put in harness to some humdrum utilitarian end—the catching of rabbits or the curing of disease" (1924:319). Not only is the "emotional aesthetic" meaning of culture different from its function, it is, for Sapir and Benedict, more basic. Boas, Sapir, and Benedict all argue that humans rationalize—or invent reasons to justify—those aspects of their culture of which they become conscious. But they remain unconscious of the formal patterns (as in the grammar of their language) that provide the ultimate ordering in culture. Thus Benedict takes care to distinguish the configurational order that she is trying to describe from the functional order of Malinowski:

> The order that is achieved is not merely the reflection of the fact that each trait has a pragmatic function that it performs—which is much like a great discovery in physiology that the normal eye sees and the normally muscled hand grasps, or . . . the discovery that nothing exists in human life that mankind has not espoused and rationalized. The order is due rather to the circumstance that in these societies a principle has been set up according to which the assembled cultural material is made over into consistent patterns in accordance with certain inner necessities that have developed within the group. (1932:2)

Benedict's phrasing continues to be evocative and imprecise—"principle," "consistent patterns," "inner necessities." Her ensuing discussion, however, drawing on Dilthey and Spengler, makes it clear that culture has become for her a question of the meaning of life, as such meanings are constructed or patterned for the members of each culture. Disparate traits, assembled into a culture from heterogeneous sources, can be understood only in terms of the particular meaningful configuration of that culture; they take their meaning from their place in the pattern, not from their origins or function:

> Traits objectively similar and genetically allied may be utilized in different configurations. . . . The relevant facts are the emotional background against which the act takes place in the two cultures. It will illustrate this if we imagine the Pueblo snake dance in the setting of our own society. Among the Western Pueblo, at least, repulsion is hardly felt for the snake. . . . When we identify ourselves with them [the snake dancers] we are emotionally poles apart, though we put ourselves meticulously into the pattern of their behavior. (6)

Although Benedict speaks here of emotional attitudes, the issue is, more broadly, one of cultural interpretation. In her example, we are asked to imagine ourselves in the place of the snake dancers. Without an understanding of the meaning of the snake in Pueblo culture, we will impose our own, Western understanding on the ethnographic material and thus misinterpret the dance, however meticulously we note its external details. Sapir made a similar argument a few years earlier in "The Unconscious Patterning of Behavior in Society," an essay that Benedict must have known. In that 1927 essay, Sapir, like Benedict, concocts a "thought experiment." He asks the reader to imagine "making a painstaking report of the actions of a group of natives engaged in some form of activity, say religious, to which he has not the cultural key." A "skillful writer," Sapir suggests, will get the external details right, but her account of the significance of the activity to the natives "will be guilty of all manner of distortion. . . . It becomes actually possible to interpret as base what is inspired by the noblest and even holiest of motives, and to see altruism or beauty where nothing of the kind is either felt or intended" (1927:546–47). He goes on to speculate about how it is that natives can regularly reproduce in their behavior cultural patterns of which they have no conscious awareness. By contrast, Benedict's discovery of cultural patterning leads her to issue a programmatic call to her colleagues to reorient field research in order to document the patterns of particular cultures (Benedict 1932:7). For her, the anthropologist's ability to master pattern was never in doubt. It was the anthropologist's business to stand aside and describe in objective terms the cultural patterns that make life meaningful for the peoples under study.

Yet Benedict's interpretive method is fundamentally comparative and hermeneutic (see Boon 1999:23–42). It thus implies the impossibility of objective descriptions of individual cultures—or, more precisely, of descriptions constructed by an observer occupying neutral ground. In the "Configurations" article, as in *Patterns of Culture* and *The Chrysanthemum and the Sword* (1946), Benedict never describes cultures in isolation. Rather, she delineates their characteristic configurations or patterns by way of contrast with the patterns of other cultures. Thus a Benedictian description of a culture depends as much upon which culture the observer-writer chooses as the relevant point of comparison as it does upon the "facts" of the culture in question. As I have shown, the essay on psychological types is largely taken up with elaborating on the distinction between the Apollonian pueblos and their Dionysian neighbors. A similar method is developed to a high art in "Configurations." There Benedict rehearses again the Apollonian-Dionysian distinction. Not content to stop there, however, she introduces other, crosscutting contrasts:

> In the face of the evident opposition of these two . . . types of behavior it is at first sight somewhat bizarre to group them together over against another type in contrast to which they are at one. It is true nevertheless. In their different contexts, the [Apollonian] Southwest and the [Dionysian] Plains are alike in not capitalizing ideas of pollution and dread. . . . In contrast with the non-Pueblo Southwest, for instance, these two are alike in realistically directing their behavior toward the loss-situation instead of romantically elaborating the danger situation. (1932:9)

Benedict goes on to elaborate this realist-romantic distinction in a long review of attitudes toward the dead. She is now working with three cultural configurations: Apollonian realists (Pueblo), Dionysian realists (Plains), and Dionysian romantics (non-Pueblo Southwest). But each discrete type comes into being, as it were, only by way of a contrast deliberately elaborated by the anthropologist. In other words, Pueblo and Plains, distinguished by the Apollonian-Dionysian contrast, turn out to be similar, as realists, when opposed to other cultures that can be characterized as romantics. Finally, Benedict introduces a fourth configuration, that of the "megalomaniacal" Northwest Coast cultures. These peoples, too, are Dionysian, but their institutionalization of the "pursuit of personal aggrandizement" represents a new crosscutting of the Dionysian temperament. This yields a configuration that can be contrasted as significantly to the Dionysian realists of the Plains as to the Apollonian Pueblos (1932:18).

At this point, it is worth noting that the cultural configurations that serve as the apparently holistic units in Benedict's comparisons are themselves synthetic, built by the anthropologist from multiple ethnographic sources. Consider, for example, the following sketch of a Dionysian-romantic ritual:

> Years ago in the government warfare against the Apache the inexorable purification ceremonies of the Pima almost canceled their usefulness to the United States troops as allies. Their loyalty and bravery were undoubted, but upon the killing of an enemy each slayer must retire for twenty days of ceremonial purification. He selected a ceremonial father who cared for him and performed the rites. This father had himself taken life and been through the purification ceremonies. He sequestered the slayer in the bush in a small pit where he remained fasting for sixteen days. . . . Among the Papago the father feeds him on the end of a long pole. His wife must observe similar taboos in her own house. (1932:16)

The footnotes to this passage list four sources, including Benedict's field notes, from which the account is constructed. From the mass of details afforded by the sources, she begins with one that emphasizes the practical consequences of an interpretive contrast. The ethnographer, Frank Russell, had noted, "The bravery of the Pimas was praised by all army officers . . . but Captain Bourke and others have complained of their unreliability, due solely to their rigid observance of this religious law" (1908:204). Just as Americans might read the Western horror of snakes into the Pueblo snake dance, and thus misunderstand it, so U.S. Army officers had mistranslated Piman religiosity as "unreliability." It is with this maximal contrast that Benedict chooses to begin her portrait of the rituals.

As Benedict's account develops, she individualizes general information, bringing readers closer to the authentic existence of the natives. "The Pima" (plural) becomes two people acting out a particular ritual: "He selected a ceremonial father. . . . This father had himself taken life." As the narration takes us through the by now personalized ritual, Benedict injects a "culture trait" from elsewhere: a custom of the Papago that is strikingly illustrative of the Dionysian-romantic horror that Benedict wishes to stress. Note that the narration returns without explicit transition from the Papago father to the Piman wife (see Russell 1908:205). To be sure, the Papago were "closely related" to the Pima. Moreover, the implicit epistemology of Benedict's comparative method justifies her lumping together similar or related groups in order to contrast them, as a holistic culture configuration, to other peoples grouped together as representative of an opposing configuration. Yet the synthetic nature of the culture configurations that she first described in these articles of 1930 and 1932 is belied by much of the rhetoric and organization of *Patterns of Culture*, the first book in which she spoke to the public in the coherent voice of a scientist and professional writer.

The Anthropologist as Modernist Persona

Ruth Benedict's most widely known work, read by several generations of American college students, presents her theory of culture illustrated with three apparently neatly bounded, holistic cultures. It is this image of a world of discrete cultures that undergraduates most easily retain. However, a close reading of *Patterns of Culture* will show that Benedict's comparative hermeneutic is vigorously at work, even in a book whose core consists of three separate chapters devoted to three unproblematically separate cultures. This is obvious in chapter 4, "The Pueblos of New Mexico," which is an expanded version of the 1930 and 1932 articles, continuing the presentation of the Pueblos in terms of the Apollonian-Dionysian contrast. Her contrastive method is also apparent in the final two chapters, devoted to the problem of the individual and society. There, Benedict becomes a subtle but pointed critic of American culture, discussing American aggressiveness and competition in the comparative light of Pueblo sobriety and Northwest Coast megalomania (1934a:244–45, 248, 273–77). In other words, her own culture became an important contrastive focus in her work. Indeed, her final book, *The Chrysanthemum and the Sword*, is more than a study of patterns of Japanese culture, as its subtitle proclaims. Beyond that, it is a sustained contrast between American individualism and Japanese hierarchy in which almost every assertion about Japan is brought home by means of contrastive material on the United States (see Geertz 1988:102–28).

But to return to *Patterns of Culture*: the comparative aspects of the narrative notwithstanding, the book can easily be read as a description of three distinct cultures. The sixth chapter, "The Northwest Coast of America," elaborates the discussion that Benedict began in the 1932 article. Now, however, the mediating configurations of that essay—Dionysian realists and romantics—have been eliminated, as has the argument about crosscutting configurational dimensions. The sixth chapter thus presents the Pueblos' Dionysian opposite, but it does so in such a way that the hermeneutic construction of a contrast is hidden, and cultural differences are made to seem solely a function of "objective" differences in two "on-the-ground" cultures. Moreover, chapter 5, based on Reo Fortune's Melanesian material from Dobu (Fortune 1932), presents an example drawn from the opposite side of the globe, in place of the mediating North American examples that Benedict used earlier. Thus is the geographical and configurational gradualism of the "Configurations" article replaced by three apparently well-separated and starkly contrasted culture wholes.

An individualizing vision, then, prevails in *Patterns of Culture*, despite the hermeneutic twist implicit in Benedict's comparative method. The holistic culture sought by alienated modernists is there discovered in portraits of three "collective individuals." That term is peculiarly apt, given Benedict's characterization of cultures as "individual psychology thrown large upon the screen, given gigantic proportions and a long time span" (1932:24; see also 1934a:46). Indeed, I would argue that modern social theory (dating from at least the eighteenth century) swings between reified conceptions of the individual (as in utilitarianism) and reified conceptions of society and culture (as in most twentieth-century sociology and anthropology). The modernists' quest for what Sapir called genuine culture was motivated in part by their perception that an atomistic, rationalistic science had destroyed tradition. But the modernists' genuine culture cannot, in the final analysis, be discovered by a social science that constructs cultural wholes on individualistic principles. Indeed, embodied in governmental policies, modernist social science paradoxically leads away from holism to the routinization of all aspects of social life, bureaucratically fragmented and administered (see also Handler 1988).

The individualistic premises implicit in the theory of cultural integration are linked to Benedict's notion of detachment. In *Patterns of Culture*, Benedict discovered the authentic, holistic cultures she sought and from which the modern world excluded her as a participant. She describes the Apollonian, anti-individualistic Pueblos with an almost utopian longing, for in them, apparently, the surrender of individuality to society is not even problematic. Here there is no question of conventional ceremonies' repressing individual feelings (recall Benedict's rejection of funerals and weddings in her own society). But even in cultures that demanded that individuals assert themselves, as on the Northwest Coast, the thorough determination of individual personality by cultural configuration meant that individuals were unself-conscious in their individualism. Sapir, in his essay on genuine culture, writes of cultural authenticity in terms of sincerity, but, as I have shown, Benedict objects to the argument: "It seems to me that cultures may be built solidly and harmoniously upon fantasies, fear-constructs, or inferiority complexes and indulge to the limit in hypocrisy and pretensions" (1932:26). Her rejection of sincerity perhaps reflects the search for that intense yet detached cultural participation that she described in her journal. Sincerity implies self-consciousness, and Benedict sought worlds in which meaningfulness and participation could exist without such awareness. The Northwest Coast potlatcher could pursue megalomaniacal successes unhindered by modernist self-doubt.

Detachment was also to be found in the persona of the scientist. As an anthropologist-narrator, Benedict wrote into being the holistic, genuine cultures that no longer existed in the modernist's world. At the same time, she preserved her own individuality, controlling and inviolate as a narrative voice (see also Levenson 1984:207). It seems clear that the voice of the scientist and the genre of scientific writing worked for Benedict: through them she achieved the "hard" personality that she desired but could not achieve as a writer of poetry and biography. In her anthropological writing, she did not eliminate all reference to herself, to the *I*. But that *I* was now a scientist, a cultural anthropologist working within an established community of scholars possessed of their own techniques and discourse. For example, in the first chapter of *The Chrysanthemum and the Sword*, the authorial voice identifies itself in a variety of terms, shifting among them gracefully and apparently unproblematically. "In June, 1944, I was assigned to the study of Japan. . . . As a cultural anthropologist . . . I had confidence in certain techniques and postulates which could be used. . . . The anthropologist has good proof in his experience that even bizarre behavior does not prevent one's understanding it. . . . The student who is trying to uncover the assumptions upon which Japan builds its way of life has a far harder task than statistical validation" (1946:3, 6, 10, 17). Thus, despite the book's Tocquevillian hermeneutic method—Japan and the United States are each interpreted in terms of what the other is not—the narrative is presided over by an apparently objective persona. Indeed, that persona is more than objective: it is detached, its existence grounded either in its own individuality or in the universal comprehension of science (see also Tyler 1987:42).

Ruth Benedict's conquest of a voice and a personality as she moved through biography and poetry to anthropology might be summarily described in the words of James Joyce's young artist:

> The personality of the artist, at first a cry or a cadence or a mood and then a fluid and lambent narrative, finally refines itself out of existence, impersonalises itself, so to speak. . . . The artist, like the God of the creation, remains within or behind or beyond or above his handiwork, invisible, refined out of existence, indifferent, paring his fingernails. (1916:215)

This is a famous passage, one "indelible in the memory of readers of a certain age," as Lionel Trilling puts it (1971:7). Ruth Benedict was of that modernist age, and in her anthropological writing she achieved the integral personality that she and so many of her contemporaries sought. The achievement of integrity depended upon writing about—or writing into existence—cultures that could be seen to be whole, holistic, and authentic. That postcolonial, postmodern anthropology has produced a spate of biographies, histories, and literary-critical analyses of our ancestors testifies, perhaps, to an inauthenticity that we perceive in ourselves and that we try to escape by writing the storied lives of others.

CHAPTER 6

American Culture in the World

Margaret Mead's *And Keep Your Powder Dry*

An underlying tension in Boasian anthropology opposes scientific rationality to the recognition of a world of differing cultures, hence of differing ways of thought, even differing rationalities. As Boas moved "from physics to ethnology" (Stocking 1965a), from the natural sciences to cosmology, he came to a profound awareness of the power of cultures in human affairs. That developing awareness was rooted in part in German romanticism stemming from Herder. As Boas put it, much later in his career, in a 1916 letter to the *New York Times* in which he decried anti-German sentiments expressed by Americans during World War I: "In my youth I had been taught in school and at home not only to love the good of my own country but also to seek to understand and respect the individualities of other nations" (Stocking 1974a:332). Yet, as Stocking has pointed out, "Boas never abandoned entirely a nineteenth-century liberal belief in a singular human progress in 'civilization' that was based ultimately on the cumulation of rational knowledge" (1979:45). Science, then, led to an appreciation of— indeed, a theory about—cultural diversity and alternative cultural logics. At least for Boas, science did not thereby renounce its claim to privileged status among modes of human knowledge—even though the scientific study of other cultures made possible a newly critical awareness of the biases inherent in even the scientist's perspective.

This tension—between recognition of the provisionality of all human knowledge, on the one hand, and allegiance to science and to scientific expertise, on the other—permeates the work of Boas and his students. Reading the cultural criticism of relativistic anthropologists, one is led to ask about the epistemological and moral presuppositions that, often implicitly, ground their judgments. Granted that cross-cultural comparison leads to a new and relativistic awareness of values, how does one justify those values that one chooses to privilege as a cultural critic? Granted that natives everywhere invent rationalizations to justify or explain customs that are ultimately nonrational, upon what scientific bases can a cultural critic advance practical solutions to problems of value? Having examined such questions in the lives and works of Sapir and Benedict, I turn now to Margaret Mead's portrait of American national character.

And Keep Your Powder Dry

Margaret Mead came under the influence of Boas and Benedict in the fall of 1922, the first term of her senior year at Barnard College. "I entered my senior year committed to psychology," she wrote in her autobiography (1972:111), but a course with Boas and his teaching assistant, Benedict, led her to opt for graduate work in anthropology. She claimed that Boasian relativism was congruent with the values that she had been taught by her parents, both of whom were social scientists and educators. Anthropology also appealed to her because her teachers were animated by a sense of mission—to document human cultural diversity before it succumbed to the global spread of modern culture. She chose anthropology over psychology and sociology when Benedict convinced her that "anthropology had to be done *now*. Other things could wait" (114). Mead's first field trip, to Samoa, resulted in *Coming of Age in Samoa* (1928) and brought its young author lasting fame.

It has been said that Mead wrote *And Keep Your Powder Dry* (1942) in three weeks. She wrote it as a contribution to the war effort at a time when many anthropologists saw it as their duty to throw themselves into the battle for democracy (Howard 1984:236; see also Mead 1979; Yans-McLaughlin 1986; Novick 1988:293–95). As Philip Gleason notes (1984), the ongoing search for an American identity and culture was given new life by the "mighty democratic revival" engendered by World War II. Opposition to fascism and a reaffirmation of the democratic faith combined with a growing cognizance of the Boasian theory of culture to create renewed interest in American national culture, holistically understood. Like Benedict's book on Japan, Mead's study of the United States was intended to help policy makers plan the U.S. war effort in a way that used its citizens' capabilities most effectively. To that end, Mead offered an assessment of the "assets and . . . liabilities," the "strengths and . . . weaknesses," of the American national character (Mead 1942:15, 164).

And Keep Your Powder Dry was not based on systematic fieldwork or research on American culture. Rather, Mead combined the insights she had gained in the anthropological study of non-Western cultures with impressions of American culture drawn from her personal experience and, increasingly, from her professional activities and the travels that they entailed. Mead's biographer, Jane Howard, has commented critically on the book's "slapdash, flippant quality" (1984:274–87). Similarly, Gleason has described the book as "a loose and rambling affair written in a style of impressionistic omniscience." Worse, according to him, the book offered little that was new to discussions of American identity and culture, though he points out that Mead's analysis, grounded in anthropological expertise, conferred a new legitimacy on the very idea of national character and its scientific study (Gleason 1981:506–7). And Micaela di Leonardo finds the book's "sloppiness" to be the least of its problems; she sees it as a "transition text" that documents "Mead's final jettisoning of any pretense at progressive scholarship on gender," race, and ethnicity (1998:197).

Yet despite such criticisms, which may well be justified, I find *And Keep Your Powder Dry* remarkably coherent and frequently insightful. Its coherence may be attributed, first, to the culture theory that informed it. As Mead puts it, "The anthropologist is trained to see form where other people see concrete details" (1942:5–6). Though this statement may sound like self-serving, disciplinary boasting, it is nonetheless true that Mead, Benedict, and other Boasian anthropologists had spent two or three decades learning to describe and analyze culture patterns. We may well question the presuppositions of holism and unity that anchor the culture theory of Mead and Benedict, but we can still admire their rhetorical strategy, which allowed them (as we saw in the case of Benedict) to "write up" whole cultures in coherent books and essays.

Second, *And Keep Your Powder Dry* continued a theme that ran throughout Mead's work, from *Coming of Age in Samoa* to her last writings. This theme may summarily be described as the relationship between culture change, intergenerational dynamics, and child-rearing practices. However much time Mead spent writing it, *And Keep Your Powder Dry* was not created in three weeks. Her earlier books had gained her a large audience precisely because she speculated in them on modern American culture in relationship to the "primitive" societies that she had studied in the field.

By 1942, Mead already had developed many of the ideas about American culture that she was able to write into a coherent account in a few weeks.

And Keep Your Powder Dry moves somewhat disconcertingly between an account of American national culture and character and a more detailed account of the child-rearing practices that produced them. In the book, Mead defends her attention to child-rearing practices by drawing an analogy, appropriate for wartime, between the production of children and the production of machines: "Just as one way of understanding a machine is to understand how it is made, so one way of understanding the typical character structure of a culture is to follow step by step the way in which it is built into the growing child" (38). Later (1954), Mead explained herself to critics who thought the child-rearing hypothesis overly simple: analyses of child-rearing practices did not constitute a historical account of how a culture developed nor a description of the culture's structure or central patterns; rather, such analyses showed how, given a particular culture, children were socialized to become part of that culture and to continue it. Such explanations notwithstanding, in *And Keep Your Powder Dry*, Mead blurs the distinction between an account of child-rearing practices and a description of national culture. Nonetheless, her analyses of American child-rearing practices and their relationship to national character were astute.

In her account of American culture, Mead focuses on (1) America as a moral culture, (2) perpetual movement, progress, and the lack of rigidly fixed, ascribed social places for individuals, and (3) the success ethic and conformity. Each of these topics is treated with explicit reference to American child-rearing practices and family structure, and Mead analyzes each with a constant eye to cross-cultural contrasts that make the American material unusual.

America as a Moral Culture

The relationship of twentieth-century American culture to the Puritan morality of the New England colonies had been an important topic for the progressive reformers of Mead's youth, as it had been to many before her who had written on American identity, culture, and character. Taking the relativist's stance, Mead pointed out how unusual the American conception of morality is:

> As America has a moral culture—that is, a culture which accepts right and wrong as important—any discussion of Americans must simply bristle with

words like *good* and *bad*. Any discussion of Samoans would bristle with terms for awkward and graceful, for ill bred and "becoming to those bred as chiefs." Any account of the Balinese would be filled with discussions of whether a given act would make people feel *paling*, the Balinese word for the state of not knowing where you are. . . . For none of these peoples think of life in as habitually moral terms as do Americans. (10–11)

As Benedict had done in *Patterns of Culture*, using a comparison of Pueblo Indians and modern Americans (1934a:127–29), Mead relativized a distinction that most Americans would not think to question: that between "good" and "bad." (Notice that the issue is not the conventional one of differing notions of "good" and "bad" but the very existence of the terms as important categories in the cultures in question.) Later in the book, Mead observes that long-term social failures (such as the depression) were punishing, particularly to people who saw earthly prosperity as a sign of God's grace. "Very few peoples have ever trafficked long with such an unmanageable moral code" (195). Thus, though American moralism had long been a topic for students of American culture, Mead casts that topic in a new light by treating it as a cross-culturally unusual, and perhaps unbearable, obsession.

Mead further explicates the relatively exotic, even bizarre, nature of American moralism by analyzing its relationship to family structure. Mead points out that in American nuclear families, parents, particularly mothers, are made to embody moral authority vis-à-vis children to a degree that is highly unusual:

[American] parents take the responsibility of punishing children, . . . thereby risking the children's hostility and hatred. This is a risk that the parents of very few societies have ever been willing to take; more usually they call in gods, or scare dancers, or relatives to punish their children, unwilling to take the moral responsibility of facing the child and saying, "I call this wrong . . . ." American parents are actually performing, every day, acts which would seem unthinkably brave to parents of other societies. (129)

Connected to this child-rearing pattern is a second one, "by which the parents assume the responsibility of representing themselves to their children as better than they really are." In other words, parents admonish children to uphold standards of behavior that the parents themselves do not follow. Americans typically judge this gap (between admonishment and action) as hypocritical, but Mead remarks, "This disparagement is made with no understanding of what a special invention this type of parenthood is, and of how much depends upon it." What depends upon it, according to Mead, is, first, the development of the child's conscience, which, far from being innate or universal to humans, can be produced "only [by] very special types of training" (127).

These child-rearing patterns have further consequences, for they contribute to adolescent rebellion and crisis, topics about which Mead had made herself a public authority since the publication of *Coming of Age in Samoa*. In *And Keep Your Powder Dry*, Mead connected parental authority and adolescent rebellion to other traits of American culture: when children learn that their parents are less than perfect, they are impelled to search elsewhere for standards of excellence, progress, or a better way of life. Thus American moralism, inculcated by a culturally unusual family dynamic, was connected, in Mead's analysis, to the perpetual movement of individuals in American culture.

Perpetual Movement, Progress, and the Lack of Ascribed Social Place

Like many observers of American culture, Mead draws a picture of American rootlessness, mobility, and perpetual motion by contrasting American with European systems of social class. Unlike feudal Europeans, unlike, even, their present-day descendants, Americans do not expect to remain in the towns of their birth or follow in the footsteps of their parents. Rather, they expect to move on ceaselessly, always searching for a better way of life and a higher standard of living.

Mead discusses these culture traits in terms of family dynamics. Here, she draws on a model that she used from her earliest writings to her last (Mead 1951, 1970), distinguishing three types of culture in terms of intergenerational dynamics and culture change: first, cultures in which respected elders pass on cultural wisdom and habits that are assumed to be unchanging; second, cultures that educate children to adapt to change but in customary ways; and third, cultures that face unpredictable changes that cannot be met in customary ways. Unlike the first and second types, in which adult wisdom is esteemed, in the third type of culture, adults must learn from children, as well as teach them. In other words, in modern American culture—the third type—parents become obsolete.

Mead discusses this obsolescence in pseudo-historical terms, linking it to the experience of first-, second-, and third-generation Americans. First-generation Americans had rejected the world of their parents and left Europe behind; second-generation Americans rejected their imperfectly Americanized European parents; and by the third generation, an American child is "expected to go further than his father went . . . expected to feel very little respect for the past." Correlatively, "the American parent expects his child to leave him . . . and parents see themselves not as giving their children final status and place . . . but merely as training them for a race which they will run alone" (1942:49,41). Mead wrote also of the father's "autumnal" attitude toward his children: "They are his for a brief and passing season, and in a very short while they will be operating gadgets which he does not understand and cockily talking a language to which he has no clue" (45). As this passage suggests, Mead's notion of ceaseless mobility in American culture refers as much to technological progress, seen in terms of the grand sweep of fifty thousand years of human history, as it does to intergenerational rebellion in a culture of immigrants (see Mead 1970:xv).

Success and Conformity

To be successful in American terms, Mead argues, children must surpass their parents. Lacking any sense of a fixed place in society, American individuals have been taught that the place they ultimately attain depends on their own efforts:

> Life depends, not upon birth and status . . . but upon effort, effort that will be rewarded in riches, in material goods which are the sign that the effort was made, that one has in the language of childhood been "good." The member of the middle class [in Mead's analysis, the American mainstream] . . . is taught from birth that upon his own effort will depend the valuation which is placed upon him. (55)

Thus to succeed is to be good, an equation that suggests the moralism that permeates American life. Mead further hints that the moralistic equation of success and good behavior unrealistically places "moral responsibility for success" upon individuals (75). As many observers before her (and since) have argued, this makes it difficult for impoverished citizens to imagine social reform, because they accept responsibility for their own relatively disadvantaged circumstances.

Continuing her analysis, Mead focuses on the links between family structure, moralism, success, and conformity. The American nuclear family, Mead suggests (continuing an argument initiated in her Samoan book [1928:208–13]), is unusually isolated from wider networks of kinfolk. This leads to an unhealthy intensification of the parent-child bond, which Mead cleverly explicates by commenting on American fears of adoption. From infancy, a child is taught

> that only his father and his mother are really relevant to his life. . . . Every picture a child sees, every skit over the radio, every song or popular phrase, reaffirms the importance of having a [nuclear] family, that one is not either safe or sound without one. Meanwhile . . . he encounters the phenomenon of adoption. Some children don't belong to their families at all—they are adopted. . . . The scene is set against which he can come to doubt and question his own place in his own family.

The result is Americans' exaggerated emphasis on normality, an emphasis that, Mead hints, a cross-cultural perspective would reveal to be as problematic as most Americans deem deviations from the normal family:

> From broken homes come our delinquents and our neurotics; from unbroken homes come the ordinary Americans, terribly impressed with the fragility and importance of those homes which made them into regular fellows, not children about whom other children whispered and whom teachers and neighbors commiserated. (84–86)

Overemphasis on the nuclear family combines with two other features of American family life that Mead had also stressed in earlier writings: individualistic marriage and constantly changing child-rearing methods. Because individuals often marry people from differing backgrounds and experiences, and because the methods by which their parents raised them will be considered outdated for their children, young parents know no traditional standards by which to judge the success of their new family life. In the absence of such standards, their only recourse is a continuous and anxious assessment of other young families:

> To compensate for this [uncertainty], she [the young wife] insists on conformity. Their house, their car, their clothes, their patterns of leisure time,

shall be as much like other people's as possible. . . . But inside the walls of that home, there is no one to tell her, or to tell her husband, whether their expectations are too high or too low, no one to quote from the experience of other generations, no yardstick, no barometer. (87–88)

Moreover, children too are "valued in comparative terms" (88). They soon learn that their parents' love is conditional upon their comparing well to their peers, and growing "normally" becomes an achievement: "To the anxiety with which small boys in many if not all cultures . . . view grown men and wonder if they will ever be as tall and strong, is added in America . . . the anxiety as to whether they will be successful in keeping their parents' love" (90). This conflation of love and success, combined with the absence of traditional standards, leads to "dependence upon externals for the validation of success" (95). And the primary source of external validation becomes the school, which measures children in terms of routinized grades and test scores that are based, Mead argues, on no absolute values. Thus American children become conformists, ready to measure their worth in terms of a "meaningless, quantitative scale, on which all human beings become comparable and so inevitably cheap" (113).

Despite Mead's strictures against American conformity, her purpose in *And Keep Your Powder Dry* is to point out national strengths, as well as weaknesses, in order to plan rationally for war. The war itself mobilized intellectuals like Mead in a defense, even celebration, of American values. Thus the final chapters of the book veer away from criticism of American culture to optimistic pronouncements about postwar reconstruction and the uses of social science for social engineering. In these chapters, Mead ignores Americans' conformity and stresses their need for participation in the democratic process—because, as she puts it, Americans are "a people who trust themselves more than their parents—and for parents read: leaders" (164–65). She also asserts that social science can be used, not merely to control and manipulate people but "to promote a degree of human freedom which will itself provide the ground within which more science and more freedom will grow" (183).

Finally, Mead sketches her vision of a world order based on tolerance for human differences. This vision, too, was a theme both she and Ruth Benedict had explored before in their discussions of deviance. Both anthropologists had argued that deviance and normality varied across cultures. From such variation, they concluded that traits considered deviant in a particular culture—such as homosexuality in the United States—elsewhere might be useful or socially adaptive. Thus a deviant in one culture might be a paragon of virtue, or at least a normal individual, in another. Both Mead and Benedict used these arguments to plead for socially engineered tolerance, envisioning a society that would make use of diverse human abilities without branding any as deviant (Mead 1928; 1935:279–322; Benedict 1934a:251–78).

At the end of *And Keep Your Powder Dry*, Mead imagines the American success ethic and moralism placed in the service of world reconstruction. In the new world order, cultural and individual differences will be respected; indeed, Mead envisions cultural variation as a storehouse of "precious inventions" from which social engineers can draw important lessons.[1] At the same time, she asserts that some human values are better than others:

> The democratic assumption is to say: all cultures are equal in that each is a complete whole, a social invention within which man has lived with man and has found life in some way good. There is no hierarchy of values by which one culture has the right to insist on all its own values and deny those of another. . . . But though all cultures have the dignity of wholes, some of them may be utterly incompatible with living on a world scale. (239–40)

Americans, she argues, must take the lead in creating a world in which "every social limitation of human beings in terms of heredity, whether it be of race, or sex, or class," would be proscribed (155). This "job," she suggests, is one that can provide Americans with the sense of mission and challenge that is necessary to their national character. "Building the World New," as she titles her penultimate chapter, would replace conquest of the frontier as America's destiny.

---

1. The desire of Mead and other Boasians to preserve and draw on the inventions of all cultures is part of a wider "cosmopolitan" attitude examined by David Hollinger. As Hollinger shows (1985:59), cosmopolitanism was one solution to the dialectic of national character and ethnic diversity that troubled American intellectuals in the first half of the twentieth century: "The ideal is decidedly counter to the eradication of cultural differences, but counter also to their preservation in parochial form. Rather, particular cultures . . . are viewed as repositories for insights and experiences that can be drawn upon in the interests of a more comprehensive outlook on the world."

Relativism, Criticism, and Science

There is a tension in Boasian cultural criticism between social engineering and social satire, between a view of human beings as rational and a view of them as rationalizing, between, ultimately, an optimistic vision and a pessimistic one. Yet none of the Boasians fits neatly into such a dichotomy. Consider Margaret Mead's work in this regard. As I have shown, *And Keep Your Powder Dry* speaks forthrightly for social engineering to create a world organized in terms of the liberal, democratic values that Mead espoused. Moreover, Mead does not attempt to relativize those values: democracy, freedom, and science in the service of both are values that she accepts as unquestionably appropriate for the modern world. Indeed, Mead was one of the first social scientists to assume the role of public moralist, a task that earlier had fallen mainly to clerics and literary essayists.

On the other hand, in the rhetorical strategy that Mead used to propagate the values that she espoused, anthropological relativism played a key role. To dislodge her audience's conventional certitudes about adolescence, deviance, family life, and other topics, Mead told them of "exotic" cultures where human beings felicitously did otherwise than was done in the United States. Moreover, though Mead played the role of public moralist and social engineer, she was aware that social engineering was but a step from the fascistic social control that Americans were fighting. In *And Keep Your Powder Dry*, therefore, she strives to distinguish the beneficial social science that she advocates from an antidemocratic and manipulative one. Without rigorously arguing the point, she suggests that social science could be made to differ from natural science and technical control because it can include itself in the scientific equation:

> It is possible . . . that with the development of social science, with the application of real scientific inquiry to the ways of man, with techniques for freeing ourselves from the limitations imposed by our own culture, with techniques for including and allowing for the psychology of the investigator himself, the world has entered a new era. . . . It is possible that this type of social science, which is not a mere lifeless aping of the mannerisms of the natural sciences but which shapes its hypotheses to its materials and includes the repercussions of a hypothesis inside its equations, can give us premises by which we can set men free. (181–82)

Thus Mead invokes a reflexive social science as antidote to the mechanical manipulation of human beings. Though she does not develop her argument, it draws on one version of the Boasian understanding of the limits of rationality: social science is human thought and, therefore, is part of the human world that it studies. Objectivity, then, is impossible. What is necessary is a social science that takes account of itself as part of the phenomenon under study. Mead does not elaborate her vision of how such a science might proceed, but she shows herself to be aware of the problem.

Though Hiroshima caused her to revise her attitudes toward government work, Mead remained an optimistic voice for rational social planning until the end of her life. She spoke out against perceived injustices—for example, against the Vietnam War—but her rhetorical stance was always that of the social engineer, never the social satirist (Lutkehaus 1995; Yans-McLaughlin 1986:212–14; Dillon 1980; Mead 1970:xviii). Moreover, she knew that there was a professional price to be paid for her public status. As her biographer noted, "Her cavalier attitude about this hazard [writing in popular magazines for a mass audience] would impose a lifelong strain on her relations with her academic colleagues" (Howard 1984:105).

Since Mead's death in 1978, American anthropologists have turned increasingly to the study of American culture (for references, see Marcus and Fischer 1986; Moffatt 1992). A glance at current issues of the discipline's professional journals reveals a significant number of articles devoted to the analysis of American culture; such would not have been the case in Mead's day. Most of this new anthropological writing on American culture, however, is social-scientific and analytic, and, although U.S. anthropologists now aspire to "cultural criticism," none has mastered the rhetoric of the public moralist as Mead did. Today the voices of anthropologists reach nonacademic audiences only occasionally and then most frequently through mass media that cast social scientists in the role of "experts." Ironically, perhaps the most striking example of anthropological expertise made public occurred when Derek Freeman (1983) attacked Mead's Samoan research in a highly publicized book. Then anthropologists were drafted by the national media to help the public digest a sensational attack on a public figure.[2]

2. For a review of the Mead-Freeman controversy and a discussion of Mead's public stature, see Rappaport (1986). It is possible that, after Mead, the most famous American anthropologist has been Clifford Geertz. But unlike Mead, his appeal has been mainly to academics in other disciplines and to the very elite "lay" readership of such publications as the *New York Review of Books*. We should consider also the influence of

Anthropologists who today are writing on American culture continue to draw both on Boasian relativism and on a Boasian commitment to science. Like their predecessors, they espouse, sometimes passionately, beliefs in human equality, tolerance, and openness to cultural diversity. Unlike the Boasian cultural critics of the first half of the twentieth century, the current generation of anthropologists has not invented a rhetorical stance that commands public attention. Though many anthropologists today write "experimentally" in an attempt to transcend older jargons and reach new audiences, it remains to be seen whether the discipline can escape the confines of the university and the limitations of its own narrow professionalism.

---

an ethnographer like Napoleon Chagnon, whose Holt, Rinehart and Winston monograph on the Yanomamö has been read by generations of American college students (Chagon 1968). His work, too, has recently become publicly notorious, as a result of the muckraking of Patrick Tierney (2000); on this controversy, see AAA (2002).

CHAPTER 7

Critics against Culture

Jules Henry, Richard Hoggart, and the Tragicomedy of Mass Society

Similarities

In 1957, Richard Hoggart (1918–), literary critic and senior lecturer in the extramural department (adult education) at the University College of Hull, published *The Uses of Literacy*. In 1963, Jules Henry (1904–1969), anthropologist and professor in the Department of Sociology and Anthropology at Washington University, Saint Louis, published *Culture against Man*. It is probable that neither author knew of the existence of the other; at least, I have found no reference in the work of either to the other. *The Uses of Literacy* and *Culture against Man* derived from different, though related, intellectual traditions, and their fates have been different. As far as I know, no one has thought to bring them together in a single reading, as I do here.

Both books may be described as critiques of mass society and can thus be placed among a spate of such books written in the Anglo-American world during the Cold War, and they also fall within a long tradition of such work. The fount of that tradition, as I construe it, is Tocqueville's *Democracy in America*. Tocqueville figures significantly in the second part of *The Uses of Literacy* (141, 157, 161, 172, 224). Henry quotes Tocqueville twice at length in *Culture against Man* (5, 101–2), but Henry goes out of his way to tell us that "my book was practically completed before I read Tocqueville's book" (5, n. 2). Although I do not know what motivated Henry's claim, it cannot be completely accurate, for in a 1951 paper Henry quotes Tocqueville at length on a point (parental authority in modern society) that will become central to his argument in *Culture against Man* (1951:98). The original title of *The Uses of Literacy* was *The Abuses of Literacy*.

Hoggart tells us in his autobiography that he changed "abuses" to "uses" as a concession to his publisher's fears of a libel suit (1990:143–44); be that as it may, the earlier title, with "abuses," resonates with Henry's title. Both titles counter the conventionally positive connotations of their key terms—"culture" and "literacy"—by presenting them as oppressive social forces: culture can turn against people, just as literacy can abuse them.

Both works are remarkably (creatively, delightfully) "intertextual," as we would say today. Both authors routinely allude to or quote from canonical literary texts. *A Midsummer Night's Dream* provides Henry with a key motif, and Hoggart frequently draws on W. H. Auden (about whom he wrote his first book [Hoggart 1951]), Thomas Hardy, D. H. Lawrence, and George Orwell. Violating to some degree the conventions of their respective disciplines, both Henry and Hoggart make extensive use of texts from popular culture. Tweaking anthropology, Henry states at the outset:

> I doubt that there is any country in the world more suitable for anthropological study as a whole than the United States, for . . . the United States Government Printing Office is an inexhaustible source of information on everything from how to repair a home freezer to analysis of the military budget. . . . Millions of pages of *The Congressional Record* provide a running ethnography on some of our most crucial concerns; and over and over again these millions of pages are condensed into brilliant reports by nameless anthropological geniuses employed by the Government. In addition to all this are our newspapers, . . . for not only do they carry a continuous report of our daily goings-on, but even their biases, their omissions, and their trivia provide deep insights into our culture. (4)

In "primitive culture," Henry concludes, the anthropologist must "work to ferret out information," but in modern society "the printing presses inundate him with it, and his greatest task is to sort it out" (4). Throughout *Culture against Man* Henry draws on material (especially advertisements and statistics) from the *New York Times*, *St. Louis Post-Dispatch*, *Fortune*, *Esquire*, *Life*, *Time*, *Women's Day*, *McCall's*, and various trade journals, juxtaposing such publications to the standard social-scientific literature.

Texts drawn from popular periodicals are central also to *The Uses of Literacy*, which Hoggart describes in his preface as a book "about changes in working-class culture during the last thirty or forty years, in particular as they are being encouraged by mass publications" (11). Hoggart surveys and draws upon a range of newspapers, magazines, and songs that were popular, he claims, among the English working classes. There is, however, a twist: Hoggart himself wrote many of his examples. His publisher had consulted a libel lawyer, who drew up a long list of "alarums." In a meeting, Hoggart was able to counter some of the barrister's objections and make minor changes to answer others. "The sticking-point," however, "was the use of quotations from sex-and-violence novels," about which "the barrister was immovable." After the meeting, with the fate of his book in the balance, Hoggart "decided to substitute for the libellous quotations my own sex-and-violence literature, and found that kind of pastiche surprisingly easy. . . . The barrister was satisfied and Chatto set publication in motion" (1990:144–45). Thus scattered throughout *The Uses of Literacy* are "fictitious" (199) articles in which Hoggart tries to convey "the manner of writing" (194) that he aims to analyze.

Another source of intertextuality in both books is their ethnographic dimension. Hoggart, the literary critic, is the more conventional ethnographic writer. The first half of *The Uses of Literacy* is a beautifully evocative, generalizing portrayal of working-class neighborhood life. Hoggart wrote it after he had attempted what became the second half of the book, his analysis of mass publications and their effects on working-class people. "The need to provide a context" for that analysis, he tells us, "led me . . . to describe the texture of working-class life as I knew it; and that then became the first half" (1990:141). His ethnographic chapters at times allow us to glimpse the author while eavesdropping and observing—in a children's clinic (27), in the marketplace (42), in a court of law (64). But—and here is another twist—Hoggart's ethnography is primarily autobiographical, based both on his childhood and on his work as an extramural lecturer teaching adult education courses (1990:96). Drawing both from observation and memory, Hoggart lards his text with what he considers to be characteristic phrases of working-class people. He does not quote at length from interviews with informants. Instead, working-class speech becomes part of his argument, as in the following: "Towards the parson their attitude is likely to be faintly cynical; he is in with the bosses. But it is usually a cheerful cynicism with no active hostility behind it. 'It's a good racket if you can get in on it,' they will say, 'good luck to 'em'" (94).[1]

1. As in many ethnographies, Hoggart includes an appendix, "Quoted Speech." "The problem," he explains, "was to come close to the sound of urban working-class speech without either puzzling a reader or giving a misleadingly quaint air" (283).

Henry, the professional anthropologist writing about his own culture, that of the United States, does not write autobiographically, nor does he provide a holistic sketch of a local way of life, as Hoggart does. Working out of the culture and personality approach as forged by his teachers and colleagues Ruth Benedict and Margaret Mead, Henry begins *Culture against Man* with an analysis of American values, then shows how those values are played out in a variety of institutional settings. In the first section, on the central values of the culture, he draws "native voices" largely from advertisements, trade publications, and popular magazines. In the rest of the book, on American families, teenagers, elementary and high schools, and old age homes, the interpolated voices are those, first of all, of "native informants," often youngsters who had written essay responses to questionnaires; second are the voices of Henry's various field assistants, "observers," he tells us, who were "students trained by me" (306, n. 2). The field texts of Henry's assistants introduce layers of intertextuality into *Culture against Man*: Henry often is reading over the shoulders, as it were, of his assistants, who are describing themselves engaged with their informants. At times it is not clear whether the observer (quoted at length in the text) is Henry or an assistant, but usually Henry is commenting on reports written by his assistants, who are themselves directly and indirectly quoting the informants.

Both texts are explicitly comparative, though in different ways. For Hoggart, working-class culture is a distinct way of life, and its distinctiveness can be made evident by imagining middle- or upper-class reactions to it or working-class reactions to middle- or upper-class culture:

> To live in the working-classes is even now to belong to an all-pervading culture, one in some ways as formal and stylised as any that is attributed to, say, the upper-classes. A working-class man would come to grief over the right way to move through a seven-course dinner: an upper middle-class man among working-class people would just as surely reveal his foreign background by the way he made conversation . . . , used his hands and feet, ordered drinks or tried to stand drinks. (31)

Hoggart at times points out how differently outsiders and insiders might view the same working-class scene: "To a visitor they are understandably depressing, these massed proletarian areas. . . . But to the insider, these are small worlds, each as homogeneous and well-defined as a village" (52). At other times he shows how social facts vary as they manifest themselves in different classes: the neighborhood grocer, for example, has a "relation to his customers [that] is different from that of the shop-keeper in middle-class areas. There he tends to assume . . . a lower status than his customers; he may earn more than many of them do but he acts as their servant. . . . Here the shop-keeper is among his own class . . . [and] has the tastes and habits" of his neighbors, though he might well be more prosperous than they are (54). Always, Hoggart is concerned about helping his reader—"a visitor from another class"—"realise imaginatively" the unique quality of working-class life (68). And always, Hoggart evidences a double consciousness, as one of those "scholarship boys" about whom he writes so tellingly (238), the talented working-class students "uprooted from their class . . . through the medium of the scholarship system" and who thus find themselves "at the friction-point of two cultures" (239).

Although Henry (who was born into an upper-middle-class family in New York City) pays some attention to class differences in American culture, his comparative approach is global and anthropological. His is a Boasian stance, developed to a high art in the work of Benedict and Mead. In this tradition, the anthropologist's vision is informed both by a general sense of the range of all (historical and geographical) cultural possibilities (Benedict 1934a:24) and by specific cultural alternatives or oppositions. As Mead once put it, "Every single statement that an anthropologist makes is a comparative statement" (1955:9). In *Culture against Man*, comparison takes both forms, the general and the particular. In the first, Henry speaks (in terms we would today abjure) of "primitive culture" and "simpler societies" in opposition to "the modern world" (8). In making particular cross-cultural comparisons, Henry usually draws on his South American fieldwork among the Kaingang (Henry 1941) and Pilaga (Henry and Henry 1944), as in the following discussion of the social regulation of "impulses":

> [In American culture] I may drink but my young children may not; I may have sexual intercourse but my young children may not; I may tell sexy jokes but my children may not; I may smoke but not my children, et cetera. I know of no culture where such a total division is attempted between impulse release patterns in children and impulse release in adults. Among my friends the Pilaga Indians of Argentina, children of all ages attempted or had intercourse with one another, played sexual games, listened to and told sexual stories, and smoked if the adults would let them have tobacco. . . . Thus, since the Pilaga have no impulse logic according to which children are excluded

from the impulse release patterns of adults, when children engage in them they . . . are not made to feel immoral. (236–37)

In either comparative mode (the general or the particular), the point is to bring to light the arbitrariness, the peculiarity, of our own, taken-for-granted values and routines; so highlighted, they are more amenable to analysis and critique.

The writing styles of the two books differ noticeably, but the critical inclinations of both authors find expression in a similarly cutting use of language. Henry is more prone to this than Hoggart. Throughout *Culture against Man*, Henry invents pseudo-technical terms to facilitate his analysis and, I think, to express his outrage. (One reviewer noted that Henry had "a genius for phrase-making that rivals Thorstein Veblen's" [B. Berger 1963].) For example, Henry presents advertising, as the title of chapter 3 has it, "as a philosophical system," and he labels its elements "pecuniary pseudo-truth," "hyperbolic transformation," "product therapy," and so on (47, 60, 62). He describes teenagers' desperate search for "popularity," for community, as "the endless American game of interpersonal pinball" (148). A middle-class mother's inconsistent struggle with her infant to enforce a feeding schedule is "the war around the mouth" (333), and advertisers fight "wars of pecuniary claims" (56). Henry also bends lengthier tropes, conventions of anthropological writing, to his ironic purposes, as in the following section on "pecuniary philosophy as cradle snatcher": "*Homo sapiens* trains his children for the roles they will fill as adults. This is as true of the Eskimo three-year-old who is encouraged to stick his little spear into a dead polar bear as it is of an American child of the same age who turns on TV to absorb commercials; the one will be a skilled hunter, the other a virtuoso consumer" (70).

As I noted earlier, Hoggart wrote examples of some of the popular genres he wanted to critique, though these were imitations, not parodies. His most scathing figures of speech come in the second half of *The Uses of Literacy*, as he attempts to demonstrate the ways in which mass culture infiltrates, makes use of, and in the end degrades working-class values. For example, arguing that mass culture transmutes working-class egalitarianism into a leveled-down conformity, he laments, "We are encouraging a sense, not of the dignity of each person but of a new aristocracy, the monstrous regiment of the most flat-faced" (151). Elsewhere, Hoggart calls this "the band-waggon mentality" and describes "the waggon," loaded with its

barbarians in wonderland, mov[ing] irresistibly forward" (160). And his
depiction of the masses narcotized by television is as devastating, and as
bleak, as anything Henry wrote: "Nightly, dead from the eyes downwards,
they would be able to link on to the Great Mother. They might spend
their days fixing a dozen screws on each of a hundred T.V. sets, but their
nights could be passed sitting in front of one" (Hoggart 1957:157). Most
generally, both *Culture against Man* and *The Uses of Literacy* are almost
wildly idiosyncratic with respect to the state of the art in the authors' respective disciplines. Although Henry was by no means the only anthropologist of his generation to study American culture, at midcentury, American
anthropology's favored object of study was still an exotic culture, whether
that of "primitives," "peasants," racialized minorities, colonized majori-
ties, or civilizations and "great traditions" other than the Western. Henry
had impeccable primitivist credentials, having worked the summer of 1931
among Mescalero Apache, under the direction of Benedict (Modell 1983:
179; Caffrey 1989:261); Henry then completed fourteen months (1932–34)
of fieldwork with the Kaingang of Brazil (Henry 1941:xxii), followed by
twelve months (1936–37) among the Pilaga of Argentina. During World
War II, he worked first for the Mexican government and then in various
U.S. government bureaus, and he went to Japan in 1945 with the U.S. Stra-
tegic Bombing Survey. Hired in 1947 as an associate professor at Washington University, he immediately began pursuing his anthropological and
psychoanalytical interests in U.S. settings, working in counseling centers,
hospitals, and schools.[2]

2. No one has written a biography of Henry, although the 1971 obituary by Gould
provides a sketch of Henry's life. Using the obituary and Henry's publications, I have
pieced together the following information on Henry's U.S. research to the time of the
publication of *Culture against Man*: mid-1930s, observations at a psychiatric hospital,
New York City; 1947–?, research at the Washington University Child Guidance Clinic;
1951, study of a maternity ward of a large hospital; September 1951–April 1952, study of
the psychiatric unit of a private general hospital; 1953–54, research at the Sonia Shankman
Orthogenic School, Chicago; 1953 onward, studies of public school classrooms, including
elementary and high schools and lower-, middle- and upper-middle-class white children and lower-class black children (Henry 1951:87; 1952:267; 1954a:176; 1954b:141–42;
1954c:139; 1954d:34; 1955:189; 1957a:118; 1957b:148; 1959:266; 1964:21; 1965:7; 1973).
   Of his "one year of intensive research . . . and . . . second year of constant and interested close contact" at Sonia Shankman, Henry said this: "The intensive research
includes roughly 700 hours of direct observation of interaction between children and
counselors, exhaustive records of staff conferences, several hundred informal chats with

His postwar research agenda was an unusually active one, but what it shows, more than the man's sheer energy, is that Henry was focusing on mainstream American culture at a time when few anthropologists would have done so. *Culture against Man* draws on all Henry's work in various American settings, but it is more than the sum of its parts: it is an attempt to analyze the whole culture, a task that had been accomplished by Mead (1942) and also by Geoffrey Gorer (1948). But this task was one that the Boasians, interested in the delineation of integrated cultural patterns, acknowledged to be difficult in "great Western civilizations," with their "competing professional groups and cults and classes and their standardization over the world" (Benedict 1934a:17). Few anthropologists before (or since) Henry have dared holistic monographs of American culture.

But most of all, *Culture against Man* is idiosyncratic because of its critical focus and tone. At a time when U.S. anthropologists were still enthralled by science, Henry wrote in the book's first paragraph, "*This is not an objective description of America*, but rather a passionate ethnography" (3; emphasis in original). It is an ethnography, he goes on, of "conditions I deplore," of "grim situations," and though, he tells us, he will at times offer solutions to problems (see Sapir 1927:558–59), that is not his main goal. Given "the complex interrelationships in culture . . . one may regret what one describes, [but] usually he cannot make practicable suggestions for change" (3). Moreover, Henry refused to hide behind his data: "I do not *use research as proof* in any rigorous sense; rather I write about the research from an interpretive, value-laden point of view. Since I have an attitude toward culture, *I discuss data as illustrative of a viewpoint and as a take-off for expressing a conviction*" (4; emphasis in original). Two contributors to *Reinventing Anthropology* (Hymes 1972a:63 n. 6; Nader 1972:286) praised Henry's passionate engagement, but it was that book, not *Culture against Man*, that became a landmark for the "reflexive," antipositivist anthropology of the 1970s and beyond. In 1963, the discipline was not yet ready to build on *Culture against Man*.

As for *The Uses of Literacy*: from the perspective of mid-1950s departments of English literature, it must have seemed an odd and perhaps irrelevant book. Hoggart reports in his autobiography that "social scientists . . .

_____

personnel, and a continuous anthropological record of daily life in the School. The study was done by the writer on the invitation of Dr. Bruno Bettelheim, Director of the School" (1957c:725).

were generous to the book" but that "people I knew in internal departments of English kept fairly quiet about it, as though a shabby cat from
the council house next door had brought an odd—even a smelly—object
into the house" (1990:142–43). The smelly object was, of course, lowbrow
or vulgar culture, seriously and respectfully examined by an accomplished
literary critic. The book's object of analysis would have been enough to
make it odd to traditional literary scholars, but, in addition, Hoggart more
or less invented his own genre. His mix of literary analysis, ethnographic
description, personal memoir, and political conviction all but guaranteed
that *The Uses of Literacy* would be seen by "internal" (that is, those not in
extramural, or adult education, as Hoggart was) faculty as "dangerously
indisciplined," as Andrew Goodwin celebrates it in his introduction to a
1992 reprint (Goodwin 1992:xiii). But Goodwin also notes that *The Uses of
Literacy* was anchored in alternative social and intellectual traditions—
adult education and working-class improvement efforts, on the one hand,
and English cultural criticism, from Matthew Arnold to F. R. and Q. D.
Leavis, on the other (Goodwin 1992:xvi). As Hoggart himself put it:

> Here is where the experience of Raymond Williams and E. P. Thompson
> particularly comes in, and my own. For all three of us, the largish books
> which first brought us to attention were begun during those early years in
> extra-mural education. . . . The experience of adult teaching . . . shaped and
> informed the very nature of the works . . . as they developed. Raymond
> Williams's *Culture and Society* would have been a different book if it had
> been written over years spent teaching internal undergraduates in a tradi-
> tional university setting. Similarly, Edward Thompson's *The Making of the
> English Working Class* is rooted in his direct experience of taking tutorials
> with working-class adults. (1990:96)

Hoggart also tells us that, during his early years of teaching, he used to
think of Matthew Arnold, "also trying to write creatively in similarly difficult circumstances." And *The Uses of Literacy* "pays tribute" to Q. D. Leavis's
Fiction and the Reading Public (1968) while aiming "to adjust something in
[her] approach" by taking seriously working-class responses to what she
would have considered "dismissible trash" (Hoggart 1990:79, 134–35).

The foregoing has been a catalogue of similarities, but I must note one
difference between *The Uses of Literacy* and *Culture against Man:* while Hoggart's book is honored as a foundational text in cultural studies (Nelson

et al. 1992:9, Steedman 1992:613), Henry's is unread and largely forgotten. Hoggart's book has been reprinted; Henry's can be found, if at all, in used bookstores.

Richard Hoggart: Working-Class Life, High Art, Mass Culture

"Resistance" and "persist" are words that appear frequently in *The Uses of Literacy*. For Hoggart, the resistance of urban working-class culture to the pressures exerted by mass cultural products, or its persistence despite such pressures, is a largely unconscious phenomenon. As I have shown, Hoggart treats urban working-class culture as a coherent whole, as an "integrated" pattern, as Benedict might have said. But it is a pattern that is threatened. Thus Hoggart is compelled at the outset to argue negatively, to reject the notion "that there are no working-classes in England now," that all "social differences" between them and the "lower middle- to middle-classes" have been flattened, that England is a "'classless' society" (15). Offering "a rough definition" of the group that he aims to discuss, he notes the distinct urban "districts" in which its members live and that working-class people tend to rent rather than own their houses, "work for a wage, not a salary," have limited education, and work as skilled or unskilled "labourers" (19–20). He is not unmindful that his ethnographic "generalizations" cannot be expected to apply to every member of the group—especially to those who are more self-conscious and thoughtful than usual, those he calls "the purposive, the political, the pious and the self-improving." He nonetheless sticks to his project of sketching the "less tangible," largely unconsciously held attitudes of working-class life (21–22; see also Steedman 1990:285–87).

Hoggart begins his sketch of the content of working-class culture where many ethnographers begin, with language, with "common speech," "oral and local tradition" (27). He then discusses home, mother, father, and neighborhood as elements—as lived collective representations, we might say—at "the core of working-class attitudes" (32). There follow three chapters on routines, values, and worldview: "them" versus "us," "self-respect," tolerance, ways of handling money, religious beliefs, morality, aesthetic preferences, modes of entertainment, and sociality. The organization of the first half of *The Uses of Literacy* doesn't quite match that of a standard anthropological ethnography (with its chapters on kinship, economy, religion, and so on), but Hoggart's sketch can be fitted easily enough into the genre.

Crucial to Hoggart's description and analysis is the assumption (standard in anthropological theory) that the pattern of working-class culture is alive—adaptive, resistant, persistent—precisely because its "bearers," the "natives," hold to it unconsciously. The "old forms of speech" (those un-affected by the new mass culture) persist, he tells us, "in a formal manner"— "the phrases are used like counters, 'click-click-click.'" Their "tone" might suggest that they are meaningless, that "they have no connection at all with the way life is lived." But that is not quite true. They are not yet dead metaphors: people "lean upon" their aphorisms as "trustworthy . . . refer-ence[s] in a world now difficult to understand" (28–29). They similarly cling to "superstition and myth" (especially notions of good and bad luck), not examining them intellectually, "not troubled by inconsistencies" (29–30). They live their culture, in short, the way anthropologists imagine most natives do: "They believe and do not believe. They go on repeating the old tags and practising their sanctions and permissions" (30).

Hoggart finds "the core of working-class attitudes" (indeed, of working-class culture, as a pattern) in "a sense of the personal, the concrete, the local . . . embodied in the idea[s] of . . . family and . . . neighbourhood" (32). His ethnographic chapters provide myriad details, lovingly marshaled, of family and neighborhood life and of working-class people's attachment to it. But the point is generalized beyond the truism that most people are attached to home and family; Hoggart is talking about a worldview, a way of think-ing: "Other people may live a life of 'getting and spending', or a 'literary life', or 'the life of the spirit', or even 'the balanced life', if there is such a thing. If we want to capture . . . the essence of working-class life in such a phrase, we must say that it is the 'dense and concrete life', a life whose main stress is on the intimate, the sensory, the detailed and the personal" (88).

Hoggart sees a coherent aesthetic in the working-class approach to life, and, more important, he sees working-class people unconsciously reproduc-ing it as they adapt the new products of consumer culture and mass society to their homes. After fourteen dense paragraphs describing working-class homes, Hoggart tells us, "I could continue almost endlessly recalling other individual details which give this kind of domestic life a recognisable qual-ity of its own. . . . Though it may seem muddled and sprawling, the design can be seen, ensured by an unsophisticated and unconscious but still strong sense of what a home is for" (36–37). The existence of the "design" is proven (à la Ruth Benedict) by a quickly sketched contrast to "the kind of public room which may be found in many a cafe or small hotel today." Such rooms, "all tawdry and gimcrack," abound in elements (the anthropologist's "mate-rial culture traits") that one might find in a working-class home—"cold and ugly plastic door-handles; fussy and meaningless wall lamp-holders." But these items are not integrated into a coherent aesthetic: "The materials need not produce this effect; but when they are used by people who have rejected what sense of a whole they had . . . , the collapse is evident. In homes, the new things are absorbed into the kind of whole instinctively reached after" (37–38). Hoggart makes a similar argument with regard to the transmission of the central roles of "mother" and "father." Teenage girls, for example, go through "a brief flowering period . . . during which they have no responsibilities and some spare money . . . enveloped in the chrysalis of an adolescent daydream" (45–46). They work, they date, they gossip, they go to the movies, but the period ends (as does a similar one for boys) with marriage—at which time they begin "to draw upon [their] older roots":

> Most pick up a rhythm which goes back beyond the dance-tunes and the cinema's lovers. Watch the way a girl who, in view of the extent to which her taste is assaulted by the flashy and trivial, should have an appalling sense of style can impose on even the individually ugly items she buys that sense of what it is important to re-create in a living-room. Watch the way she handles a baby; not the more obvious features, the carelessness of hygiene and the trivialities, but the acceptance of a child in the crook of the arm or in a bath by the fire. (46)

Notice here that "style" manifests itself both in material culture and in interpersonal relationships, and it is "picked up" (and "embodied," as we might say today) unconsciously.

After the working-class sense of the local, the personal, and the concrete, in Hoggart's sketch of central values, comes the sense of the group, of "'Them' and 'Us,'" as the third chapter is titled. Hoggart defines "them" and "us" in terms of social class: "'Them' is the world of the bosses, whether those bosses are private individuals or . . . public officials" (62). Towards "them," working-class people evince an attitude "not so much [of] fear as mistrust" (63). Such mistrust leads to a kind of group self-reliance and an avoidance of "them." It is also related to another major working-class value, "self-respect." Self-respect, according to Hoggart, flowers into "respectability," which includes skilled workers' pride in their skill and the family pride in a home characterized by "thrift and . . . cleanliness." For Hoggart, such attitudes derive not from a "servile" imitation of the middle classes nor from status "anxiety." They stem, rather, from a determination to maintain oneself upright in a difficult world, "from a concern not to drop down, not to succumb to the environment." Working-class people hate the thought of "'going on the parish'" (66–67).

The notion of "us" speaks to what Hoggart calls "the group-sense, that feeling of being not so much an individual with 'a way to make' as one of a group whose members are all roughly level and likely to remain so" (68). This group-sense "is not a very self-conscious sense of community." Rather, it derives directly from lived experience, from "the close, huddled, intimate conditions of life" and from the knowledge "that it is important to be friendly, co-operative, neighbourly," especially given that one's worldly circumstances are precarious (68–69). Those circumstances are also limiting, and that is another source of the group-sense: "The solidarity is helped by the lack of scope for the growth of ambition" (70). Working-class life will go on in the same pattern as it always has, and people will continue to rely on family and neighborhood. All this leads to "an extensive and sometimes harsh pressure to conform." But working-class conformity is not the same as that prevalent among the middle classes oriented to the newer forms of mass consumption: "There may be little of the competitive urge to keep up with the Joneses, but just as powerful can be the pressure to keep down with the Atkinses" (72).

Limiting and precarious circumstances lead also to working-class tolerance, to a philosophy of live-and-let-live. In a passage that recalls Tocqueville, Hoggart translates this "partly stoic, partly take-life-as-it comes" attitude into an acceptance of a cosmos that is believed to be beyond one's power to change:

> When people feel that they cannot do much about the main elements in their situation, feel it not . . . with despair or disappointment or resentment but simply as a fact of life, they adopt attitudes towards that situation which allow them to have a liveable life under its shadow. . . . Such attitudes, at their least-adorned a fatalism or plain accepting, are generally below the tragic level . . . but in some of their forms they have dignity. (77–78)

Hoggart argues that "the tolerance exists along with the conservatism and conformity already described." Indeed, life in the family, in the neighborhood, in the group, which presupposes reliance on people whose circumstances are similarly limited, makes tolerance and conformity "mutually reinforc[ing]" attitudes (79). He goes on to illustrate the confluence of conformity and tolerance in a discussion of working-class attitudes toward drinking. Drinking in moderation is tolerated and even expected for working-class men—"the man who does not drink at all is a bit unusual" (81). But excessive drinking can lead to financial and familial disaster—"a near-literal home-breaking as the furniture is sold"—and it was this reality, known to all in the neighborhood, which "gave such force to the anti-drink movement" (80). Hoggart tells us that he himself "signed the pledge twice . . . with the rest of my Sunday school acquaintances." Unlike Tocqueville's solitary teetotaler, however, Hoggart was motivated (as, presumably, are those about whom he is writing) not by the desire of the uprooted to conform but by the lived experience of those well rooted in the group: Hoggart "had a drunken uncle," he tells us (81), and in his autobiography we learn that this man triggered much conflict in the family (1988:16–26). In sum, conformity in this case stems from shared values and experiences, not from the alienation of the individual in mass society.

Indeed, the concept of the abstract individual in relation to an equally abstract society is alien to the working-class people whom Hoggart describes. They do not easily engage in the kind of generalizing that Tocqueville saw as characteristic of modern individuals. They understand and respond to familial duties but not to appeals based on state, society, or citizenship: "with their roots so strongly in the homely and personal . . . and with little training in more general thinking," they cannot relate the local to the global (66). And as "the centralisation of modern life" increases, so does their isolation: "Home is carved out under the shadow of the giant abstractions" (88).

This leads to Hoggart's literary-critical analysis of working-class attitudes toward art and belief. "Working-class people are only rarely interested in theories or movements. . . . They are enormously interested in people" (89). Hoggart claims that most of them no longer attend church but that they nonetheless take seriously Christianity "as a system of ethics" to be applied in daily life: "The emphasis is always on what it is right for them to do . . . as people; people who do not see the point of 'all this dogma', but who must constantly get along with others, in groups" (97). A similar down-to-earth attitude underpins their taste in reading and music. An "overriding interest in the close detail of the human condition," Hoggart tells us, "is the first pointer to an understanding of working-class art" (100). He validates that art—in the face of its dismissal by highbrow critics—because it upholds values (of family, neighborhood, marriage, and love) that Hoggart sees both as dignified in themselves and as central to

working-class life. Thus, despite the naive realism, the stock heros and vil-
lains, the sentimentality, and the use of cliché that characterize working-
class reading materials, "there is no virtue in merely laughing at them: we
need to appreciate . . . that they may in all their triteness speak for a solid
and relevant way of life." For Hoggart, that way of life is coherent, vital,
and unself-consciously reproduced: "The world these stories present is a
limited and simple one, based on a few accepted and long-held values. It
is often a childish and garish world, and the springs of the emotions work
in great gushings. But they do work; it is not a corrupt or a pretentious
world" (107).

The second part of *The Uses of Literacy*, entitled "Yielding Place to New,"
is a treatise on the corrupting influences of an emergent mass-cultural hegemony. Hoggart argues not simply that the mass media are overrunning local
cultures, and not simply that it is concentrated economic power that underpins the mass media's success. The heart of his argument, rather, is that
the mass media and mass cultural products are able to seduce working-class
people because they have appropriated working-class values and turned
them to their own ends: "The success of the more powerful contemporary
approaches is partly decided by the extent to which they can identify themselves with 'older' attitudes" (142). Thus the working-class emphasis on the
personal and the local, on the group and the neighborhood, on self-respect
and tolerance are transmuted in mass culture into "a soft mass-hedonism,"
"an arrogant and slick conformity," "a destroying self-flattery." Mass-cultural
products are, in the end, "invitations to self-indulgence" (142).

Tolerance, for example, is absorbed into "the concept of an almost unlimited inner freedom," the slogan for which is not the older "live and let
live" but (taking a cue from Cole Porter?) "anything goes" (146–47). As
Hoggart views it, "freedom" in mass culture does not buttress chosen or
accepted values but destroys them; freedom becomes an end in itself: "It
is always freedom from, never freedom for; freedom as a good in itself,
not merely as the ground for the effort to live by other standards." It is,
he tells us, "in the interest of the organs of mass entertainment that this attitude should be maintained." Freedom and the erosion of values allow the
mass media, and producers of consumer goods in general, to commoditize
anything; there are no standards, whether moral or aesthetic, to oppose
their marketing campaigns. Modern consumers have the right to choose
or not to choose, but they are discouraged from evaluating their choices in
any terms but those of personal preference. And they are discouraged even

more strongly from condemning the choices of others: "Tolerance becomes not so much a charitable allowance for human frailty and the difficulties of ordinary lives, as a weakness, a ceaseless leaking-away of the will-to-decide on matters outside the immediate touchable orbit. . . . charity as a refusal to admit that anyone can be judged for anything. . . . In this condition people will accept almost anything without objecting" (147–48). Those who dare to object, who use their "freedom to choose so as to be unlike the majority," will be branded bigoted, dogmatic, intolerant, even undemocratic (147).

Similarly, the older group-sense, with its emphasis on self-respect and equality (both within the group and in relation to other social groups), is being transmuted into a kind of conformity that Hoggart calls "a callow democratic egalitarianism" (149). Here Hoggart is close to Tocqueville's fear of the power of the majority in democratic societies:

> From then on [since the turn of the twentieth century] has developed . . . the well-known cant of 'the common man'; a grotesque and dangerous flattery, since he is conceived as the most common or commonplace man. 'Rely on the people'; all are equal, all have a vote . . . therefore in all things, says the publicist, your attitudes are as good as anyone else's: but since you share the opinions of the great majority, you are more right than the odd outsiders. The popular papers . . . elevate the counting of heads into a substitute for judgment. (149)

Hoggart chiefly fears the "levelling-down" (153) that must follow, as he sees it, from the inability or unwillingness to make discriminations of value— "a cocksure refusal to recognise any sort of differentiation, whether of brains or of character" (150). Such an attitude debases both art and politics. Respect for the dignity of individual persons is transmuted into a refusal to tolerate anything but the least common denominator, "the lowest level of response" (153). When, in the name of "freedom," people abdicate the responsibility to make informed choices, society becomes "more and more unfree" (155).

Related to the tyranny of the majority is the transmutation of the working-class penchant for the concrete and personal into "personalisation," which Hoggart defines as "extending the personal note beyond its reasonable limits" (164). The anonymous agents of mass culture—whether radio announcers, newspaper writers, or salespeople—can reach working-class consumers by addressing them in personalizing terms. Personalized appeals to unknown customers—inviting readers, listeners, or customers to "join their 'gang'"—enable the mass marketers to create "a fake intimacy . . . a phoney sense of belonging" (164). Hoggart illustrates this in his analysis of commercial music. In the first part of *The Uses of Literacy*, he describes "club-singing" (public singing in working-men's clubs) as expressive of feelings and experiences that are at once personal and shared; in the second part, he argues that those styles, rooted in working-class culture, are being appropriated and corrupted by "the claustrophobically personal manner" of the new popular music:

> In the older manner the singing was both personal and public or communal. The personal emotions were wholeheartedly accepted and also felt to be common to all. In the later manners there is a huge, public effect and the use of echo-chambers makes this more impressive than the effect which can be gained in a large variety-hall; and there is an enforced intimacy like a close-up on an immense screen. The singer is reaching millions but pretends that he is reaching only 'you', and this is a deterioration from the communally-felt personal emotion of the . . . [older] manner. The would-be personal is many times larger than life and has lost its sanction in the group. (188)

Hoggart also decries what he sees as the increasing "fragmentation" and "bittiness" of the public offerings of mass culture. Today we might also use the word "commodification" in reference to the same processes. Consumer culture chops up all reality into small, easily packaged and marketed bits. Consumers are not expected to exercise their faculties in order to consume such offerings: "The reader must feel intimately one with the dream that is being presented to him, and he will not feel this if he has to make an effort to think about the weight of a word, or puzzle over a nuance, or follow even a moderately involved sentence-structure" (166).

Here we are close to a traditional ("traditional," even at the time *The Uses of Literacy* was written) critique of popular or mass culture, one that deems it shallow and lazy in comparison to higher forms of culture as represented, say, in "great literature." Indeed, despite Hoggart's admiration for working-class culture, the center of gravity of his evaluative stance is to be found in a distinctly high-cultural literary modernism. A telltale sign of this perspective is his deployment of the contrast between what is imagined to be "hard" and what "soft" (or analogous pairs like strong/weak and solid/thin). The corruption of working-class culture by mass culture is depicted as a "softening-up" (198). The "oral tradition," for example, is said still to be connected to "a more muscular tradition of speech" (28), but it is weakening. The new popular newspapers show "a considerable decline from the sinewy sensationalism of Elizabethan vernacular writers" (276). The new popular songs are "soft-in-the-middle" (188), and the self that they depict is that of "a hollow little man clinging to a mask" (187). In general, "the newer mass art" constitutes "a candy-floss world," to use phrases from the title of chapter 7 (171). In part 1, in a literal conflation of reading matter and food, Hoggart described the characteristic Sunday smell of working-class homes: "the *News of the World*-mingled-with-roast-beef" (37). In contrast, mass art provides "only the constant trickle of tinned-milk-and-water which staves off the pangs of a positive hunger and denies the satisfactions of a solidly-filling meal" (195).

From the modernist perspective that Hoggart endorses, true art conveys the felt intensity of experience by making the medium transcend itself, by using it to say something that has never before been said and, in the process, rendering the depicted object accessible (for the first time) to a reader who is willing to work to attain it. The creative writer, says Hoggart, tries "to mould words into a shape which will bear the peculiar quality of his experience" (174). He uses Faulkner's *Sanctuary* as an example (one about which he is ambivalent; as Goodwin notes [1992:xxiii], *The Uses of Literacy* is marked by "a strong current of anti-Americanism"). Published in 1931, *Sanctuary* is, according to Hoggart, "an early pot-boiler," one that may well have served as a model for a "new style" of "gangster-fiction novel," a lowbrow genre that he finds "dead," "trite," thin, and banal. Yet one can see in *Sanctuary* "the marks of a serious and disinterested creative writer," one whose "language stretches and strains to meet the demands of the emotional situation," one whose "words and images become alive as they explore its nature . . . [and] suggest its complexity" (203–6).

Popular art does not do this. Even the popular working-class genres that Hoggart praises succeed, according to him, because they reproduce features of a collective culture that people can "identify with," as we might say today:

Presumably most writers of fantasy for people of any class share the fantasy worlds of their readers. They become the writers rather than the readers because they can body those fantasies into stories and characters, and because they have a fluency in language. Not the attitude to language of the creative writer . . . but . . . a 'gift of the gab', and a facility with thousands of stock phrases which will set the figures moving on the highly conventionalised stage of their readers' imaginations. They put into words and intensify the day-dreams of their readers, often with considerable technical skill. Their relation to their readers . . . is more direct than that of the creative writer. They do not create an object-in-itself; they act as picture-makers for what is behind the readers' daydreams but what cannot have a local habitation and a name because of imaginative inability. (174)

The same analysis appears in Hoggart's admiring portrait of the pianist in working-men's clubs: "He must know the exact idiom in which to play. This involves not only knowing the established songs and how to play them, but which of the new songs are catching on and, more important, how to play them so that, though their main lines are kept, they are trans-muted into the received idiom" (128).

Above all, then, working-class or popular art is a "received idiom." As I have shown, Hoggart stresses the unconscious reproduction of the pattern of working-class culture; indeed, he suggests that it is that unconsciousness that guarantees both its authenticity and its survival. This is close to a tra-ditional anthropological attitude toward what is imagined to be traditional or folk cultures: these are worlds where individuals reproduce their culture without ever developing much critical awareness of it. In the extreme form of the model, individuals as such do not yet exist. Artists, for example, are depicted not as imaginative individuals but as passive agents of the tradi-tion; it is the tradition that is treated (in, for example, a museum exhibit) as an individuated artist, to be compared to other traditions in a region or on an evolutionary scale. The artist as hero, or as alienated critic, or as rev-olutionary, is seen to emerge only at a "higher" stage of social develop-ment—usually, of course, in the modern West (see also Errington 1998).

Hoggart reserves a special chapter for "the uprooted and the anxious," working-class people who have somehow gotten beyond their milieu, typified, above all, in the figure of "the scholarship boy" (238). Hoggart has a decided notion of what constitutes, as Durkheim might have said, social health: the crucial issue, for Hoggart, is "the importance of roots, of unconscious roots, to all of us as individuals" (258–59). In his initial discussion of the central collective representations of mother, father, and home, Hoggart noted, "Working-class men and women have a host of jokes about marriage, but not against marriage. They are not harassed by the ambivalences of some more self-conscious people. . . . Working-class people still accept marriage as normal and 'right'" (51). When working-class people move out of their milieu, they become, in his depiction, not enterprising cultural mediators or brokers between two worlds (as "cultural middlemen" are sometimes depicted in anthropological literature) but "transplanted stock," fragile, ill at ease, and, in extreme cases, "psychotic" (239–40). "Under the stimulus of a stronger critical intelligence" (239) than that of their class compatriots, they have achieved enough education, enough culture, to make them dissatisfied with their natal milieu, but they have not achieved cultural mastery of the new one. They can wield the terms of a higher culture but only imitatively; they deploy that culture to climb socially or to buttress their insecurities, but they cannot "carry it easily," that is, unself-consciously and creatively (248). Just as he read working-class culture from the details of home furnishing, Hoggart reads—in high-modernist terms—the cultural dis-ease of these people from their interior decorating:

> The homes of some of those who achieve even an apparent poise tell as much as anything else. They have usually lost the cluttered homeliness of their origins; they are not going to be chintzy. The result is often an eye-on-the-teacher style of furnishing like their favourite styles in literature. . . . Each room echoes a thousand others among those who sought cultural graduation at the same time, and so most of them have an anonymous public air. . . . There is little healthy untidiness, natural idiosyncrasy, straight choice of what is personally liked. . . . 'Never a good or a real thing said' by the room, because the room is not yet a part of the actuality of life. (254)

"The actuality of life" can be found, then, in traditional working-class culture but not, apparently, in the ascendant mass culture. The latter proposition brings us to Jules Henry.

Jules Henry: Pseudo-Self and Society

Whereas *The Uses of Literacy* is grounded both in literary modernism and in Hoggart's experience as a participant-observer in English working-class culture, *Culture against Man* is grounded both in the general tradition of Boasian anthropology and in a specific development within it, the interest in culture and personality that engaged Henry's teachers and colleagues. Henry's doctoral dissertation, written under Boas and Benedict, was a grammatical analysis of Kaingang texts—that is, a piece of Boasian anthropological linguistics that Henry clearly saw as a fieldwork tool (Henry 1935: 172). But by the time of his second stint of field research, among the Pilaga, he was fully involved in the culture and personality movement, with its direct links to the New York Psychoanalytic Institute and Freudian theory (Manson 1986). According to Harold Gould, Henry "attended [Abram] Kardiner's seminars and Karen Horney's lectures, . . . became interested in David Levy's ideas concerning the universality of sibling rivalry, and developed an interest in the cross-cultural uses of the Rorschach Test" (Gould 1971:790). Jules and Zunia Henry were among the first to carry out systematic "projective" testing in anthropological field-work, specifically, to use ethnographic observations as a check on "the use of a . . . technique developed in our own culture" (Henry and Henry 1944:1). There is direct continuity between the Pilaga work, with its con-cern for the psycho-dynamics of family relationships, and Henry's later research in the United States; as Gould put it, "What is perhaps most sig-nificant in the professional development of Jules Henry . . . is the commit-ment he made to the conjoining of depth psychology with ethnography" (1971:790). To this I should add that in Henry's work, psychoanalytic con-cerns were always informed by Boasian culture theory.

In *Culture against Man*, Henry sometimes speaks of "the American character" (6), but his central focus is not "national character" but the configuration of "American culture" and its effects on "the self." Although he makes passing reference to culture change, his book is primarily a syn-chronic analysis of American culture in the 1950s; it is not an after-and-before comparison, as is *The Uses of Literacy*. Henry nonetheless posits, as I will show, a model of traditional American and Judeo-Christian culture as a point of comparison at crucial moments of his analysis.

Henry's model of culture is, in many ways, a grimmer version of that of his teacher, Benedict. Benedict had noted in passing in *Patterns of Culture* that a culture "manifests the defects of its virtues" (1934a:246), and she was a harsh critic of certain aspects of American culture. But she was also capa-ble of seeing great beauty in a cultural pattern, as expressed, for example, in her lyrical conclusion to the chapter on the pueblos (1934a:128–29). Henry carried out intensive research in three cultures, and, in his depictions, all seem equally grim. Readers of *Culture against Man* might infer from his occasional references to the Pilaga that Henry is a romantic who unam-bivalently esteems "primitive" culture, but a quick reading of the Pilaga ethnography will dispel such an inference. Though by their own report the Henrys had good relations with the villagers among whom they lived (1944:3–5), they describe the basic mechanisms of Pilaga social life as almost dysfunctional: "Although people distribute most of the food they obtain by their own work to other members of the household, the primary sanction for giving is not praise or expectation of return, but fear—fear of being called stingy, fear of being left alone, fear of sorcery." This leads to a "cycle of feeling" that "produce[s] great tension and hostility": "Reluctance to share is accompanied by reluctance to beg. Reluctance to beg leads to exclusion from sharing, and produces resentment and, in turn, leads to reluctance to share." The result, according to the Henrys, is that "Pilaga customs of food distribution strengthen hostility to a degree rare among primitive societies" (1944:9). And the picture becomes even bleaker as the Henrys outline the "cultural position" of women ("in so many ways inferior to that of the men") and, especially, children who, once weaned, find themselves "without status and deprived of warmth, . . . poor hostile little flounderer[s]" (1944:10, 17).

In *Culture against Man,* Henry begins with the Benedictine notion that "every culture has its own imaginative quality and each historic period, like each culture, is dominated by certain images." He veers immediately, however, to the dark side of the force: "And every culture and every period . . . has its phantasms, is ruled by its Great Nightmares. The nightmares of the ancient Hebrews were the Philistines and their own God," just as his contemporary Americans cowered before "the encompassing Fear Incarnate, Russia" (8). Henry's broadest generalizations about culture maintain this emphasis on the negative: "Human culture," he tells us, tends "to provide remedies for the conflict and suffering it creates," and "Man *wrings* from culture what emotional satisfactions he obtains from it." This reverses Benedict's dictum about virtues and vices; in Henry's view, the vices seem to come first. Indeed, he discusses the issue in evolutionary terms: "It is the misery man himself creates that urges him up the evolutionary tree." Hence the title of the book—man uses culture against himself "while he works on his ultimate problem—learning to live with himself" (10–11, emphasis in original).[3]

3. Despite his use of words like "primitive," I would not describe Henry as a cultural evolutionist. Nonetheless, the willingness to think about contemporary human cultures in relationship to human evolution in general distinguishes anthropologists of many stripes from their colleagues in other disciplines, like English literature and cultural studies, who are also concerned with culture and cultural criticism. Henry's

Henry's invocation of evolutionary terms seems less grounded in older anthropologies than in a particular conception of, and concern for, the self. For Henry, societal arrangements speak to biological and social needs but not to the needs of the self: "The very efficiency of human beings in ordering relationships for the satisfaction of these external needs has resulted in the slighting of . . . the satisfaction of complex psychic needs; everywhere man has . . . had to force from an otherwise efficient society the gratification of many of his inner needs." The result is that society is "a grim place to live . . . a place where, though man has survived physically he has died emotionally" (12).

This pessimistic theory of culture accords with a distinction that Henry posits at the outset between "values" and "drives" in American culture:

> Values are different from what I call drives, and it is only a semantic characteristic of our language that keeps the two sets of feelings together. To call both competitiveness and gentleness "values" is as confusing as to call them both "drives." Drives are what urge us blindly into getting bigger, into going further into outer space and into destructive competition; values are the sentiments that work in the opposite direction. Drives belong to the occupational world; values to the world of the family and friendly intimacy. (14)

The form of this argument goes back to Boas's essay on alternating sounds (Boas 1889), which showed that a range of phenomena that one language classified under one rubric might be classified under more than one by another language (Stocking 1974a:1–4). A more proximate example is *The Chrysanthemum and the Sword*, in which Benedict repeatedly argues that English terms collapse value distinctions that Japanese culture makes explicit, and vice versa (Benedict 1946:99, 105, 127, 133, 146). In any case, Henry takes the trouble to separate "drives" and "values" so that he can distinguish between aspects of American culture he deems life affirming and those he considers destructive. It is, we might say, *his* values that are at issue.

---

occasional recourse to evolutionary tropes is encompassed, in my opinion, by his Boasian relativism. As in Benedict's work, his generalizations about culture and evolution are exemplified by widely distanced cultures, and it seems clear both that he treats all the cultures he mentions as equally contemporary and that he never relies on race to explain cultural differences.

The basic drives of American culture are, in Henry's view, those for achievement, competition, profit, and mobility, on the one hand, and those for "security and a higher standard of living," on the other (13). The first group of drives animates the elites, "the cultural maximizers," while the masses are persuaded to settle for those of the second group. But both elites and masses are, as Henry depicts them, victims of "a driven culture" (13), one that makes insatiable demands on individuals who become, as a result, insatiable and driven, restless and insecure. Those "urges" that Henry calls "values"—"such as gentleness, kindliness, and generosity"—are not esteemed in American culture (13); they are relegated to the private, familial domain, but even families, in Henry's vision, are grim places to live.

Henry's catalogue of drives, and his argument about the dominance of drives over values, are well integrated, in his model, with two central features of the cultural system and the social life that it organizes. The first feature is what he terms "the absence of production-needs complementarity and . . . [of] a property ceiling" (10). This is a "fateful" difference between the primitive world, with its "assumption of a fixed bundle of wants," and the modern, with its "assumption of infinite wants." "In primitive culture . . . one does not produce what is not needed. . . . There is thus a traditional and . . . stable relationship not only between production and material needs, but also between production and psychological ones: the craftsman does not try to invent new products . . . nor to convince his customers that they require more or better than they are accustomed to" (8–9). Modern America, in contrast, is marked by a perpetual "imbalance among products, machines, wants, consumers, workers, and resources" (17). This is a central feature of the culture; indeed, as Henry puts it, "were the main factors in the economy ever to come into balance, the culture would fall apart" (18).[4]

The second feature is the demise of traditional, stable social relationships in the face of the unprecedented social and personal mobility that industrial society requires. Once again, Henry highlights the American material by contrasting it with primitive societies, as well as with "the great cultures of Asia." In these, "a person is born into a personal community, a group of

4. The argument about traditional craft workers recalls Tocqueville's chapter "In What Spirit the Americans Cultivate the Arts." The anthropological argument about the relationship between production and need, culturally defined, is later elaborated in Sahlins's well-known essay "The Original Affluent Society" (1972:1–39). Sahlins favorably reviewed *Culture against Man* in *Scientific American* (Sahlins 1964).

intimates to which he is linked for life by tradition; but in America everyone must create his own personal community." The American child, Henry argues, "must be a social engineer" in order to construct and maintain a community of friends. But since children and families are always scattering to the four winds as parents "move from job to job, up and down the social ladder," personal communities are fleeting (147–48). As in the realm of the economy, where incessant change is the rule, in the domestic domain Americans are expected continually to make new friends and lose old ones. The debilitating effects on the self of this structuring of both public and private life is Henry's ultimate concern.

The economy drives, deprives, and ultimately uses up the self in a number of ways. The two "commandments" of the modern American economy are, according to Henry, "create more desire" and "thou shalt consume." In its ceaseless drive to expand, industry (abetted by its accomplice, advertising) opens "the modern Pandora's box," "the storehouse of infinite need," creating products never before imagined that consumers have to be taught to desire: "There is probably nothing to which industrialists are more sensitive in America than consumer desires. . . . The slightest sign of a decline in consumer demand makes the business world anxious, but this very petulance in the consumer stimulates the manufacturer to throw new products on the market" (19–20). Both elites, the cultural maximizers, and masses, the ordinary workers, must be trained to "heroic feats of consumption" (44); the elites are additionally trained to consume themselves, that is, to be "hard-driving," constantly growing, achieving, and surmounting challenges.

Here it is necessary to speak of Henry's notion of the self. It is as central to *Culture against Man* as the modern artist is to *The Uses of Literacy*, although Henry's concept is even less well defined than Hoggart's. Henry's model of the self is the tripartite Freudian one of id, superego, and ego (44). But mostly, Henry defines the self negatively in *Culture against Man*; that is, he posits and presupposes a healthy self, but the discussion concerns the ways in which American culture denies health to the self. The description of "the job and the self" in reference to ordinary workers is crucial in this regard:

> Most people do the job they have to do regardless of what they want to do; technological drivenness has inexorable requirements, and the average man or woman either meets them or does not work. With a backward glance at the job-dreams of his pre–"labor force" days the young worker enters the

occupational system not where he would, but where he can; and his job-dream, so often an expression of his dearest self, is pushed down with all his other unmet needs to churn among them for the rest of his life. The worker's giving up an essential part of himself to take a job, to survive, and to enjoy himself as he may is the new renunciation, the new austerity: it is the technological weed that grows where the Vedic flower bloomed. What makes the renunciation particularly poignant is that it comes after an education that emphasizes exploitation of all the resources of the individual, and which has declared that the promise of democracy is freedom of choice. (25)

Although Henry's chapters on teenagers include discussions of youthful dreams for self-realization, and although Henry lists "love, kindness, quietness, contentment, fun, frankness, honesty, decency, relaxation, simplicity" (14) as values that nourish the self, he does not articulate a model in *Culture against Man* of what the "dearest self," the "essential" self, is. Rather, as in this passage, we see the self deprived and destroyed.

The renunciation of self that the economy requires of workers dovetails with the commandments to desire and to consume: "The average American has learned to put in place of his inner self a high and rising standard of living, because technological drivenness can survive as a cultural configuration only if the drive toward a higher standard of living becomes internalized; only if it becomes a moral law, a kind of conscience. The operator, truck driver, salesclerk, or bookkeeper may never expect to rise much in 'the firm,' but he can direct his achievement drive into a house of his own, a car, and new furniture" (25). Thus the masses retreat into a passive consumerism that is lodged in the private world of home, family, and fun. Workers lack "involvement" in their work (a condition, Henry argues, that industry bemoans yet requires, since it must be able to hire and fire employees at the drop of a hat, to keep up with the ever-changing market). At the same time, workers pursue fun and family with a "grim resolve." "Fun," Henry tells us, "is an underground escape from the spiritual Andersonville in which technological drivenness has imprisoned us. In fun the American saves part of his Self from the system that consumes him" (43). Yet the pursuit of fun is in itself exhausting, and "Europeans think we work too hard at having fun" (44).

Like fun, family in American culture is positively imagined yet in actuality often joyless. "It is in his family life," Henry writes, "that the American tries to make up for the anxieties and personality deprivations suffered in the outer world. . . . It is only when he has a family that a man can fully come into his pseudo-self, the high-rising standard of living, for on whom but his family does a man shower the house, car, clothes, refrigerator, TV, etc., which are [its] material components?" Moreover, the values that are not "maximized"—indeed are all but ignored—in the public realm "must be sought in the family." As a consequence, "it must serve therapeutic and personality-stabilizing needs which . . . are overwhelming" (128). Given this analysis, it is no surprise that Henry's depiction of family life is bleak. In the "normal" families that populate chapters 5 through 8 (on "Parents and Children," "The Teens," "Rome High School and Its Students," and "Golden Rule Days: American Schoolrooms"), we watch "the child tug at each parent as his impulses hammer at him, and his parents yield or resist as they are swayed by their own impulses toward their children" (134). In chapter 9, "Pathways to Madness: Families of Psychotic Children" (elaborated into a massive book, published posthumously [Henry 1971]), the vision becomes nightmarish. Based on "500 hours of direct observation in the homes of families that had a psychotic child" (1963:323)—homes where, for example, a mother calls her child "'a human garbage pail' and keeps the garbage bag and other refuse in his high chair when he is not in it" (327)— the chapter shows how the pathologies of the culture can be transmitted through parents to children, with devastating results.

Friendship, like family, is another casualty of modern culture. The social engineering that children must do to maintain a personal community leads directly, in Henry's analysis, to the conformity of mass society. Among American teenagers, "conformity and the wish to be popular" are "insurance against uncertainty in interpersonal relations": "When the personal community is unstable and must be constantly worked on and propped up, individual idiosyncrasies become dangerous and must be ruled out" (148). Americans, in effect, must market themselves to one another, and the standards they use to evaluate themselves and others become external to the self (see also Mead 1942:95), deriving ultimately from something like Tocqueville's (and Hoggart's) public opinion.

Henry's chapter on elementary school classrooms is replete with ethnographic examples of routines that teach children to conform. As in his work on families with psychotic children, here Henry is acutely aware of Batesonian double binds: "The first lesson a child has to learn when he comes to school is that lessons are not what they seem. He must then forget this and act as if they were" (291). Lessons that are ostensibly about a particular subject matter are in fact training for the presentation of properly conforming selves (G. Bateson et al. 1956; Henry 1971:135). In an observed music period, for example, the humanistic enrichment that music should provide is secondary to the frenzied competition among the pupils for the teacher's approval. Another teacher triggers a similar competition merely by asking which of the boys would like to hang up the visiting ethnographer's coat. Immediately, a "forest" of "waving hands" appears:

> Although the teacher could have said, "Johnny, will you please hang up [the observer's] coat?" she chose rather to activate all the boys, and thus give *them* an opportunity to activate their Selves, in accordance with the alienated Selfhood objectives of the culture. The children were thus given an opportunity to exhibit a frantic willingness to perform an act of uninvolved solicitude for the visitor; in this way each was given also a chance to communicate to the teacher his eagerness to please her "in front of company." (293–94; emphasis in original)

In Henry's analysis, education everywhere inculcates the "central preoccupations" of cultures; in American classrooms, which "deal with masses of children," one such preoccupation is the conformity that mass society demands. Thus American schools "reduc[e] . . . all [children] to a common definition" (321) and teach them to accept that definition of themselves.

I noted earlier that Henry sees the differences between "traditional" or "primitive" and modern societies to be "fateful" (9). Technological drivenness and the consumer economy, which have invaded even the domains of family and fun, are restructuring, according to Henry, the historically derived bases of American culture: "Together they lead the attack on the key bastion of the Indo-European, Islamic, and Hebrew traditions—the impulse control system—for the desire for a million things cannot be created without stimulating a craving for everything" (20). Or, in Freudian terms, Henry argues that "Super Ego values (the values of self-restraint)" are losing ground "to the values of the Id (the values of self-indulgence)." The result is "the loss of self" (presumably, Henry means here the loss of the true self, whatever that may be) and the creation of "a glittering modern pseudo-self, the high-rising standard of living, waxing like the moon in a *Midsummer Night's Dream* of impulse release and fun" (127).

Although Henry mourns "loss of self," he does not preach the necessity of a return to "traditional" values. As a Boasian, he knows that value systems are relative to particular times and places and that they change. Still, there are moments when he explicitly abandons relativism, notably in his chapter on advertising. In general, the chapter argues that advertisers will "monetize" anything—"space, time, the President, the Holy Bible and all the traditional values" (81)—in order to sell products (here the similarity to Hoggart's arguments is clear). But as Henry marshals his examples of monetization, he speaks not of new meanings for old concepts but of debased and untruthful ones, as if words and values have correct meanings that cannot be changed:

> Ancients of our culture sought clarity: Plato portrays Socrates tirelessly splitting hairs to extract essential truth from the ambiguities of language and thought. Two thousand years later we are reversing that, for now we pay intellectual talent a high price to amplify ambiguities, distort thought, and bury reality. All languages are deductive systems with a vast truth-telling potential imbedded in vocabulary, syntax, and morphology, yet no language is so perfect that men may not use it for the opposite purpose. One of the discoveries of the twentieth century is *the enormous variety of ways of compelling language to lie.* (91; emphasis in original)

Here there is a curious intertwining of Boasian relativism (specifically, the Sapir-Whorf hypothesis: "All languages are deductive systems") and moral absolutism. But as in Henry's discussions of the essential self, it is difficult to know what exactly he means by "truth." At any rate, when in the chapter on advertising he says that "the meanings of words, like the significance of values, have become soft and shapeless" (90), he returns us to Richard Hoggart.

Differences

Relativism is a problem for Richard Hoggart. As I have shown, his interpretation of conformity concerns, above all, the abandonment of standards of value. There is little discussion of the rootlessness of a mobile society, of anomie, of social routines that inculcate standardized selfhood—issues that inform Henry's notion of conformity and, even more so, Tocqueville's. For Hoggart, conformity is a function of mass marketing: if consumers can be trained to accept what everyone else accepts, to respect no standard but that of mass approval, then producers (especially those in the culture industries) can achieve economies of scale that will allow them to dominate the market. Moreover, when mass approval is the only standard of judg-ment, producers aim at the lowest common denominator; they have little interest in products that are difficult to digest (to use one of Hoggart's food metaphors), that can appeal only to a discriminating, and thus a small, audience.

Hoggart has held to this position remarkably consistently, as his collec-tion of essays, *The Tyranny of Relativism*, published almost four decades after *The Uses of Literacy*, shows. The old authorities, Hoggart argues, are in disrepute (some of them rightly so, he adds), and "the contemporary ground-level is relativism." "It is an amenable ground," he continues, for "technologically advanced" and "consumer-driven" societies that are "run by means of persuasion. . . . Such societies need relativism; it is the perfect soil for their endless and always changing urges" (1998:6). Hoggart recognizes what many conservative critics in the American culture wars overlook—that relativism is not simply a tool that the left, or the counterculture, uses against the establishment; it is used by the right as well (see also Gable and Handler 1996:575–76; Blake 1999:429–30; Sahlins 2003). Indeed, Hoggart's main targets are the Thatcherites, the mass media, the elites. In the con-sumer society, "those on the Right . . . can move happily," for they know that relativism and the abandonment of standards lead to a "leveling" that is, as he puts it, "bogus." The leveling and conformity that he decries do not infringe on the "privileges" of the rich. Instead, they render the masses incapable of "thoughtful" critique (1998:7)—as in the case of the introduc-tory anthropology students whom I discussed in the introduction, who too quickly conclude that relativism makes value judgments impossible.

Although Jules Henry was as harsh a critic of the consumer society as Richard Hoggart, and although Henry, like Hoggart, often comes across as a defender of traditional values, his notion of relativism, anchored in the Boasian epistemology of culture, is more complex than that of Hoggart. In a paper called "Anthropology in the General Social Science Course" (1949), published many years before *Culture against Man*, Henry set out a position that informs, it seems to me, the "passionate ethnography" of that book. Henry's key argument is that values cannot be judged abstractly, for they are formulated and applied always in culturally specific situations. It is in this sense that values are relative—that is, they "are related to the par-ticular form of social totality in which they have their being and to what people need and feel to be their needs at the time, in terms of the social situation as a whole." Anthropologists can teach students about other value

systems, to "drive home the lesson of the relation of value premises to cultural wholes." They can also teach students to examine values "in terms of
their consequences" for people's "physical and spiritual well-being." But to
do so "they will have to shift from the safe ground of cultural relativism to
the less secure one of judgment-making; for . . . when we examine values
in terms of consequences . . . we must take a stand" about our own definitions of "well-being." Anthropologists may appropriately "indorse a set of
values," but "we cannot blithely insist that other cultures adopt our value
system. There is this much good in the fact of cultural relativity: it makes
us understand that a way of life cannot be lightly interfered with and that,
in meeting people across the globe, we must meet them on a level of understanding that will eventually make sense to them and to us" (1949:308).
That Henry was willing to "indorse" (and condemn!) particular values in
his own society is clear from *Culture against Man*. But for him, relativism
is not the root problem but a form of anthropological wisdom that can
inform, without determining, value judgments.

For Hoggart, the opposite of relativism is "discrimination" in judgment,
and one of the main themes of *The Uses of Literacy* is that aesthetic discriminations vary across social classes. Indeed, Hoggart's work presupposes
class distinctions in ways that Henry ignores. Hoggart does not start with
a notion of unitary English or British culture; rather, he posits distinct class
cultures, on the one hand, and an increasingly hegemonic mass culture,
largely American in inspiration, on the other. For Hoggart, upward mobility is possible (the "scholarship boy") but it does not alter fundamental class
formations. Finally, the politics of culture that he espouses entails at once
recognizing the virtues of class-based cultural value systems that traditional elites have despised, and extending a kind of Arnoldian culture—
"the best which has been thought and said in the world," in Arnold's famous
phrase (1868:6)—to people of all classes.

Henry, in contrast, starts with the notion of a unitary American culture
(and his description of its contents more or less matches Hoggart's understanding of the contents of mass culture). Henry recognizes class distinctions, but his framework of analysis is based on the relationship of "culture"
and "personality," that is, of the individual and society. When, for example,
he discusses upward mobility, he does not dwell on the clash of class-based
cultural styles and the consequent dis-ease of the social climber, as Hoggart does, but on the "fit" between personality type and cultural configuration, as in the notion of the "cultural maximizer." From this perspective

("typically American," we might say), class barriers to upward mobility are less important than the personality-based "drive" (or the lack of it) of each individual.

Both anthropology and the world have changed since the publication of *Culture against Man*. For anthropologists, a not insignificant change in their academic world stems from the emergence of cultural studies as a field in its own right, a development due in no small part to the work of Richard Hoggart and the influence of *The Uses of Literacy*. The relationship between anthropology and cultural studies is multistranded, with practitioners variously situated within their own field making alliances with, or arguing against, their counterparts in the other discipline. In some respects, the comparative reading, offered here, of *Culture against Man* and *The Uses of Literacy* can serve as a map to this interdisciplinary terrain, even at the turn of the twenty-first century. In the next essay, I continue this mapping project with a comparative reading of Raymond Williams and George Stocking.

CHAPTER 8

Raymond Williams, George Stocking, and Fin-de-siècle U.S. Anthropology

For anthropologists in the United States, most of whom are heirs (whether they admit it or not [see Darnell 2001]) to the Boasian tradition of cultural history and analysis, one of the most immediately off-putting attributes of that array of approaches that have come to be called cultural studies is the name itself. As many anthropologists see it, if a new discipline, or a new trend across disciplines, can get away with calling itself cultural studies, then it poses a direct challenge to the scholarly authority of anthropology—for anthropology, as one origin story tells us, institutionalized itself within the U.S. academy by putting the culture concept on the intellectual map and making itself responsible for that concept and its purported relationship to "the world out there." However narrow (and historically oversimplified) such a view may be, it has the virtue of enticing us to reconsider, yet again, our intellectual roots, our complex relationship to the culture concept, and the relationship of that concept to the worlds that we study and write about.

As a step toward such reconsideration, in this chapter I initiate a comparison of the works of Raymond Williams and George Stocking, two scholars who have done much, since the late 1950s, to shape culture theory in anthropology and cultural studies, respectively. In teaching culture theory to a mixed audience of graduate students of anthropology and literature, I usually begin with Williams's *Culture and Society* (1958) and Stocking's *Race, Culture, and Evolution* (1968). Both books present (among other things) revisionist histories of the culture concept, and both can be considered (after the fact) to be foundational texts in the disciplines that sprung up in their wake, cultural studies and the history of anthropology. The comparative reading that I propose here is intended, then, to facilitate thinking about the uses of the culture concept in both anthropology and cultural studies and, more generally, about the intellectual positioning of the two disciplines vis-à-vis each other.

The comparison proceeds in two "moments." The first concerns the role that Matthew Arnold plays in *Culture and Society* and *Race, Culture, and Evolution*. Using the figure of Arnold as an entry into these two works will allow me to sketch, comparatively, the quite different historical narratives that each author constructs to contextualize his analysis of the culture concept. The second moment of comparison concerns the degree to which each author may be considered to have used (however unintentionally) historical analysis to contribute to ongoing debates in culture theory. Considering the transformation of history into theory will allow me to return in the end to the question of anthropology vis-à-vis cultural studies. I do this by comparing the uses of culture theory in the two disciplines—in cultural studies, to critique classism, racism, and sexism; in anthropology, to interpret global human diversity.

Historicizing Matthew Arnold's Culture

Among the names listed in the fifteen-page index of *Race, Culture, and Evolution* and the nine-page index of *Culture and Society*, there are just a dozen in common: Arnold, Darwin, Freud, Goethe, Herder, Humboldt, Lenin, Marx, Plekhanov, Schiller, Adam Smith, and Herbert Spencer. Of those twelve authors, both Stocking and Williams treat only one in detail: Matthew Arnold. Williams devotes an entire chapter to J. H. Newman and Matthew Arnold, and one essay in *Race, Culture, and Evolution* is entitled "Matthew Arnold, E. B. Tylor, and the Uses of Invention."

Williams places Matthew Arnold in what he sees as an English tradition of thought about the culture concept that runs from Edmund Burke and William Cobbett at the end of the eighteenth century to T. S. Eliot and George Orwell in the early twentieth. The immediate foil for Williams's Arnold is John Henry Newman. Williams aligns Newman with such thinkers as Samuel Taylor Coleridge, who championed the notion of "the ideal perfection . . . of the intellect," as Newman put it, and "the harmonious development of . . . our humanity," as Coleridge himself put it, in opposition to utilitarian theories of rationalized education aimed at "training men to carry out particular tasks" (Williams 1958:111). This lineage of thinkers, this "tradition" of thought, begins, for Williams, with Burke. It begins at the end of the eighteenth century and arises in response to the great social upheavals that came to be called "revolutions," the French and the industrial. In *Culture and Society*, Williams's analysis of that tradition begins in a way that has come to seem characteristic of his modus operandi, that is, with a discussion of five key words: "industry," "democracy," "class," "art," and "culture." For Williams, the histories of those words are keys to understanding societal trends and transformations of the broadest import; indeed, their individual histories follow the same "general pattern," and that pattern "can be used as a special kind of map by which it is possible to look again at those wider changes in life and thought to which the changes in language evidently refer" (xiii). As the title of his book indicates, Williams finds "culture" to be quintessential among his list of key words:

> The development of *culture* is perhaps the most striking among all the words named. It might be said, indeed, that the questions now concentrated in the meanings of the word *culture* are questions directly raised by the great historical changes which the changes in *industry, democracy* and *class* . . . represent. . . . The development of the word *culture* is a record of a number of important and continuing reactions to these changes in our social, economic and political life, and may be seen, in itself, as a special kind of map by means of which the nature of the changes can be explored. [xvi–xvii]

For Williams, then, the development of the culture concept, in England at least, is to be understood as a response to the great transformation of society in the wake of the industrial revolution. More specifically, and beginning with Burke, the term "culture" stands for "a position in the English mind from which the march of industrialism and liberalism was to be continually attacked" (11). Burke himself did not use "culture" as the key word of that position; he spoke instead of government, nation, civil society, and the state. Within "the tradition," it was Arnold, according to Williams, who "was to name . . . the work of perfection . . . as Culture" (111). As is well known, even by some anthropologists (see Kroeber and Kluckhohn 1952:29), Arnold's notion of culture referred to the harmonious development of the intellectual and spiritual faculties of all the members of a society. Moreover, Arnold conceived of culture as an antidote to the England of his time, that is, to a society he deemed too exclusively devoted to the "external" and practical pursuits of economic development. There is a long tradition of speculation preceding Arnold concerning the internal and the external in relation to human development—ultimately, the material and spiritual aspects of the human condition. There is a long tradition after him, too, that associates modern industrial society with the external, the mechanical, and the spurious and sees "genuine culture" as the antidote to those ills.

But there is another aspect of Arnold's culture that Williams pointedly criticizes: its elitism, its narrow range. Arnold, of course, is famous for defining culture as "the best which has been thought and said in the world" (1868:6). Arnold reserved for himself and his fellow intellectuals the right to formulate the standards by which "the best" was to be known. He also argued that an abandonment of those standards and of that culture led to anarchy (see Herbert 1991). And, most important in Williams's view, when Arnold surveyed the rising Victorian working classes, he saw not culture, a different culture, or even a desire for more culture but the threat of anarchy:

> The Hyde Park railings were down, and it was not Arnold's best self which rose at the sight of them. Certainly he feared a general breakdown, into violence and anarchy, but the most remarkable facts about the British working-class movement . . . are its conscious and deliberate abstention from general violence, and its firm faith in other methods of advance. . . . I think it had more to offer to the "pursuit of perfection" than Matthew Arnold . . . was able to realize. (125)

Williams's critique of Arnoldian culture, then, is less concerned with its aesthetic elitism—what anthropologists might disparage as its "opera-house" quality (Wagner 1975:21)—than with its class biases. Arnold could not transcend his position within the English class structure to see that English workers, too, "had" culture. Nor could he see what we would today call the hegemonic implications of his use of the culture concept—that to enshrine, in the context of ongoing class conflict, certain particular standards of art, thought, and conduct as universally valid is to rule out of bounds other ways of being and thinking and thereby to deny legitimacy to the aspirations of those who do not agree with you. One can see from this brief discussion the seeds of much of the work in cultural studies that has followed from Raymond Williams—that is, the concern for varieties of culture that anthropologists sometimes, but literary critics almost never, took seriously and the additional concern (largely ignored by anthropologists) of the class politics of the culture(s) so understood.

Matthew Arnold assumes a different place in the work of George Stocking, where Arnold appears not in his own right but as a foil for E. B. Tylor; indeed, Stocking devotes only seven pages to Arnold, though those pages are dense and, to use one of Stocking's favorite words, suggestive. Stocking's essay, "Matthew Arnold, E. B. Tylor, and the Uses of Invention" (1963), can be "multiply contextualized" in terms of two of Stocking's larger projects (1992:4). First, as Stocking tells readers playfully at the outset, it is an attempt to replace anthropology's myths about its past with history. The myth in this case concerns the invention of the culture concept by Tylor in 1871, and, in this essay and others, Stocking proceeds somewhat in the manner of Williams in quest of a key word: culture. More generally, the rhetorical tactic and the intellectual strategy—the replacement of myth by history, or presentism by historicism, or house histories by professional ones—are central to Stocking's work, a point to which I shall return.

A second project that the essay announces, at least in Stocking's introduction to the 1968 version, is an alternatively contextualized version of the origins of Victorian anthropology, in response to the 1966 publication of J. W. Burrow's *Evolution and Society* (see also Stocking 1967:381–83; 1987). It is in that alternative version that the opposition of Arnold and Tylor will become salient, but I will begin with the myth and history of the origin of the culture concept.

For Stocking, the principal (or, perhaps, proximate) mythmakers are Kroeber and Kluckhohn, who argued in their remarkable 1952 compendium of definitions of the culture concept that Tylor invented the "modern," that is, anthropological, notion of culture in 1871, even though his definition was not widely adopted until the 1920s:

> The word with its modern technical or anthropological meaning was established in English by Tylor in 1871, though it seems not to have penetrated to any general or "complete" British or U.S. dictionary until more than fifty years later—a piece of cultural lag that may help to keep anthropologists humble in estimating the tempo of their influence on even the avowedly literate segment of their society. (Kroeber and Kluckhohn 1952:9)

Kroeber and Kluckhohn added that Tylor "was deliberately establishing a science by defining its subject matter. That he made this definition the first sentence of a book shows that he was conscious of his procedure" (150–51).

This is the myth that Stocking wishes to demolish, and, as he does so, Arnold as foil to Tylor becomes an important character. There is, however, more at stake, for this particular myth about the culture concept is symptomatic of the larger problem of presentism, or the history of anthropology written by anthropologists who not only are not historians but who use history, however unconsciously, to advance their own theoretical agendas. And even more generally, the problem of the myth/history of the culture concept bears on anthropology's relationship to the humanities and to cultural studies, an issue to which I will return at the end of this essay.

Stocking argues that Kroeber and Kluckhohn are wrong—that in Tylor's 1871 work, *Primitive Culture*, he did not invent the modern conception of culture; rather, "he simply took the contemporary humanist idea of culture and fitted it into the framework of progressive social evolutionism" (1963:87). In Stocking's reading, the thrust of Tylor's argument was to make culture, in addition to material civilization, a progressive, as opposed to a degenerative or discontinuous, process. It is that move that makes Arnold significant and also makes significant a chapter in the history of anthropology that Burrow overlooked but that Stocking has dealt with at length—namely, the continuing importance in the early nineteenth century of the biblical "paradigm for research on the cultural, linguistic, and physical diversity of mankind" (Stocking 1963:71).

The biblical view led some scholars to argue against the idea of evolutionary social progress; they interpreted existing "primitive" peoples not as representative of early stages of human history but as evidence for "degeneration" (Stocking 1973). Tylor, needless to say, was not a degenerationist. To the contrary, as Stocking puts it, "Tylor's anthropological thought was part of the nineteenth-century positivist incarnation of the progressionist tradition which [the degenerationists] attacked" (1963:76). Moreover, while it was not explicitly degenerationist, Arnold's major statement on culture, published as a book three years before Tylor's *Primitive Culture* and widely discussed at the time, presented Tylor with a serious challenge. Arnold, it will be recalled, defined culture in opposition to civilization. For him, culture meant the harmonious development of humanity's highest faculties; it was the process of "getting to know . . . the best which has been thought and said in the world" as well as the inner balance resulting from such knowledge (Arnold 1868:6). Moreover, Arnold saw England's advanced industrial civilization as lacking in culture, and he was contemptuous of it:

The people who believe most that our greatness and welfare are proved by our being very rich, and who most give their lives and thoughts to becoming rich, are just the very people whom we call Philistines. Culture says: "Consider these people, then, their way of life, their habits, their manners, the very tones of their voice; look at them attentively; observe the literature they read, the things which give them pleasure, the words which come forth out of their mouths, the thoughts which make the furniture of their minds; would any amount of wealth be worth having with the condition that one was to become just like these people by having it?" (Arnold 1868:52)

In sum, Arnold's culture constitutes what Raymond Williams called "a position in the English mind from which the march of industrialism and liberalism was to be continually attacked" (1958:11). But, as Stocking argues, Tylor was spurred by Arnold's attack to mount a defense not only of England's material civilization but of its culture—to show, that is, that progress in the material and spiritual aspects of civilization, or culture, advanced through human history together.

Thus, in Stocking's reading, what Arnold separated—culture and civilization—Tylor reunited and conflated. Stocking, in short, uses Arnold to puncture Kroeber and Kluckhohn's origin myth. The latter ignored what Stocking sees as the crucial equation, in Tylor's famous definition, of culture and civilization: "In this very synonymity, which some modern renditions obscure by an ellipsis of the last two words, Tylor begs the whole question of relativism and in effect makes the modern anthropological meaning of 'culture' impossible" (1963:73). In sum, Kroeber and Kluckhohn saw Tylor as the inventor of the modern culture concept, in contrast to a Victorian humanist such as Arnold, who for them represented an outmoded and dying tradition of thought. But Stocking sees both Tylor and Arnold as engaged in a debate that goes back to the eighteenth century and shows us that neither transcended that debate to achieve the twentieth-century anthropological definition of culture—though surprisingly, as Stocking notes, Arnold came closer to it in some ways than did Tylor (Stocking 1963:88–90; see also Young 1995:45–50).

So, the Matthew Arnold of Raymond Williams and the Matthew Arnold of George Stocking are characters in different narrative projects. Williams's narrative runs from Burke to Eliot and is concerned with a tradition of literary thought critical of the industrial revolution in England. (Indeed, Williams goes so far as to derive the modern anthropological conception of culture from that literary tradition: "The sense of 'culture' as 'a whole way of life' . . . in twentieth-century anthropology . . . depends . . . on the literary tradition" [1958:233].) Stocking's project is a history of anthropology, both as an intellectual tradition and as an institutionalizing discipline, from the Enlightenment to the mid-twentieth century. Thus the two projects are different in their narrative trajectories and have different theoretical potentials, as well.

History into Theory

By the end of *Culture and Society*, Williams is no longer writing as an intellectual historian but as a politically engaged theoretician. As such, he wants to transform the key words with which he began *Culture and Society*—"culture," "class," "art," "democracy"—into analytic tools that will serve his political and critical purposes. In particular, he proposes a high modernist definition of "culture" that is focused on the dialectic of individual creativity and established cultural patterns; for example, in a 1957 essay entitled "Culture Is Ordinary," he writes:

> Culture is ordinary: that is the first fact. Every human society has its own shape, its own purposes, its own meanings. Every human society expresses these, in institutions, and in arts and learning. The making of a society is the finding of common meanings and directions, and its growth is an active debate and amendment under the pressures of experience, contact, and discovery, writing themselves into the land. The growing society is there, yet it is also made and remade in every individual mind. The making of a mind is, first, the slow learning of shapes, purposes, and meanings, so that work, observation and communication are possible. Then, second, but equal in importance, is the testing of these in experience, the making of new observations, comparisons, and meanings. A culture has two aspects: the known meanings and directions, which its members are trained to; the new observations and meanings, which are offered and tested. These are the ordinary processes of human societies and human minds, and we see through them the nature of a culture: that it is always both traditional and creative; that it is both the most ordinary common meanings and the finest individual meanings. (Williams 1989:4)

It is worth noting how similar this passage is to T. S. Eliot's 1921 essay, "Tradition and the Individual Talent" (1921:47–59) or to Edward Sapir's essay from the same period, "Culture, Genuine and Spurious" (1924a). What is at stake in all these essays is the play of creative individuality and inherited cultural forms, with the former dependent on the latter for its development but with that development leading, ultimately, to the transformation of the inherited culture—leading, that is, to the creation of new culture (see also Eldridge and Eldridge 1994:45–75; McGuigan 1993).

What distinguishes Williams from such predecessors as Eliot and Sapir is his elaborate and provocative attempt to combine this modernist theory of culture with a Marxian critique of the interaction of culture and social class. Thus at the end of *Culture and Society* and in its sequel, *The Long Revolution* (1961), Williams presents carefully reasoned analyses of terms such as "mass society," "mass media," "popular culture," and "cultural democracy," and he goes on to consider the history of the relationship of public education to Britain's class hierarchy, as well as the history of the institutionalization of hegemonic cultural forms like "standard English" and various literary genres. His political and critical goals are clear: to attack those highbrow critics who ridicule popular or mass culture and who attribute its failings to the impoverished sensibilities of the working classes; to turn the tables on those critics by pointing out the distinction between, on the one hand, the culture created by heavily capitalized and increasingly centralized mass media and, on the other, genuinely popular cultural forms that express something of the lived experiences—the "structure of feeling" (Williams 1961:48)—of the working classes, as well as their resistance to an imposed mass culture; and to argue for a cultural democracy in which all shall have access to education and mass media and, therefore, the possibility for cultural creativity and self-expression.

This set of arguments, it seems to me, constitutes a striking development, starting as it did in a kind of standard intellectual history and transforming itself into what literary people came to call "theory," or cultural critique. However much Williams may be criticized today for his attention to class at the expense of gender and race (Gilroy 1991:49–50), and even for his British, not to mention Welsh, nationalism (Williams 1989:99–104), it is clear why cultural studies scholars find *Culture and Society* to be a groundbreaking work (Nelson et al. 1992:9; Steedman 1992:613).

Turning now to George Stocking as a culture theorist: Stocking's contribution to culture theory in anthropology depends on the interaction of two factors, both of which figure prominently in his running commentary on his own work. The first factor is his unique position as "house historiographer" in the Department of Anthropology at the University of Chicago and, more generally, as a historian among and of anthropologists (Stocking 1992:9); the second is the relationship of his project to two epistemological stances that he terms "historicism" and "presentism."

As to the first of these, even before the publication in 1968 of *Race, Culture, and Evolution* and his appointment in the same year to the Department of Anthropology at the University of Chicago, Stocking was referring to himself, both playfully and ironically, as "an outsider with no present commitment" to any particular faction within the "tribe" of anthropologists, a group within which he nonetheless saw himself as having an "honorary" status (1967:382–83; see also 1968:1). These metaphors recur in the retrospective commentaries of his 1992 volume, *The Ethnographer's Magic.* "I have always felt myself ultimately an outsider to the anthropological tribe," he writes. "I have always thought of myself, *au fond*, as an historian" (1992:13, 343). He mentions his "marginal relation to the discipline of anthropology" and, even more emphatically, his "irreducible marginality to . . . anthropology" (4, 276). He calls anthropology "my adopted discipline" (277). He even goes so far as to speculate that his interest in the history of anthropological fieldwork stems from some sort of psychological overcompensation: "Given my outsider's status, and my failure actually to have done fieldwork, one might suspect . . . a certain sublimation: lacking, even rejecting, the real experience, I sought instead to experience it vicariously" (15).

Yet, there is another strain of self-reflective commentary in *The Ethnographer's Magic.* For if Stocking assures us that he sees himself "as essentially an historian," he nonetheless admits, "I am by departmental affiliation an anthropologist" (5, 6). Or, more complexly, at times he describes himself—again, both playfully and ironically—as an ethnographer of anthropologists. As he notes, "Some of my colleagues [at Chicago] were inclined to think of my participation in the life of the department as itself a kind of fieldwork . . . and sometimes I, too, have glossed my departmental membership, and other . . . professional experiences, as . . . analogues of the fieldwork experience" (12). But the anthropological fieldworker, as we all know, is the quintessential marginal person, caught between (at least) two worlds and charged with an impossible task—that denoted by the contradictory expression "participant-observation." No wonder, then, that Stocking describes himself as aspiring to the neutrality of observer status when "divisive issues" threaten the internal peace of the anthropological tribe yet that he also acknowledges that at times he can become "a committed participant" (6, 277).

The ambiguity of the fieldworker's position—neutrality combined with engagement—is in some respects analogous to the tension between historicism and presentism that has long been a crucial historiographical and epistemological issue for Stocking. In his early yet definitive essay "On the Limits of 'Presentism' and 'Historicism' in the Historiography of the Behavioral Sciences," Stocking presented both attitudes as ideal types while recognizing that individual historians combine strands from both. He defined historicism as "commitment to the understanding of the past for its own sake" (1965b:212) and presentism as the study of the past for present-day purposes—or, in the case of present-day practitioners who study the history of their own particular discipline, presentism amounts to "theoretical polemic in the guise of history" (1966b:284).

In relation to these terms, Stocking has consistently described himself as an advocate of historicism and as one who has tried to adhere to the methods that it requires. At the same time, he has come to acknowledge presentist influences on his own work:

> The programmatic "historicism" I advocated in 1965 has long since been qualified by my residence among anthropologists and by further historiographical reflection. These have made me more appreciative of the role of present interest in the definition of a field for historical inquiry, of the various modes by which historical understanding may be cultivated, and of the different standards by which it may be evaluated. (1992:9)

Indeed, the interplay of presentism and historicism in Stocking's work is exactly what we would expect, given his ideas about what it is to do good history. In much of his work, the historicist injunction to understand the past for its own sake has meant trying to understand anthropological ideas and perspectives as these occurred, or presented themselves over time, in the minds of now-dead practitioners. Thus Stocking tells us that the goal of his studies of "well-known anthropologists" is "to recapture their understanding historically" (8–9). Or, speaking specifically of his work on Boas and the culture concept, he writes, "The problem . . . is to recreate a pattern of thought on the nature of culture in an individual mind" (1966a:196).

If this goal implies a rather straightforward realism, the key technique that Stocking uses to achieve it suggests a more complicated epistemology. That technique is what he calls "contextualization." "I have never thought of myself as an historian of ideas per se," he tells us, but "of ideas as manifested by human actors within ever-broadening circles of context" (1992:115). He goes on to define the historian's "juicy bits" as "particular passages into which more meaning than the author perhaps intended is now compressed, which by explication and contextualization may be made powerfully illuminating" (213).

Earlier, I gave an example of this technique of contextualizing juicy bits: Stocking's reading of the first sentence of Tylor's *Primitive Culture* in the context of Matthew Arnold's polemic on culture and anarchy. The example reminds us that any particular act of historical contextualization itself has a context (Fabian 1995). In this case, the context of Stocking's contextualization is the "myth" of Tylor as inventor of the anthropological culture concept, a myth codified by Kroeber and Kluckhohn and against which Stocking constructed his interpretation of Tylor's contribution. But to say that acts of contextualization themselves have contexts is to open the door to presentist influences, as, I believe, Stocking would admit. Consider again his remarks on re-creating Boas's thinking about culture. Qualifying the sentence quoted earlier, about re-creating the pattern of thought, he explains:

> As in all historical reconstruction, a solution has been facilitated by knowledge of the pattern which eventually emerged—by my knowledge of the present state of anthropological thought on culture. In the present case, it has been facilitated by the prior reconstruction of a portion of the pattern out of which Boas' thought in turn emerged. Working between these "fixed" points of pattern, with the indications of change which the patchwork of Boas' composition itself suggested, and always in relation to the corpus of his work, I have re-created (or perhaps created) the changing pattern of Boas' thought on culture during a certain period in his life. (1966a:196–97)

So, part of the historian's work involves data—even "hard" data like "the corpus" of Boas's work—and one may perhaps distinguish skilled historians from the less skilled by their ability to "control" interesting data, to find unread documents, or to make connections between bodies or types of documents that other historians have failed to bring together. But the process of interpreting the data thus amassed (assuming for the moment they are merely amassed and not somehow "constructed") can never be adequately conceptualized in terms of a simple realism or even a simple historicism. As Stocking notes in the passage just quoted, what counts as a historical problem in the history of anthropology depends at least in part on the current state of anthropological knowledge as well as on earlier historical research.

The point may perhaps be clinched by returning to an issue that I discussed earlier, that of the historian's stance toward "myth." In addition to anthropologists' myths about the genesis of the culture concept, Stocking has concerned himself with the myth of fieldwork, particularly in reference to Bronislaw Malinowski. I should note, preliminarily, that Stocking's attempt to historicize that myth proceeds by means of contextualization—that is, in his words, by placing "Malinowski's Trobriand adventure in the context of earlier British fieldwork" (1992:17). But the project aroused a particular criticism: Stocking tells us that "deconstructively inclined" colleagues have questioned his claim to uphold a distinction between myth and history, for his own work on Malinowski "tended . . . to reduce a certain version of the 'history' of British social anthropology to the status of 'myth'" (214). Stocking's defense against this charge is worth quoting at length:

> Regarding the myth/history distinction: while I am conscious of its epistemologically problematic status, I am committed to a notion of the historian's craft which assumes that a distinction between myth and history, or between more and less mythical views of history, is worth attempting in the practice of historiography—at the same time that one recognizes that much of what we deal with as historians is perhaps irreducibly "mythistorical." (214)

Again, what happens to the epistemological distinction between historicism and presentism if Stocking is willing to conflate, as he does here, a "distinction between myth and history," on the one hand, with "more or less mythical views of history," on the other? To me, the conclusion seems inescapable: "contextualization" involves both the past contexts (more or less recoverable) of historians' data and the present contexts (more or less available to conscious awareness) that impinge on historians' organization and interpretation of those data. And what will count as a more or less mythical version of history will always depend on the present, socially constructed state of opinion and knowledge in the discipline. Abstract pronouncements about the nature of myth versus the nature of history are not very useful: it is more interesting to ask why in certain contexts, at certain moments, one person's interpretations (those, for example, of Raymond Williams or George Stocking) seem magisterial, unimpeachable, superb in comparison to those of others.

If, then, I refuse to endorse a strict separation between historicism and presentism in the history of anthropology, I nonetheless do not think that my stance is one unendorsed, or unendorsable, by George Stocking. With more time, it might be useful to contextualize Stocking's rhetorical deployment of those notorious terms with regard to his approach to an emerging field of scholarship in the early 1960s. But that is not my topic here; rather, it remains to say something about Stocking as a culture theorist among anthropologists.

Returning for a moment to Raymond Williams, it seems to me that as a culture theorist he is important not so much for having developed new concepts—his notion of culture was, as I have said, conventionally modernist—but for elaborating those concepts in a Marxian framework, applying them to noncanonical materials, and bringing his synthesis to bear on the discourse of an established discipline, English literature, which before him had largely ignored the issues that he raised. In saying this, I do not mean to make light of Williams's achievements, nor am I unaware of the Gramscian turn in Marxist theory to which Williams contributed (Williams 1977). I want, rather, to suggest that the work of an important innovator such as Williams might more usefully be understood in terms of an idea like recontextualization—bringing disparate concepts and disciplinary discourses together in unexpected ways—than in terms of ideas like "discovery" or "invention."

Surely, then, we may think in similar ways of that master of recontextualization, George Stocking, as a culture theorist. The current relationship of U.S. anthropology to Boas provides an initial example. Stocking writes: "One of the most satisfying compliments I ever received came when one of his [Boas's] late students said to me, 'You gave us back Boas'" (1992:9). But I would go beyond this anecdote to suggest that those anthropologists of my generation who consider themselves, as I do, to be Boasians, yet whose genealogical links to the apical ancestor are tenuous, have constructed our claim to kinship on the basis (not merely fictive) of the work of the tribal outsider, George Stocking. We learned to read Boas and the Boasians by reading Stocking. Indeed, Stocking's historical recontextualization of Boas's work has not only made Boas available to many younger anthropologists, it has provided an organized and authoritative reading of him. That Stocking's reading may itself become an object for revisionist scholarship (for example, Evans 2005) only underscores the point that the historian's re-creation of the pattern of Boas's thought is itself an important contribution to anthropological culture theory. Ironically, then, Stocking's Boas has become a presentist presence in anthropology, despite the best historicist intentions of its creator.

Anthropology vis-à-vis Cultural Studies

By way of a conclusion, let me sketch one further example of the ways in which George Stocking's work can contribute to current anthropological debates. Briefly, I want to revisit the issue that I raised at the outset of this chapter, that is, the relationship of anthropology and cultural studies. Cultural studies often bewilders or infuriates anthropologists, who see its practitioners as poaching on their turf while almost completely ignoring the contributions of anthropologists. My present opinion on this matter is that despite use of the term "culture" by people in cultural studies, they are for the most part interested in questions that too many anthropologists (especially since World War II) have ignored—that is, they are occupying new territory, not poaching on ours. Their questions concern the politics of "high culture," "mass culture," and "popular culture," terms that inflect the culture concept in directions that anthropologists tend to avoid (think for a moment of the absence of Matthew Arnold from the anthropological canon). Their questions concern hegemony and the relationship of culture to social stratification in modern societies along axes of class, race, and gender. Their questions presuppose the Boasian critique of race and then go on to examine the politics of racism—another set of issues that, until quite recently, postwar U.S. anthropologists largely (although not completely) overlooked.

The lack of attention, in postwar anthropology, to these issues has stemmed, I think, from the Whiggishness of our historical perspective, which has allowed us to believe that, in the progress of knowledge, culture replaced race as the correct way to understand human social variation and that anthropological culture replaced the culture of Matthew Arnold. But Stocking's work on race, culture, and evolution—that is, his construction of a history that interrelates rather than separates those terms—might remind us that in the wider society all three terms, and the discourses connected to them, remain intertwined and alive. For, as Stocking's work shows, race and culture have been alternative yet interrelated answers to anthropology's fundamental question: How are we to understand global human diversity?

Those of us who learned our Boas from Stocking find in the early twentieth century a key moment in the history of anthropology—the moment when culture replaced race as the privileged explanation that anthropologists (although not necessarily scholars in other fields [Segal 2000]) offered for the puzzle of human social diversity. To us, the return to biological explanations since the mid-1980s—whether in sociobiology, the Freeman-Mead debate (Freeman 1983; cf. Rappaport 1986), *The Bell Curve* (Herrnstein and Murray 1994; cf. Jacoby and Glauberman 1995), or evolutionary psychology—can only seem reactionary. Yet, as readers of Stocking, we should have been prepared for such a turn. In the second essay of *Race, Culture, and Evolution*, "French Anthropology in 1800," Stocking sketches a key transition analogous to the contemporary, unwelcome turn to sociobiology and evolutionary psychology—when Enlightenment notions of the relativity of different civilizations gave way to the new nineteenth-century French anthropology of race (see also Stocking 2001:3–23). Coupling "French Anthropology in 1800" with Stocking's essays on Boas might help us to see that the concepts of race and culture represent something like an enduring (synchronic) duality, which, from our various presentist perspectives, appears in the (diachronic) form of historical progress (from "race" to "culture") or retrogression (from "culture" to "race").

Or, one might think of the deployment of the two linked concepts not diachronically, in historical time, but synchronically, in social space. For example, in his autobiography, *Dusk of Dawn*, W. E. B. Du Bois describes how "race" was taught in the various educational institutions that he attended at the end of the nineteenth century. Du Bois notes that, in elementary school, "It came only in the matter of geography when the races of the world were pictured." At Fisk, he writes, "The problem of race was faced openly and essential racial equality asserted." When he transferred to Harvard to complete his undergraduate education, he "began to face scientific race dogma . . . evolution and the 'Survival of the Fittest.'" Finally, in graduate school "at Harvard and again in Germany, the emphasis again was altered, and race became a matter of culture and cultural history" (1940:97–98).

I dare say that one could find people having similar experiences at the turn of the twenty-first century. For example, the logic of contemporary multiculturalism, in which racist notions seem to be reborn in discourses ostensibly about culture (see Wetherell and Potter 1992), exhibits a similar configuration of what we might call, taking a cue from James Clifford (1988:224), "the race-culture system." The point is simply that the anthropological culture concept has not vanquished racism or even race as an explanation of human social diversity, nor is it likely to in the near future.

Rather, the two terms seem profoundly intertwined, as much of the history of anthropology suggests. As that history further shows, even within anthropology there are many different versions of the culture concept, some more useful for critiquing ideological formations such as racism and nationalism, some less so (see Brightman 1995). The versions of culture theory that are useful in this regard are those critical not only of the essentializing and naturalizing implications of the race concept but of the way in which the culture concept can carry the same implications. In sum, to transcend race-culture discourses it is not enough to replace "race" with "culture." Culture has to be theorized in terms that, as Clifford put it, "preserv[e] the concept's differential and relativist functions and that avoi[d] the positing of . . . essences" (1988:274–75).

Using the culture concept to relativize any and all foundational assumptions is not, as far as I understand it, the project of cultural studies practitioners. They are, however, interested in particular cultures of class, race, and gender as resources for a critique of unmarked, hegemonic values. To put it another way: cultural studies focuses on certain subordinated "positions" within the dominant structure of modern (or postmodern) Western societies. Its practitioners use the cultures of, or "knowledges" associated with, those positions to critique and relativize the dominant system (see Lave et al. 1992:277–78). But they are not interested in culture theory per se, as anthropologists have been and continue to be. That is why cultural studies practitioners ignore the literature that anthropologists have produced (in more than a century of work) on such diverse issues as the relationship of human evolution and culture, the theory of the symbol and of human "symboling," and even the relationship between ecology and culture (useful, one would think, for the kinds of Marxian theorizing engaged in by many cultural studies scholars).

Nor is the field of cultural studies particularly interested in global cultural diversity and the ethnographic record that anthropologists have laboriously constructed to document and interpret it. There has, of course, been a cultural studies critique of the entanglement of anthropological knowledge production in colonialist regimes—a critique that anthropologists themselves have been quick to take seriously. But that sort of work falls easily into the mainstream of cultural studies, with its concern for dominance and subordination (based, in this case, on race) within modern societies. Cultural studies rarely ventures beyond those issues to look seriously at anthropological interpretations, however compromised, of other cultures.

In the end, then, it is clear that anthropologists have learned much from cultural studies, and it is probable that we will continue to learn from it. It is also clear that the histories of the two disciplines are distinct. On the other hand, it is not at all certain how they will interface in the future. The Williams-Stocking contrast is certainly symptomatic of past differences (as is the Hoggart-Henry contrast). Williams, more than many of his successors, thought and wrote about the culture concept in a way that qualifies his work, in my estimation, as "culture theory." But the thrust of his theorizing led specifically to discussions of culture and class, culture and hegemony, and culture and democracy within British society—and it is that aspect of his work that has been developed by his successors. Stocking, the culture theorist malgré lui, helped anthropologists to reinvigorate a long tradition of culture theory within the discipline by making Boasian culture theory, and especially Boas's own work, relevant again. But like anthropological culture theory, Stocking's most explicitly theoretical musings—on presentism and historicism as historiographical problems—are phrased as a concern for general issues in interpretive social science, not as specific questions about power and knowledge in a particular society. That questions about historiographical and anthropological theory are also questions about power and knowledge in a particular society is an assertion to which, I believe, both Stocking and Williams, as well as their followers, would assent. And that is a point of convergence between anthropology and many of the approaches represented by the rubric "cultural studies."

REFERENCES

AAA (American Anthropological Association). 2002. *El Dorado Task Force Papers*, 2 vols. Washington, DC: American Anthropological Association.

Abrams, M. H. 1953. *The Mirror and the Lamp: Romantic Theory and the Critical Tradition*. Oxford: Oxford University Press.

Abu-Lughod, Lila. 1991. Writing against Culture. In Richard Fox, ed., *Recapturing Anthropology*, 137–62. Santa Fe, NM: School of American Research Press.

Aldington, Richard. 1920. Standards of Literature. *Poetry* 16:164–68.

Anderson, Benedict. 1983. *Imagined Communities: Reflections on the Origin and Spread of Nationalism*. London: Verso.

ANMM. Archives of the National Museum of Man. Ottawa, Canada.

Arnold, Matthew. 1868 [1963]. *Culture and Anarchy*. Cambridge: Cambridge University Press.

Arnold, Thurman. 1937. *The Folklore of Capitalism*. New Haven, CT: Yale University Press.

Aron, Raymond. 1965. *Main Currents in Sociological Thought*. Vol. 1. Translated by Richard Howard and Helen Weaver. New York: Basic Books.

Austen, Jane. 1969. *Pride and Prejudice*. Ed. R. W. Chapman. Oxford: Oxford University Press.

Banner, Lois. 2003. *Intertwined Lives: Margaret Mead, Ruth Benedict, and Their Circle*. New York: Alfred A. Knopf.

Bateson, Gregory, Don D. Jackson, Jay Haley, and John H. Weakland. 1956. Toward a Theory of Schizophrenia. *Behavioral Science* 1(4):251–64. (Reprinted in G. Bateson, *Steps to an Ecology of Mind*, 201–27. San Francisco: Chandler, 1972.)

Bateson, Mary Catherine. 1984. *With a Daughter's Eye: A Memoir of Margaret Mead and Gregory Bateson*. New York: William Morrow.

Bellah, Robert, Richard Madsen, William Sullivan, Ann Swidler, and Steven Tipton. 1985. *Habits of the Heart: Individualism and Commitment in American Life*. Berkeley: University of California Press.

Benedict, Ruth. 1923. *The Concept of the Guardian Spirit in North America*. Menasha, WI: American Anthropological Association.

———. 1924. A Brief Sketch of Serrano Culture. *American Anthropologist* 26:366–92.

———. 1930. Psychological Types in the Cultures of the Southwest. In Mead 1959: 248–61.

———. 1932. Configurations of Culture in North America. *American Anthropologist* 34:1–27.

———. 1934a. *Patterns of Culture*. Boston: Houghton Mifflin.

———. 1934b. Anthropology and the Abnormal. In Mead 1959:262–83.

———. 1946. *The Chrysanthemum and the Sword: Patterns of Japanese Culture*. Boston: Houghton Mifflin.

Berger, Bennett M. 1963. Explorations of a Driven Society: Review of *Culture against Man*, by Jules Henry. *New York Times Book Review*, October 20: 54.

Berger, M. 1947. Jazz: Resistance to the Diffusion of a Culture-Pattern. *Journal of Negro History* 32:461–94.

Blake, Casey. 1990. *Beloved Community: The Cultural Criticism of Randolph Bourne, Van Wyck Brooks, Waldo Frank, and Lewis Mumford*. Chapel Hill: University of North Carolina Press.

———. 1999. The Usable Past, the Comfortable Past, and the Civic Past: Memory in Contemporary America. *Cultural Anthropology* 14(3):423–35.

Boas, Franz. 1887. The Study of Geography. *Science* 9:137–41. (Reprinted in Boas, *Race, Language, and Culture*, 639–47. New York: Macmillan, 1940, and in G. W. Stocking, ed., *Volksgeist as Method and Ethic*, 9–16. Madison: University of Wisconsin Press.)

———. 1889. On Alternating Sounds. *American Anthropologist* 2:47–53. (Reprinted in Stocking 1974a:72–77.)

———. 1904. The History of Anthropology. *Science* 20:513–24. (Reprinted in G. W. Stocking, ed., *The Shaping of American Anthropology, 1883–1911: A Franz Boas Reader*, 23–36. New York: Basic Books, 1974.)

———. 1911a. *The Mind of Primitive Man*. New York: Macmillan.

———. 1911b. Introduction to *Handbook of American Indian Languages, Part I*. Bulletin No. 40. Bureau of American Ethnology. Washington, DC: Government Printing Office.

———. 1925. What Is a Race? *Nation* 3108:89–91.

Boon, James. 1999. *Verging on Extra-vagance: Anthropology, History, Religion, Literature, Arts . . . Showbiz*. Princeton, NJ: Princeton University Press.

Bourne, Randolph. 1914 [1969]. Our Cultural Humility. In *History of a Literary Radical*, 31–43. New York: Biblo and Tannen.

———. 1915. The Heart of the People. *New Republic* 35:233.

———. 1917a. The Cult of the Best. In Bourne 1977:193–96.

———. 1917b. Twilight of Idols. In Bourne 1977:336–47.

———. 1917c. The Puritan's Will to Power. In Bourne 1977:301–6.

———. 1977. *The Radical Will: Selected Writings, 1911–1918*. Edited by Olaf Hansen. New York: Urizen Books.

Bradley, Phillips. 1945. A Historical Essay. In Tocqueville 1945:389–487.

Brightman, Robert. 1995. Forget Culture: Replacement, Transcendence, Relexification. *Cultural Anthropology* 10:509–46.

Bunzl, Matti. 1996. Franz Boas and the Humboldtian Tradition. In G. W. Stocking, ed., *Volksgeist as Method and Ethic*, 17–78. Madison: University of Wisconsin Press.

———. 2004. Boas, Foucault, and the "Native Anthropologist": Notes Toward a Neo-Boasian Anthropology. *American Anthropologist* 106(3):435–42.

Burke, Kenneth. 1938 [1973]. The Virtues and Limitations of Debunking. In *The Philosophy of Literary Form*. Berkeley: University of California Press.

Burrow, John. 1966. *Evolution and Society: A Study in Victorian Social Theory*. Cambridge: Cambridge University Press.

Caffrey, Margaret. 1989. *Ruth Benedict: Stranger in This Land*. Austin: University of Texas Press.

Cassirer, Ernst. 1932 [1951]. *The Philosophy of the Enlightenment*. Translated by Fritz C. A. Koelln and James Pettergrove. Princeton, NJ: Princeton University Press.

Ceaser, James. 1990. *Liberal Democracy and Political Science*. Baltimore: Johns Hopkins University Press.

Chagnon, Napoleon. 1968. *Yanomamö, the Fierce People*. New York: Holt, Rinehart and Winston.

Clayton, Bruce. 1984. *Forgotten Prophet: The Life of Randolph Bourne*. Baton Rouge: Louisiana State University Press.

Clifford, James. 1988. *The Predicament of Culture: Twentieth-century Ethnography, Literature, and Art*. Cambridge, MA: Harvard University Press.

Cohler, Anne. 1988. *Montesquieu's Comparative Politics and the Spirit of American Constitutionalism*. Lawrence: University Press of Kansas.

Cowan, William, Michael Foster, and E. F. K. Koerner, eds. 1986. *New Perspectives on Edward Sapir in Language, Culture, and Personality*. Amsterdam: John Benjamins.

Croce, Benedetto. 1902 [1909]. *Aesthetic as Science of Expression and General Linguistic*. Translated by Douglas Ainslie. London: Macmillan.

Crunden, Robert M. 1972. *From Self to Society, 1919–1941*. Englewood Cliffs, NJ: Prentice-Hall.

Darnell, Regna. 1990. *Edward Sapir: Linguist, Anthropologist, Humanist*. Berkeley: University of California Press.

———. 2001. *Invisible Genealogies: A History of Americanist Anthropology*. Lincoln: University of Nebraska Press.

Deacon, Desley. 1997. *Elsie Clews Parsons: Inventing Modern Life*. Chicago: University of Chicago Press.

Di Leonardo, Micaela. 1998. *Exotics at Home: Anthropologies, Others, American Modernity*. Chicago: University of Chicago Press.

Dillon, Wilton. 1980. Margaret Mead and Government. *American Anthropologist* 82:319–39.

Dorsey, James. 1884. *Omaha Sociology*. Third Annual Report of the Bureau of Ethnology. Washington: Government Printing Office.

Drescher, Seymour. 1988. More Than America: Comparison and Synthesis in *Democracy in America*. In Eisenstadt 1988:77–93.

Du Bois, W. E. B. 1940 [1995]. *Dusk of Dawn: An Essay toward an Autobiography of a Race Concept.* New Brunswick, NJ: Transaction Books.

Dumont, Louis. 1965. "The Individual" in Two Types of Society. *Contributions to Indian Sociology* 8:7–61.

————. 1970. Religion, Politics, and Society in the Individualistic Universe. In *Proceedings of the Royal Anthropological Institute of Great Britain and Ireland*, 31–45. (Reprinted in revised form in Dumont 1977:47–60.)

————. 1977. *From Mandeville to Marx: The Genesis and Triumph of Economic Ideology.* Chicago: University of Chicago Press.

————. 1983. *Essais sur l'individualisme.* Paris: Editions du Seuil.

————. 1986. *Essays on Individualism: Modern Ideology in Anthropological Perspective.* Chicago: University of Chicago Press.

————. 1994. *German Ideology: From France to Germany and Back.* Chicago: University of Chicago Press.

Durkheim, Emile. 1933. *The Division of Labor in Society.* Translated by George Simpson. New York: Free Press.

Eisenstadt, Abraham, ed. 1988. *Reconsidering Tocqueville's Democracy in America.* New Brunswick, NJ: Rutgers University Press.

Eldridge, John, and Lizzie Eldridge. 1994. *Raymond Williams: Making Connections.* London: Routledge.

Eliot, T. S. 1921 [1960]. *The Sacred Wood.* New York: Alfred A. Knopf.

Errington, Shelly. 1998. *The Death of Authentic Primitive Art and Other Tales of Progress.* Berkeley: University of California Press.

Evans, Brad. 2005. *Before Cultures: The Ethnographic Imagination and American Literature.* Chicago: University of Chicago Press.

Fabian, Johannes. 1983. *Time and the Other: How Anthropology Makes Its Object.* New York: Columbia University Press.

————. 1995. Ethnographic Misunderstanding and the Perils of Context. *American Anthropologist* 97:41–50.

Fernández Casas, María Xosé. 2004. *Edward Sapir en la Lingüística actual. Verba, Anuario Galego de Filoloxía,* Anexo 54. Chile: University of Santiago de Compostela.

Fortune, Reo. 1932. *Sorcerers of Dobu.* New York: E. P. Dutton.

Frank, Waldo. 1929. *The Re-Discovery of America.* New York: Charles Scribner's Sons.

Freeman, Derek. 1983. *Margaret Mead and Samoa: The Making and Unmaking of an Anthropological Myth.* Cambridge, MA: Harvard University Press.

Gable, Eric, and Richard Handler. 1996. After Authenticity at an American Heritage Site. *American Anthropologist* 98(3):568–78.

Geertz, Clifford. 1966. The Impact of the Concept of Culture on the Concept of Man. In Geertz 1973:33–54.

————. 1973. *The Interpretation of Cultures.* New York: Basic Books.

————. 1988. *Works and Lives: The Anthropologist as Author.* Stanford, CA: Stanford University Press.

Ghosh, Gautam, ed. 2001. Vulnerability and Translation: Reflections in the Aftermath of September 11. *Anthropological Quarterly* 75:92–184.

Gilroy, Paul. 1991 [1987]. *"There Ain't No Black in the Union Jack": The Cultural Politics of Race and Nation*. Chicago: University of Chicago Press.

Gleason, Philip. 1981. Americans All: World War II and the Shaping of American Identity. *Review of Politics* 43:483–518.

———. 1984. World War II and the Development of American Studies. *American Quarterly* 36:343–58.

Goffman, Erving. 1963. *Stigma: Notes on the Management of Spoiled Identity*. Englewood Cliffs, NJ: Prentice-Hall.

Goldschmidt, Walter, ed. 1979. *The Uses of Anthropology*. Washington, DC: American Anthropological Association.

Golla, Victor, ed. 1984. *The Sapir-Kroeber Correspondence*. Survey of California and Other Indian Languages, Report No. 6. Berkeley: University of California.

Goodwin, Andrew. 1992. The Uses and Abuses of In-Discipline. In Richard Hoggart, *The Uses of Literacy*, xii–xxxix. New Brunswick, NJ: Transaction.

Gorer, Geoffrey. 1948. *The American People: A Study in National Character*. New York: W. W. Norton.

Gould, Harold. 1971. Obituary of Jules Henry. *American Anthropologist* 73(3):788–97.

Grimshaw, Anna, and Keith Hart. 1993. *Anthropology and the Crisis of the Intellectuals*. Cambridge, UK: Prickly Pear Press.

Grossberg, Lawrence, Cary Nelson, and Paula Treichler, eds. 1992. *Cultural Studies*. New York: Routledge.

Guillory, John. 1993. *Cultural Capital: The Problem of Literary Canon Formation*. Chicago: University of Chicago Press.

Hall, Robert. 1969. Sapir and Croce on Language. *American Anthropologist* 71:498–99.

Handler, Richard. 1986. The Aesthetics of Sapir's *Language*. In Cowan et al. 1986:433–51.

———. 1988. *Nationalism and the Politics of Culture in Quebec*. Madison: University of Wisconsin Press.

———. 1997. Interpreting the Predicament of Culture Theory Today. *Social Analysis* 41(3):72–83.

———. 2004. Afterword: Mysteries of Culture. *American Anthropologist* 106(3):488–94.

Handler, Richard, and Daniel Segal. 1990. *Jane Austen and the Fiction of Culture: An Essay on the Narration of Social Realities*. Tucson: University of Arizona Press. (The second edition was published by Rowman and Littlefield in 1999.)

Hansen, Olaf, ed. 1977. *The Radical Will: Selected Writings [of Randolph Bourne], 1911–1918*. New York: Urizen Books.

Hartman, Geoffrey. 1970. Romanticism and "Anti-Self-Consciousness." In Harold Bloom, ed., *Romanticism and Consciousness*, 46–56. New York: W. W. Norton.

Hegeman, Susan. 1999. *Patterns for America: Modernism and the Concept of Culture*. Princeton, NJ: Princeton University Press.

Henry, Jules. 1935. A Kaingang Text. *International Journal of American Linguistics* 8:172–218.

———. 1941 [1964]. *Jungle People*. New York: J. J. Augustin.

———. 1949. Anthropology in the General Social Science Course. *Journal of General Education* 3:304–8.

———. 1951. The Inner Experience of Culture. *Psychiatry* 14:87–103.

———. 1952. Child Rearing, Culture and the Natural World. *Psychiatry* 15:261–71.

———. 1954a. Laughter in Psychiatric Staff Conferences: A Sociopsychiatric Analysis. *American Journal of Orthopsychiatry* 24:175–84.

———. 1954b. The Formal Structure of a Psychiatric Hospital. *Psychiatry* 17:139–51.

———. 1954c. The Problems of Invariance in the Field of Personality and Culture. In Francis Hsu, ed., *Aspects of Personality and Culture*, 139–60. New York: Abelard-Schuman.

———. 1954d. Docility, or Giving Teacher What She Wants. *Journal of Social Issues* 11:33–41.

———. 1955. Culture, Education, and Communications Theory. In George Spindler, ed., *Education and Anthropology*, 188–207. Stanford, CA: Stanford University Press.

———. 1957a. Attitude Organization in Elementary School Classrooms. *American Journal of Orthopsychiatry* 27:117–33.

———. 1957b. Working Paper on Creativity. *Harvard Educational Review* 27:148–55.

———. 1957c. The Culture of Interpersonal Relations in a Therapeutic Institution for Emotionally Disturbed Children. *American Journal of Orthopsychiatry* 27:725–34.

———. 1959. The Problem of Spontaneity, Initiative and Creativity in Suburban Classrooms. *American Journal of Orthopsychiatry* 29:266–79.

———. 1963. *Culture against Man*. New York: Random House.

———. 1964. Space and Power in a Psychiatric Unit. In Albert Wessen, ed., *The Psychiatric Hospital as a Social System*, 20–34. New York: Charles C. Thomas.

———. 1965. Hope, Delusion, and Organization: Some Problems in the Motivation of Low Achievers. (U.S. Department of Health, Education, and Welfare) *Bulletin*, no. 31:7–16.

———. 1971. *Pathways to Madness*. New York: Random House.

———. 1973. *On Sham, Vulnerability and Other Forms of Self-Destruction*. New York: Random House.

Henry, Jules, and Zunia Henry. 1944. *Doll Play of Pilaga Indian Children: An Experimental and Field Analysis of the Behavior of the Pilaga Indian Children*. Research Monographs, No. 4. New York: American Orthopsychiatric Association.

Herbert, Christopher. 1991. *Culture and Anomie: Ethnographic Imagination in the Nineteenth Century*. Chicago: University of Chicago Press.

Herrnstein, Richard, and Charles Murray. 1994. *The Bell Curve: Intelligence and Class Structure in American Life*. New York: Free Press.

Hoggart, Richard. 1951. *Auden: An Introductory Essay*. London: Chatto and Windus.

———. 1957. *The Uses of Literacy*. London: Chatto and Windus.

———. 1988. *Life and Times: A Local Habitation, 1918–40*. Vol. 1. London: Chatto and Windus.

———. 1990. *Life and Times: A Sort of Clowning, 1940–59*. Vol. 2. London: Chatto and Windus.

———. 1998. *The Tyranny of Relativism: Culture and Politics in Contemporary English Society*. New Brunswick, NJ: Transaction Publishers. (Originally published as *The Way We Live Now*. London: Chatto and Windus, 1995.)

Hollinger, David. 1985. *In the American Province: Studies in the History and Historiography of Ideas.* Bloomington: Indiana University Press.

Holt, Thomas. 2000. *The Problem of Race in the Twenty-First Century.* Cambridge, MA: Harvard University Press.

Howard, Jane. 1984. *Margaret Mead: A Life.* New York: Simon and Schuster.

Hulme, T. E. 1924. *Speculations: Essays on Humanism and the Philosophy of Art.* New York: Harcourt, Brace.

Hymes, Dell. 1961. Review of *The Anthropology of Franz Boas,* edited by Walter Goldschmidt. *Journal of American Folklore* 74:87–90.

———. 1969. Modjeska on Sapir and Croce: A Comment. *American Anthropologist* 71:500.

———. 1970. Linguistic Method in Ethnography: Its Development in the United States. In Paul Garvin, ed., *Method and Theory in Linguistics,* 249–325. The Hague: Mouton.

———. 1972a. The Use of Anthropology: Critical, Political, Personal. In Hymes 1972b:3–79.

———, ed. 1972b. *Reinventing Anthropology.* New York: Pantheon.

Hymes, Dell, and John Fought. 1975. *American Structuralism. Current Trends in Linguistics* 13:903–1176. (See also 1981 Mouton reprint of *American Structuralism.*)

Irvine, Judith, ed. 1994. *The Psychology of Culture: A Course of Lectures by Edward Sapir, 1927–1937.* Reconstructed by J. Irvine. Berlin: Mouton de Gruyter. (Reprinted in *The Collected Works of Edward Sapir,* 3:385–686. Berlin: Mouton de Gruyter, 1999.)

Jacoby, Russell, and Naomi Glauberman, eds. 1995. *The Bell Curve Debate: History, Documents, Opinions.* New York: Times Books.

Jardin, Andre. 1988. *Tocqueville: A Biography.* Translated by L. Davis. New York: Farrar, Straus and Giroux.

Joyce, James. 1916 [1956]. *A Portrait of the Artist as a Young Man.* New York: Viking.

Kenner, Hugh. 1971. *The Pound Era.* Berkeley: University of California Press.

Kent, Pauline. 1999. Japanese Perceptions of *The Chrysanthemum and the Sword. Dialectical Anthropology* 24:181–92.

Koerner, E. F. K., ed. 1984. *Edward Sapir: Appraisals of His Life and Work.* Amsterdam: John Benjamins.

Kroeber, A. L. 1917. The Superorganic. In Kroeber 1952:22–51.

———. 1952. *The Nature of Culture.* Chicago: University of Chicago Press.

———. 1959. Reflections on Edward Sapir, Scholar and Man. In Koerner 1984:131–39.

Kroeber, A. L., and Clyde Kluckhohn. 1952. *Culture: A Critical Review of Concepts and Definitions.* Papers of the Peabody Museum of American Archaeology and Ethnology, Vol. 47, No. 1. Cambridge, MA: Peabody Museum.

Lamberti, Jean-Claude. 1989. *Tocqueville and the Two Democracies.* Translated by A. Goldhammer. Cambridge, MA: Harvard University Press.

Langbaum, Robert. 1957. *The Poetry of Experience: The Dramatic Monologue in Modern Literary Tradition.* New York: Random House.

Lapsley, Hilary. 1999. *Margaret Mead and Ruth Benedict: The Kinship of Women.* Amherst: University of Massachusetts Press.

Lave, Jean, Paul Duguid, Nadine Fernandez, and Erik Axel. 1992. Coming of Age in

Birmingham: Cultural Studies and Conceptions of Subjectivity. *Annual Review of Anthropology* 21:257–82.

Lears, T. J. Jackson. 1981. *No Place of Grace: Antimodernism and the Transformation of American Culture, 1880–1920*. New York: Pantheon.

———. 1983. From Salvation to Self-Realization: Advertising and the Therapeutic Roots of the Consumer Culture, 1880–1930. In R. W. Fox and T. J. J. Lears, eds., *The Culture of Consumption*, 1–38. New York: Pantheon.

Leavis, Q. D. 1968. *Fiction and the Reading Public*. London: Chatto and Windus.

Lee, Dorothy. 1949. Ruth Fulton Benedict (1887–1948). *Journal of American Folklore* 62:345–47.

———. 1959. *Freedom and Culture*. Englewood Cliffs, NJ: Prentice-Hall.

Levenson, Michael. 1984. *A Genealogy of Modernism: A Study of English Literary Doctrine, 1908–1922*. Cambridge: Cambridge University Press.

Levi-Strauss, Claude. 1972. Structuralism and Ecology. Gildersleeve Lecture delivered March 28, 1972, Barnard College, New York. *Barnard Alumnae*, spring: 6–14. (Reprinted in Levi-Strauss, *The View from Afar*, 101–20. New York: Basic Books, 1985.)

Lewis, Wyndham. 1927 [1957]. *Time and Western Man*. Boston: Beacon.

Lindberg, Kathryne. 1987. *Reading Pound Reading: Modernism after Nietzsche*. New York: Oxford University Press.

Lowie, Robert. 1956. Comments on Edward Sapir, His Personality and Scholarship. In Koerner 1984:121–30.

———, ed. 1965. *Letters from Edward Sapir to Robert H. Lowie*. Berkeley: privately printed.

Lutkehaus, Nancy. 1995. Margaret Mead and the "Rustling-of-the-Wind-in-the-Palm-Trees School" of Ethnographic Writing. In Ruth Behar and Deborah Gordon, eds., *Women Writing Culture*, 186–206. Berkeley: University of California Press.

McGuigan, Jim. 1993. Reaching for Control: Raymond Williams on Mass Communication and Popular Culture. In W. J. Morgan and P. Preston, eds., *Raymond Williams: Politics, Education, Letters*, 163–88. New York: St. Martin's Press.

Mandelbaum, David, ed. 1949. *Selected Writings of Edward Sapir in Language, Culture, and Personality*. Berkeley: University of California Press.

Manent, Pierre. 1994. *An Intellectual History of Liberalism*. Translated by R. Balinski. Princeton: Princeton University Press.

———. 1996. *Tocqueville and the Nature of Democracy*. Translated by J. Waggoner. Lanham, MD: Rowman and Littlefield.

Manganaro, Marc. 2002. *Culture 1922: The Emergence of a Concept*. Princeton, NJ: Princeton University Press.

Mansfield, Harvey, and Delba Winthrop. 2000. Editors' introduction to Tocqueville 2000:xvii–lxxxvi.

Manson, William. 1986. Abram Kardiner and the Neo-Freudian Alternative in Culture and Personality. In Stocking 1986:72–94.

Marcus, George, and Michael Fischer. 1986. *Anthropology as Cultural Critique: An Experimental Moment in the Human Sciences*. Chicago: University of Chicago Press.

Mascia-Lees, Fran, and Susan H. Lees, eds. 2002. In Focus: September 11, 2001. *American Anthropologist* 104:713–82.

May, Henry. 1956. Shifting Perspectives on the 1920s. *Mississippi Valley Historical Review* 43: 405–427.

———. 1959. *The End of American Innocence: A Study of the First Years of Our Own Time, 1912–1917*. New York: Alfred A. Knopf.

Mead, Margaret. 1928. *Coming of Age in Samoa*. New York: William Morrow.

———. 1935 [1950]. *Sex and Temperament in Three Primitive Societies*. New York: William Morrow.

———. 1942. *And Keep Your Powder Dry: An Anthropologist Looks at America*. New York: William Morrow.

———. 1951. *The School in American Culture*. Cambridge. MA: Harvard University Press.

———. 1954. The Swaddling Hypothesis: Its Reception. *American Anthropologist* 56: 395–409.

———. 1955. Theoretical Setting—1954. In M. Mead and M. Wolfenstein, eds., *Childhood in Contemporary Cultures*, 3–20. Chicago: University of Chicago Press.

———, ed. 1959. *An Anthropologist at Work: Writings of Ruth Benedict*. Boston: Houghton Mifflin.

———. 1970. *Culture and Commitment: A Study of the Generation Gap*. New York: Natural History Press.

———. 1972. *Blackberry Winter: My Earlier Years*. New York: William Morrow.

———. 1979. Anthropological Contributions to National Policies during and Immediately after World War II. In Goldschmidt 1979:145–57.

Modell, Judith. 1983. *Ruth Benedict: Patterns of a Life*. Philadelphia: University of Pennsylvania Press.

Modjeska, C. N. 1968. A Note on Unconscious Structure in the Anthropology of Edward Sapir. *American Anthropologist* 70:344–47.

Moffatt, Michael. 1992. Ethnographic Writing about American Culture. *Annual Review of Anthropology* 21:205–29.

Monroe, Harriet. 1917. What May War Do. *Poetry* 10:142–45.

———. 1920a. Those We Refuse. *Poetry* 15:321–25.

———. 1920b. Men or Women? *Poetry* 16:146–48.

———. 1938. *A Poet's Life*. New York: Macmillan.

Montaigne, Michel de. 1580–88 [1976]. Of Custom, and Not Easily Changing an Accepted Law. In *The Complete Essays of Montaigne*. Translated by Donald Frame. Stanford, CA: Stanford University Press.

Murphy, Robert. 1971. *The Dialectics of Social Life: Alarms and Excursions in Anthropological Theory*. New York: Basic Books.

———. 1991. Anthropology at Columbia: A Reminiscence. *Dialectical Anthropology* 16:65–81.

Murray, Stephen. 1981a. The Canadian "Winter" of Edward Sapir. *Historiographica Linguistica* 8:63–68.

———. 1981b. Sapir's Gestalt. *Anthropological Linguistics* 22:8–12.

———. 1986. Edward Sapir in "The Chicago School" of Sociology. In Cowan et al. 1986:241–87.

Nader, Laura. 1972. Up the Anthropologist—Perspectives Gained from Studying Up. In Hymes 1972b:284–311.

———. 2001. Breaking the Silence: Politics and Professional Autonomy. In Ghosh 2001:161–69.

Nelson, Cary, Lawrence Grossberg, and Paula Treichler. 1992. Cultural Studies: An Introduction. In Grossberg et al. 1992:1–16.

Newman, Stanley. 1951. Review of *Selected Writings of Edward Sapir*, edited by David Mandelbaum. *International Journal of American Linguistics* 17:180–86.

Nolla, Eduardo. 1990. Introduction de l'editeur. In Tocqueville 1990, xiii–lxxxi.

Novick, Peter. 1988. *That Noble Dream: The "Objectivity Question" and the American Historical Profession*. Cambridge: Cambridge University Press.

Parker, Tom. 1984. *In One Day*. Boston: Houghton Mifflin.

Pater, Walter. 1873 [1919]. *The Renaissance*. New York: Macmillan.

Penny, H. Glenn, and Matti Bunzl, eds. 2003. *Worldly Provincialism: German Anthropology in the Age of Empire*. Ann Arbor: University of Michigan Press.

Perry, Helen. 1982. *Psychiatrist of America: The Life of Harry Stack Sullivan*. Cambridge, MA: Belknap.

Pierpont, Claudia Roth. 2000. *Passionate Minds: Women Rewriting the World*. New York: Alfred A. Knopf.

———. 2004. The Measure of America: How a Rebel Anthropologist Waged War on Racism. *New Yorker,* March 8: 48–63.

Pierson, George. 1938 [1996]. *Tocqueville in America*. Baltimore: Johns Hopkins University Press.

Pike, Kenneth. 1967. *Language in Relation to a Unified Theory of the Structure of Human Behavior*. The Hague: Mouton.

PMP. *Poetry* Magazine Papers (1912–35). Department of Special Collections, University of Chicago Library.

Pound, Ezra. 1914a. The Renaissance. In Pound 1954:214–26.

———. 1914b. The Prose Tradition in Verse. In Pound 1954:371–77.

———. 1918. A Retrospect. In Pound 1954:3–14.

———. 1954. *Literary Essays*. Norfolk, CT: New Directions.

———. 1971. *Selected Letters, 1907–1941*. London: Faber and Faber.

Preston, Richard. 1966. Edward Sapir's Anthropology: Style, Structure and Method. *American Anthropologist* 68:1105–27.

———. 1980. Reflection's on Sapir's Anthropology in Canada. *Canadian Review of Sociology and Anthropology* 17:367–75. (Reprinted in Koerner 1984:179–94.)

Putnam, Robert. 2000. *Bowling Alone: The Collapse and Revival of American Community*. New York: Simon and Schuster.

Rabinow, Paul, and William Sullivan, eds. 1979. *Interpretive Social Science*. Berkeley: University of California Press.

Raleigh, J. H. 1957. *Matthew Arnold and American Culture*. Berkeley: University of California Press.

Rappaport, Roy. 1986. Desecrating the Holy Woman: Derek Freeman's Attack on Margaret Mead. *American Scholar* (summer): 313–47.

Richter, Melvin. 1970. *Essays in Theory and History: An Approach to the Social Sciences.* Cambridge, MA: Harvard University Press.

———. 1988. Tocqueville, Napoleon, and Bonapartism. In Eisenstadt 1988, 110–45.

Riesman, David. 1950. *The Lonely Crowd: A Study of the Changing American Character.* New Haven, CT: Yale University Press.

Rosenblatt, Daniel. 2004. An Anthropology Made Safe for Culture: Patterns of Practice and the Politics of Difference in Ruth Benedict. *American Anthropologist* 106(3): 459–72.

Rosenfeld, Sophia. 2001. *A Revolution in Language: The Problem of Signs in Late Eighteenth-Century France.* Stanford, CA: Stanford University Press.

Russell, Frank. 1908. The Pima Indians. *Twenty-sixth Annual Report of the Bureau of American Ethnology.* Washington, DC: Government Printing Office.

Sacks, Harvey. 1992. *Lectures on Conversation.* Oxford: Blackwell.

Sahlins, Marshall. 1964. An Anthropologist's Criticism of Contemporary U.S. Society: Review of *Culture against Man* by Jules Henry. *Scientific American* 210 (May):139–42.

———. 1972. *Stone Age Economics.* Chicago: Aldine-Atherton.

———. 1976. *Culture and Practical Reason.* Chicago: University of Chicago Press.

———. 2003. Artificially Maintained Controversies: Global Warming and Fijian Cannibalism. *Anthropology Today* 19(3):3–5.

Sapir, Edward. 1916. Time Perspective in Aboriginal American Culture: A Study in Method. In Mandelbaum 1949:389–462.

———. 1917a. *Dreams and Gibes.* Boston: Poet Lore.

———. 1917b. The Twilight of Rhyme. *Dial* 63:98–100.

———. 1917c. Realism in Prose Fiction. *Dial* 63:503–6.

———. 1917d. Do We Need a "Superorganic"? *American Anthropologist* 19:441–47.

———. 1917e. "Jean Christophe": An Epic of Humanity:Review of *Jean-Christophe,* by Romain Rolland. *Dial* 62:423–26.

———. 1918a. Reproof. *Dial* 64:102.

———. 1918b. Representative Music. In Mandelbaum 1949:490–95.

———. 1919a. Unsigned review of *The Foundations and Nature of Verse,* by C. F. Jacob. *Dial* 66:98, 100.

———. 1919b. Randolph Bourne. *Dial* 66:45.

———. 1920a. The Heuristic Value of Rhyme. In Mandelbaum 1949:496–99.

———. 1920b. Review of *Primitive Society,* by Robert Lowie. *Freeman* 1:377–79.

———. 1920c. Primitive Humanity and Anthropology: Review of *Primitive Society,* by Robert Lowie. *Dial* 69:528–33.

———. 1921a. *Language: An Introduction to the Study of Speech.* New York: Harcourt, Brace.

———. 1921b. The Musical Foundations of Verse. *Journal of English and Germanic Philology* 20:213–28.

———. 1922a. Mr. Masters' Later Work: Review of *The Open Sea,* by E. L. Masters. *Freeman* 5:333–34.

———. 1922b. A Symposium of the Exotic: Review of *American Indian Life,* edited by E. C. Parsons. *Dial* 73:568–71.

————. 1922c. Review of *Introducing Irony*, by Maxwell Bodenheim. *New Republic* 31:341.

————. 1922d. Poems of Experience: Review of *Collected Poems*, by E. A. Robinson. *Freeman* 5:141–42.

————. 1922e. A Peep at the Hindu Spirit: Review of *More Jataka Tales*, by E. C. Babbitt. *Freeman* 5:404.

————. 1922f. An Orthodox Psychology: Review of *Psychology: A Study of Mental Life*, by R. S. Woodworth. *Freeman* 5:619.

————. 1924a. Culture, Genuine and Spurious. In Mandelbaum 1949:308–31.

————. 1924b. The Grammarian and His Language. In Mandelbaum 1949:150–59.

————. 1925a. Sound Patterns in Language. In Mandelbaum 1949:33–45.

————. 1925b. Emily Dickinson, A Primitive: Review of *The Complete Poems of Emily Dickenson*, and *The Life and Letters of Emily Dickenson*, by M. D. Bianchi. *Poetry* 26:97–105.

————. 1925c. Let Race Alone. *Nation* 3112:211–13.

————. 1927. The Unconscious Patterning of Behavior in Society. In Mandelbaum 1949:544–59.

————. 1928a. Review of *The Book of American Negro Spirituals*, edited by J. W. Johnson. *Journal of American Folklore* 41:172–74.

————. 1928b. Observations on the Sex Problem in America. *American Journal of Psychiatry* 8:519–34.

————. 1929a. Review of *The Re-Discovery of America*, by Waldo Frank. *American Journal of Sociology* 35:335–36.

————. 1929b. The Skepticism of Bertrand Russell: Review of *Skeptical Essays*, by Bertrand Russell. *New Republic* 57:196.

————. 1929c. Franz Boas: Review of *Anthropology and Modern Life*, by Franz Boas. *New Republic* 57:278–79.

————. 1929d. "The Discipline of Sex." *American Mercury* 16:413–20. (Reprint, with minor changes and the first five paragraphs omitted, of Sapir 1928b.)

————. 1930a. Review of *Our Business Civilization*, by J. T. Adams. *Current History* 32:426–28.

————. 1930b. What Is the Family Still Good For? *American Mercury* 19:145–51.

————. 1931a. Custom. In Mandelbaum 1949:365–72.

————. 1931b. Fashion. In Mandelbaum 1949:373–81.

————. 1932. Cultural Anthropology and Psychiatry. In Mandelbaum 1949:509–21.

————. 1934a. The Emergence of the Concept of Personality in a Study of Cultures. In Mandelbaum 1949:590–97.

————. 1934b. Personality. In Mandelbaum 1949:560–63.

————. 1938a. Why Cultural Anthropology Needs the Psychiatrist. In Mandelbaum 1949:569–77.

————. 1938b. Review of *The Folklore of Capitalism*, by Thurmand Arnold. *Psychiatry* 1:145–47.

————. 1939. Psychiatric and Cultural Pitfalls in the Business of Getting a Living. In Mandelbaum 1949:578–89.

Schleifer, James. 1980. *The Making of Tocqueville's* Democracy in America. Chapel Hill: University of North Carolina Press.

Schneider, David. 1968. *American Kinship: A Cultural Account.* Englewood Cliffs, NJ: Prentice-Hall.

———. 1995. *Schneider on Schneider: The Conversion of the Jews and Other Anthropological Stories.* Transcribed and edited by Richard Handler. Durham: Duke University Press.

Segal, Daniel. 2000. "Western Civ" and the Staging of History in American Higher Education. *American Historical Review* 105:770–805.

Silverstein, Michael. 1986. The Diachrony of Sapir's Synchronic Linguistic Description. In Cowan et al. 1986:67–106.

———. 2004. Boasian Cosmographic Anthropology and the Sociocentric Component of Mind. In Richard Handler, ed., *Significant Others: Interpersonal and Professional Commitments in Anthropology,* 131–57. Madison: University of Wisconsin Press.

SN. Edward Sapir. 1917–1919. Suggestive Notes. Ms. diary. Transcribed by Regna Darnell.

Stassinos, Elizabeth. 1998. Ruthlessly: Ruth Benedict's Pseudonyms and the Art of Science Writ Large. Ph.D. diss., Department of Anthropology, University of Virginia.

Steedman, Carolyn. 1990. Stories. In Terry Lovell, ed., *British Feminist Throught: A Reader.* 281–95. Oxford: Basil Blackwell.

———. 1992. Culture, Cultural Studies, and the Historians. In Grossberg et al. 1992: 613–22.

Stille, Alexander. 2003. Experts Can Help Rebuild a Country. *New York Times,* July 19: A15, A17.

Stocking, George W. 1963. Matthew Arnold, E. B. Tylor, and the Uses of Invention. *American Anthropologist* 65:783–99. (Reprinted in Stocking 1968:69–90.)

———. 1965a. From Physics to Ethnology. *Journal of the History of the Behavioral Sciences* 1:53–66. (Reprinted in Stocking 1968:133–60.)

———. 1965b. "On the Limits of 'Presentism' and 'Historicism' in the Historiography of the Behavioral Sciences." *Journal of the History of Behavioral Sciences.* 1:211–18. (Reprinted in Stocking 1968:1–12.)

———. 1966a. Franz Boas and the Culture Concept in Historical Perspective. *American Anthropologist* 68:867–82. (Reprinted in Stocking 1968:195–233.)

———. 1966b. The History of Anthropology: Where, Whence, Whither? *Journal of the History of the Behavioral Sciences* 2:281–90.

———. 1967. Anthropologists and Historians as Historians of Anthropology: Critical Comments on Some Recently Published Work. *Journal of the History of the Behavioral Sciences* 3:376–87.

———. 1968. *Race, Culture, and Evolution: Essays in the History of Anthropology.* New York: Basic Books.

———. 1973. From Chronology to Ethnology: James Cowles Prichard and British Anthropology, 1800–1850. In James Cowles Prichard, *Researches into the Physical History of Man,* ix–cx. Chicago: University of Chicago Press.

———. 1974a. The Basic Assumptions of Boasian Anthropology. In G. W. Stocking, ed., *The Shaping of American Anthropology, 1883–1911: A Franz Boas Reader*, 1–20. New York: Basic Books. (Reprinted in Stocking 2001:24–48.)

———. 1974b. The Boas Plan for American Indian Linguistics. In Dell Hymes, ed., *Studies in the History of Linguistics*, 454–84. Indiana: Bloomington University Press. (Reprinted in Stocking 1992:60–91.)

———. 1976. Ideas and Institutions in American Anthropology: Toward a History of the Interwar Period. In G. W. Stocking, ed., *Selected Papers from the* American Anthropologist, *1921–1945*, 1–44. Washington, DC: American Anthropological Association. (Reprinted in Stocking 1992:114–77.)

———. 1979. Anthropology as *Kulturkampf*: Science and Politics in the Career of Franz Boas. In Goldschmidt 1979:33–50. (Reprinted in Stocking 1992:92–113.)

———, ed. 1986. *Malinowski, Rivers, Benedict and Others*. Madison: University of Wisconsin Press.

———. 1987. *Victorian Anthropology*. New York: Free Press.

———. 1989. The Ethnographic Sensibility of the 1920s and the Dualism of the Anthropological Tradition. In Stocking, ed., *Romantic Motives*, 208–76. Madison: University of Wisconsin Press. (Reprinted in Stocking 1992:276–341.)

———. 1992. *The Ethnographer's Magic and Other Essays in the History of Anthropology*. Madison: University of Wisconsin Press.

———. 1996. Boasian Ethnography and the German Anthropological Tradition. In G. W. Stocking, ed., *Volksgeist as Method and Ethic*, 3–8. Madison: University of Wisconsin Press.

———. 2001. *Delimiting Anthropology: Occasional Inquiries and Reflections*. Madison: University of Wisconsin Press.

SUP. Sapir's unpublished poems, transcribed by William Cowan, Department of Linguistics, Carleton University. Author's personal files.

Susman, Warren. 1984. *Culture as History: The Transformation of American Society in the Twentieth Century*. New York: Pantheon.

Symons, Arthur. 1919. *The Symbolist Movement in Literature*. Rev. ed. New York: E. P. Dutton.

Tierney, Patrick. 2000. *Darkness in El Dorado*. New York: W. W. Norton.

Tocqueville, Alexis de. 1945 [1835, 1840]. *Democracy in America*. Translated by Henry Reeve. New York: Alfred A. Knopf.

———. 1990 [1835, 1840]. *De la democratie en Amerique. Premiere edition historico-critique*. Edited by Eduardo Nolla. Paris: Librairie Philosophique J. Vrin.

———. 2000 [1835, 1840]. *Democracy in America*. Translated by Harvey Mansfield and Delba Winthrop. Chicago: University of Chicago Press.

Trilling, Lionel. 1939 [1954]. *Matthew Arnold*. New York: Columbia University Press.

———. 1971. *Sincerity and Authenticity*. Cambridge, MA: Harvard University Press.

Tyler, Stephen. 1987. *The Unspeakable: Discourse, Dialogue, and Rhetoric in the Postmodern World*. Madison: University of Wisconsin Press.

Tylor, E. B. 1871. *Primitive Culture*. 2 vols. London: J. Murray.

Urban, Gregory. 2001. *How Culture Moves through the World*. Minneapolis: University of Minnesota Press.

Vaughan, Leslie. 1997. *Randolph Bourne and the Politics of Cultural Radicalism*. Lawrence: University Press of Kansas.

Voegelin, Carl. 1952. Edward Sapir. *Word Study* 27:1–3.

Wagner, Roy. 1975. *The Invention of Culture*. Englewood Cliffs, NJ: Prentice-Hall.

Weber, Max. 1905. *The Protestant Ethic and the Spirit of Capitalism*. Translated by T. Parsons. New York: Charles Scribner's Sons.

Wetherell, Margaret, and Jonathan Potter. 1992. *Mapping the Language of Racism: Discourse and the Legitimation of Exploitation*. New York: Columbia University Press.

Williams, Raymond. 1958 [1983]. *Culture and Society: 1780–1950*. New York: Columbia University Press.

———. 1961. *The Long Revolution*. New York: Columbia University Press.

———. 1977. *Marxism and Literature*. Oxford: Oxford University Press.

———. 1989. *Resources of Hope: Culture, Democracy, Socialism*. London: Verso.

Winters, Yvor. 1946 [1971]. *Edwin Arlington Robinson*. New York: New Directions.

Wolin, Sheldon. 2001. *Tocqueville between Two Worlds: The Making of a Political and Theoretical Life*. Princeton, NJ: Princeton University Press.

Yans-McLaughlin, Virginia. 1986. Science, Democracy, and Ethics: Mobilizing Culture and Personality for World War II. In Stocking 1986:184–217.

Yelvington, Kevin. 2003. A Historian among the Anthropologists: Review of *Delimiting Anthropology*, edited by George Stocking. *American Anthropologist* 105:367–71.

Young, Robert. 1995. *Colonial Desire: Hybridity in Theory, Culture and Race*. London: Routledge.

INDEX